Cutting-edge
Cabinetmaking

Cutting-edge

Cabinetmaking

Robert Ingham

GUILD OF MASTER
CRAFTSMAN PUBLICATIONS

Dedication

To my brother George, an inspirational designer and maker. With thanks to Geoff Hines and Reg Henstock, who kick started my interest and passion for making, and everyone at Parnham College for keeping me focused and expanding my knowledge.

First published 2007 by
Guild of Master Craftsman Publications Ltd
Castle Place, 166 High Street,
Lewes, East Sussex BN7 1XU

All photographs taken by the author, except for those listed below: Peter Williams (imagephotographic.co.uk): front cover, back cover (bottom right and top middle), pages 2, 9, 18, 31, 41, 47, 99, 125, 186 and 205. GMC/Anthony Bailey: 45, 60, 62, 111, 114. Philip Pickin: 70, 76, 79. Bill Clayden: 113. Robert Seymour: 115, 123. Eye Imagery: 203.

Illustrations by Simon Rodway

ISBN: 978-1-86108-518-4

A catalogue record for this book is available from the British Library.

Production Manager: Jim Bulley
Managing Editor: Gerrie Purcell
Editor: Virginia Brehaut
Managing Art Editor: Gilda Pacitti
Designer: Chloë Alexander

Set in Avenir and Janson Text

Colour origination by Alta image
Printed and bound in China by Sino Publishing

Contents

Part One The Principles of Construction

Preparation

Joints

Assembly

Part Two Pushing The Boundaries

Part Three Gallery

Foreword

I first met Robert when he was on the cusp of launching his solo career from Wales. His innovative approach to work has made him an internationally renowned maker at the cutting edge of his craft – someone who is passionate about what he does and how he practises it. Passing on his knowledge to others comes naturally whether it is through teaching directly or writing about his work. *Furniture & Cabinetmaking* would not be the magazine it is without Robert's input and it has been a privilege as well as a great learning experience to work with him over the years.

This book is a body of work that represents the thinking behind the man and the man behind the thinking. It is a technical tour de force that is original and thought provoking and should guide you as well as inspire you on to greater making challenges.

Colin Eden-Eadon

Colin Eden-Eadon
Editor, *Furniture & Cabinetmaking* magazine

Introduction

Where do ideas come from? I am often asked this question when my work is seen at shows but it can be difficult to give a clear answer.

THE TENDENCY IS OFTEN TO ANSWER IN CLICHÉS such as 'developing a vocabulary of forms', or even 'keeping one's eyes open' and 'being receptive to all of the influences and inspiration from a variety of sources'. I do not think that this question expects a definitive answer, but I am quite sure that a lot of people who start with an interest in making, and develop a good level of practical skill, feel a degree of frustration when they see the work of a designer-maker and wonder how they can produce work of a challenging nature themselves.

▼ Bedside tables in ripple sycamore – simplicity is at the heart of the design.

◆ Learning design

PERSONALLY, I DO NOT THINK THAT DESIGN CAN be taught. However, there *are* basic canons that form the foundations of design and are essential to a complete understanding of it. When I was at college training to be a craft teacher I learned how to use the tools of design such as drawing, drafting and rendering – and I was under the illusion that I was learning 'how to design'. As students, we got a lot of our inspiration from our colleagues. The college library held a collection of photographs of student work from previous years and

these formed the basis of our designs (in those days we were not encouraged to develop our own ideas). I was aware of a strong stylistic influence that had its roots in Arts and Crafts furniture, and anything else was deemed to be inappropriate.

*We all see things, but few of us really know **how** to look.*

▲ Stunning jewellery casket in weathered ripple sycamore and purpleheart.

◆ The canons of design

AROUND THIS TIME I BECAME AWARE OF THE canons of design and such notions as 'fitness for purpose' and 'form follows function', but I can't say that I really understood what they meant. I graduated from teacher training college with a distinct feeling that my design education was lacking. In the colleges of art, design education was going through a radical shake-up. Applied art was being addressed for industrial applications, and my brother, who had followed this route, showed me his portfolio. I decided that this was what I needed. I enrolled in a course that led to the National Diploma in Design, hoping to 'learn' how to design furniture. Some time later, in conversation with my brother and other designers who had followed a similar path, I came to the conclusion that what I had learned and developed was the ability to see,

through learning how to draw, but I still had a long way to go before I could call myself a 'designer'. This is an appropriate point at which to highlight the canons of design, which I mentioned earlier. They are, in no particular order of importance: aesthetics, proportion, function, materials and construction.

◆ Aesthetics

ALTHOUGH MOST USERS OF ARTEFACTS WOULD place function at the top of their list of priorities when evaluating a piece, it is likely that their first association with an object is through their eyes. Long before one gets an opportunity to use an object, one sees it, quite often from some distance. For many designers, appearance is the most important aspect of design, or the starting point in its development. We all see things, but few of us really know *how* to look. This is an aspect of design education that can be taught.

In my opinion, the skill of looking can be enhanced and accelerated if looking is accompanied by the activity of drawing. It is an excellent way of developing a visual vocabulary. As such, in the formative period of your involvement with design, a sketchbook is an extremely valuable tool – not only to record specific examples of objects that represent design inspiration, but to expand your visual vocabulary on as broad a level as possible by drawing all kinds of things from nature, artefacts, science, engineering, architecture – in fact anything that interests and intrigues you. Draw what you see in as representative a way as possible. I found that as my design vocabulary increased I sketched less and less, not because I didn't want to, but because I had difficulty justifying the time it involved.

▼ Drawers and pivoting compartments makes function an important starting point of design.

◆ Proportion

B Y THIS TIME MANY OTHER INFLUENCES WERE contributing to my awareness. I started to become more interested in proportion – and this is an aspect of design that can be taught. If you look back at the history of art there have been many attempts to establish rules to govern proportion. Amongst them perhaps the most well known is the Golden Section. When I was struggling with the imposition of design from the Arts and Crafts movement as a student, I became aware of the stylistic proportions that were being encouraged by Scandinavian designers with their strong emphasis on long and low pieces of furniture. I vividly remember a heated disagreement with an eminent designer who questioned the proportions of a sideboard that I had designed which was long and low. In his opinion there was only one proportion that was suitable and he actually stated its dimensions. In my own work today I do not think of proportion in terms of rules but as an amalgam of influences that I bring to bear on a design.

Wood is probably the most challenging of all craft materials.

◆ Function

FUNCTION IS ONE OF THE MOST IMPORTANT aspects of a design. It is essential that an object performs well in use. Not only is this about practicality or fitness for purpose but it should also include such considerations as the maintenance of the object both in the present and in the future. I like to think that my work will survive and if it functions successfully and is used, it will require maintenance and restoration. This is a consideration that I build into my designs. In fact, I include a written provenance with every piece I design. In addition to information about the design, which will inform future generations, I include information about the maintenance of the piece and about the materials and any special processes so that future restorers will have a clearer understanding and be able to respond to any work that may be necessary.

◆ Materials

I AM A WOODWORKER AT HEART AND AM FASCINATED by the challenge of wood. But I am also fascinated by any material that I can manipulate as a craftsman and welcome opportunities to combine materials. It is amazing how a combination of interesting timbers can be further enhanced by the appearance of a small amount of colour when a piece of patinated metal or a piece of stone is added. Here I must say something about balance. With an extensive vocabulary there is a risk that the design can suffer from excess. Knowing what to include and what to leave out requires a lot of thought and I have no doubt that experience plays a big part in this process. The saying 'keep it simple stupid' – or 'KISS' – is well worth bearing in mind when you have a lot of ideas fighting around for expression in your mind.

◆ Construction

WOOD IS PROBABLY THE MOST CHALLENGING of all craft materials. No two pieces of wood are alike – even from one end of a board to the other the density, texture, colour and many other features can vary considerably. This is probably why working in wood is so process-intensive. It lends itself to the learning and development of techniques.

For a long time I had difficulty stating my design philosophy. I struggled with the intellectual arguments that the design community put forward comparing one point of view with another and tried hard to identify with any one movement. I believe strongly that the influences of your early experiences form the bedrock of your ideas. Teaching design and craftsmanship, and learning so much from interaction with my students, helped me to clarify my thoughts. Now I am able to say that my work as a designer is 'construction-centred' and my starting point is influenced by how a piece will be made. I use all kinds of ways to achieve results, from sketching to model-making, from visual research to abstract thought, but what I find the most challenging is how the piece is to be made.

▼ Dressing table with pivoting drawers in steamed Swiss pear and weathered ripple sycamore – proportion and subtle use of materials achieve a quiet harmony.

The workshop

An ideal workspace should not only contain all of the technical essentials; it should also be an inspirational environment in which to work and enhance your creativity.

Following my retirement from 20 years as principal at Parnham College, my wife Andrea and I decided to relocate to the Welsh countryside. I deliberately set aside time to design and plan a new working space, drawing on my experience as both a maker and teacher, and deciding on what I would ideally like to have in it. I considered every aspect of my work when I was designing the workshop, and I now have dedicated areas for each of the different functions. A great deal of thought and care over many months produced what is, in my mind, an almost perfect environment for furniture-making.

The workshop stands at the bottom of the garden, perched on stilts overhanging a hillside of mature trees. The building is clad in tongue-and-groove boarding and painted dark green to blend with the surrounding landscape. There were problems associated with digging foundations into the side of a hill and the building had to be built on piles, some of which extend three metres into the hillside. It was an expensive operation, but the views are stunning and I think it was worth the effort.

Layout of the workshop

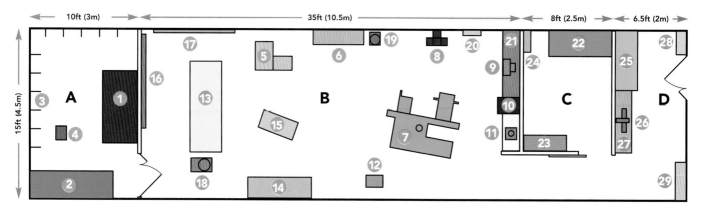

A – TIMBER STORE
1. Interwood 2m x 1m two-platen veneer press
2. Veneer and board material storage racks
3. Vertical timber storage racks
4. De-humidifier

B – MAIN WORKSHOP
5. Hitachi CB 75F band resaw
6. Felder AF 22 wall-mounted dust extractor
7. Felder BF 741 combination dimension saw, planer thicknesser and spindle moulder
8. Meddings MF4 pillar drill
9. Hegner HSM300 disc sander
10. Inca Euro 260 bandsaw

11. APTC bobbin sander
12. De-humidifier
13. Workbench – under bench tool cupboard on castors to facilitate mobility
14. Router station – two routers mounted on router tables
15. Component trolley
16. Tool cupboard
17. Cramp rack
18. Vacuum cleaner dedicated to hand-held power tools
19. Workshop vacuum cleaner
20. Drill and screw cupboard
21. Cupboard and worktop – storage for veneers, vacuum bag press, compressor

C – SPRAY ROOM
22. P&J spray booth
23. Drying shelves
24. Lacquer store cupboard

D – METAL WORKSHOP
25. Boxford 330 TR lathe
26. Rishton Promill–35 milling machine
27. Workbench and storage
28. Metalwork tool cupboard
29. Photographic equipment cupboard

▲ Although a striking modern building, the workshop blends into the Welsh countryside.

◆ An inspirational space

I HAVE A STRONG BELIEF THAT THE AESTHETICS OF the working environment are just as important as the technical aspect. My workshop is roughly 10,770 sq ft (1,000 sq m,) and while that is not a great deal of space, I designed it in a way that makes it feel spacious, with white-painted walls reflecting the maximum of light. The west-facing wall is nearly all glass with magnificent views of the Welsh mountains, which serves as a constant source of inspiration. In the main area of the workshop interior colour-coding is used for all the matching cupboards. Everything is made from easy-to-clean melamine. If you take a meticulous approach to your work, this should be reflected in an immaculately tidy workplace.

◆ The bench

MY WORKBENCH SITS AT ONE END OF THE workshop, away from the wall, and is surrounded on two sides by cupboards and racking for my sash cramps and G clamps, with between 50 and 100 all set out ready to use. One set of these I made myself – finding that even

the smallest size of cramp commercially available proved to be cumbersome and heavy for my small boxes. There are no bench dogs, but there are two adjustable battens on one side and one end of the bench, which I use for pushing against when planing. Underneath is a mobile piece of furniture, the tool chest – I find the convenience

▼ There is a home for everything.

▲ Working at the bench.

▲ Regimented ranks of cramps.

of wheeled stands for several of my machines a real boon – the band resaw and the router set-up are both wheeled, which allows for far greater flexibility when doing things such as gluing-up large pieces. To one end of the bench is a trolley in which I keep the components of whatever piece I am currently working on, so that the surface is clear for work.

▼ Another mobile piece of equipment – a chest for hand tools.

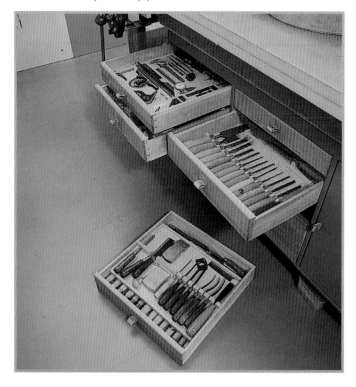

◆ Timber store

BEHIND THE BENCH IS THE TIMBER STORE IN which I keep a good supply of exotic woods and veneers along with solid boards – all of which are stored vertically and protected by a de-humidifier. It is here that my platen veneer press is housed. I take all my own photographs and use the workshop as my studio, so to the left of the door is my photographic cupboard. Further along is the spraying room fully kitted-out with an appropriate P&J extraction unit.

◆ Lifestyle

TO UPROOT ONESELF FROM A FAMILIAR SETTING and lifestyle takes courage and adaptability – the busy life of teaching at Parnham seems a long way from these Welsh hills. The only thing that I really miss is the exchange of ideas with other makers and students. Working alone can be totally engrossing but can prove hard at times.

MACHINERY

Milling machine and **lathe** I have always had a keen interest in engineering. Indeed, although I still use many traditional jointing methods, I see a lot of my work as being closer to engineering than furniture-making; almost 'wood-engineering'.

▲ The jigs and fittings are all made on the engineering lathe.

My milling machine is a Rishton Promill-35 and the lathe is a Boxford 330 TR, both of which are British. They are the kind of machines that you would expect to find in a professional tool room and are ideal for the materials that I use in my jig-making, such as Tufnol, brass and steel – it is here that I make the fittings for my furniture as well as devices for jigs for routing.

My **Felder Universal** takes pride of place in the room and is the lynchpin of my work. It was the biggest that I could feasibly fit into the space! To the left of this is a Meddings **pillar drill**, there is a grinder and two types of sanding machines, a bobbin and a disc sander. An Inca **bandsaw** with a 20in (505mm) throat sits in the middle.

▲ The Felder Universal.

I have six **routers**, and every one of them is an Elu. Two of these are mounted permanently in a double table unit – the first is one of three MOF 96Es and is permanently set up for thicknessing inlay. The second is an MOF 177E, one of two that are set up for general routing. The other four are used as roving routers, with cutters permanently in place for specific tasks for the duration of the making of a piece. This allows me to complete a moulding on a component at a later stage while carrying on with a different task on another router, saving a great deal of time and trouble changing cutters and resetting.

My **Hitachi CB 75F band resaw** is another important machine in my operations. This type of machine is usually only found in sawmills, not least because of its sheer size, and I had to import mine from the USA. I still think it was worth all the trouble as the finish is so good that I can glue down veneers straight from the saw. I like to cut my own veneers and find the process, with this machine, considerably more straightforward than using a conventional bandsaw. Much of my work is curved and is constructed with veneers and

▲ The workshop-sized band resaw – a real boon for the furniture-maker.

ply materials, such as bendy ply, which I double-veneer to avoid fractures. With these cores I also use constructional veneers that are cross-veneered to counter the spring-back that is often associated with their use. I decided to buy new machinery throughout (with the exception of my veneer press) mainly because of the logistics of tracking down individual second-hand pieces and having them delivered to this remote location.

▼ The view from my bench.

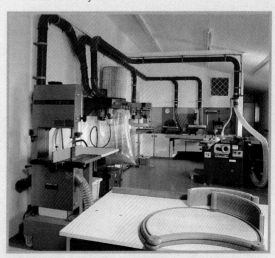

Part One:
The Principles of Construction

Shooting boards: a new approach

Cabinetmakers use shooting boards to overcome end-grain breakout and control of squareness but I have found them to be awkward to use. I decided to make my own prototype to solve the problem.

WHEN I STARTED WOODWORKING I TRIED to use the conventional horizontal shooting board with the plane held on its side, with little success. Perhaps the shooting board was worn, making control quite difficult. Trying to hold the work firmly against the stock while controlling the plane with one hand was certainly a tricky skill to master. I did not persevere at the time, preferring either to clamp a piece on to prevent breakout and hold the component in the vice or cut a small chamfer at one end and plane the piece overhead and rely on my skill with the plane. This approach worked quite well but relied on frequent checking with a try-square and a lot of trial and error. As is the case with many of the jigs that I have developed over the years the need for repetitive accuracy and efficiency of production led to an analysis of the problem and the making of a simple prototype.

▼ The 90° shooting board with the stop and bar fitted.

◆ Making a prototype

THE NEED WAS FOR A PLANING SYSTEM that held the component firmly, supported the end-grain and could be used with the plane held on top. My first attempt was made from solid wood with the stop or stock held in place with double-sided tape. Despite its temporary nature, it worked. Over a period of time I refined it by adding a cam clamp to make alignment easier. On one occasion, while teaching a summer class, we did not have time to prepare a solid wood model, so I developed the version I use today, made from MDF. Instead of using a thick piece of wood for the main body I created a wide top surface by building up an 'L' section which is the main body for the two shooting boards featured in this chapter.

◆ Construction

I CANNOT STRESS THE IMPORTANCE OF ACCURACY too strongly. It is essential to dimension the main components on a reliable circular saw on which the set-up has been tested before starting. The main body is made of MDF. The vertical section (A – see drawing on facing page) should be 1in (25mm) thick. MDF can be difficult to find in this thickness, and if you can source it you will probably have to buy a sheet, which could be quite expensive (although I must add it is a very useful size for jig-making in general). Try to buy an offcut from someone who uses MDF on a regular basis. If not, then the vertical section could be stack laminated from two layers of ²³⁄₃₂in (18mm) MDF as you will need this

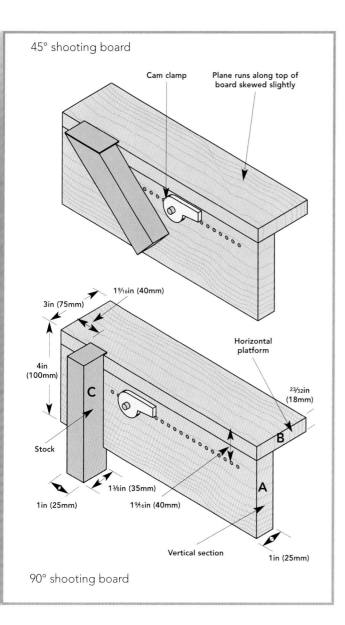

45° shooting board

Cam clamp

Plane runs along top of board skewed slightly

1⁹⁄₁₆in (40mm)

3in (75mm)

Horizontal platform

4in (100mm)

C

23⁄32in (18mm)

B

Stock

1³⁄₈in (35mm)

A

1in (25mm)

1⁹⁄₁₆in (40mm)

Vertical section

1in (25mm)

90° shooting board

◆ Stock

THE STOCK IS LOCATED IN A SHALLOW HOUSING (C – see drawing). Once again, I would recommend MDF but it could be made of a stable hardwood. Remember that solid wood moves and this could affect the stability of the shooting board. Cutting the housing is the second aspect of critical accuracy. You could rout it working with the fence of your router off the end, making a series of cuts until the width of the housing results in a snug fit with the stock. The problem with this method is the difficulty in setting the router for the final cut and the relatively small end contact with the fence. I prefer to mark two lines with a marking knife and an engineers' try-square and then freehand rout out the waste from the housing stopping about a millimetre away from the lines (see box on page 25).

To ensure a good fit between the two lines, square the first line with a marking knife and keep the try-square in place. Hold the stock against the try-square and then lightly mark the second line. Re-align the try-square with the lightly scored second line and make sure that the bevel of your marking knife compresses into what will be waste wood, and intensify the second line. When you have freehand routed the waste, you can pare back to the edges of the housing knowing that with care the chisel will locate firmly into the two knife lines, resulting in a good snug fit. For the mitre shooting board this is also by far the most suitable method. The two examples illustrated have stocks positioned for right-handed use. Position the stocks at the other end if you are left-handed.

◆ The cam clamp

WHAT MAKES THESE TWO SHOOTING BOARDS easy to use and control is the holding capability of the cam clamp. It was the big breakthrough that took my first prototype from a fumbling accessory to a reliable and highly controllable jig. Any lines that govern the dimensional limits of components can be carefully lined up with the reference surface of the top and securely held in position with the cam clamp. The most suitable material for the clamp is ¼in (6mm) thick Perspex but MDF will do the job satisfactorily.

The cam consists of a ¹⁵⁄₁₆in (24mm) radius disc with an extension to form the lever. A hole, large enough to accept a No.10 or ³⁄₁₆in (5mm) round head screw, is drilled ⁵⁄₁₆in (8mm) off centre to create the 'throw' of the cam. I form the rounded edges of my cams on my disc sander, but the curve could be formed with the careful

thickness for the horizontal platform (B – see drawing) and it is much easier to buy. Most DIY stores sell small pieces but, once again, it would be worth investing in a full sheet. The vertical section will actually benefit from the increase in thickness if it is stack laminated.

A simple butt joint between the platform and vertical section would be strong enough on its own but some form of location between the two would make the glue-up easier. Biscuits or a routed groove and a spline will do the job perfectly. I assemble this joint using my bench vice to apply pressure. Check for square with a small engineer's try-square and tap the horizontal component up or down to affect adjustment. Be extremely critical at this stage as it's much more difficult to carry out adjustments to out of square components in MDF later.

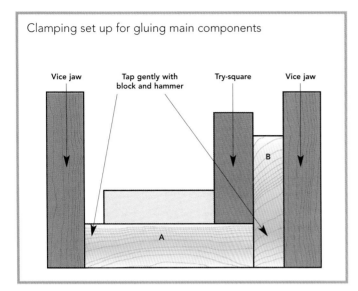

Clamping set up for gluing main components

Vice jaw Tap gently with block and hammer Try-square Vice jaw

B

A

use of a file. Finally, a series of pilot holes needs to be drilled to accommodate different component dimensions. These holes are ⅜in (10mm) apart – if they were any closer, the material in between would not be strong enough to withstand the force of the cam. To allow for greater variation a second set of holes can be drilled ⅜in (10mm) below the first row, staggered horizontally to centre in between the upper set. This second row is not shown in the drawing. In terms of sequence it would be easier to drill these holes before the platform and vertical section are glued together.

◆ Adjustable stops

FINALLY, THE ADDITION OF A BAR WHICH HAS adjustable stops can be fitted to the stock to facilitate repetitive dimensioning of components. The sliding stop moves up or down in a T-sectioned slot cut with a keyhole slot router cutter.

◆ Variable angle shooting board

MY VARIABLE ANGLE SHOOTING BOARD EMPLOYS many of the same principles as those of the square and 45° angle shooting boards. The differences lie in the changes of angle that can be accommodated and in the method of construction.

◆ Construction

THE VERTICAL SECTION MUST BE PREPARED FIRST as this component carries the controls that facilitate angle adjustments. After first preparing the component to size, carefully drill the ¼in (6mm) pivot hole. A ¼in (6mm) hexagonal nut is then embedded into a hexagonal recess sunk in the reverse surface that will be trapped in place when the vertical section and horizontal platform are glued together.

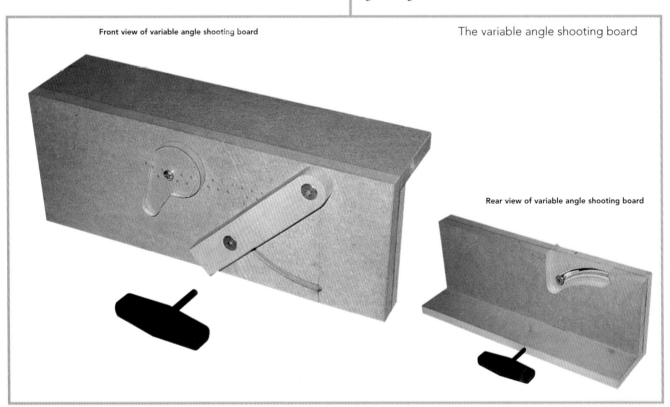

Front view of variable angle shooting board

The variable angle shooting board

Rear view of variable angle shooting board

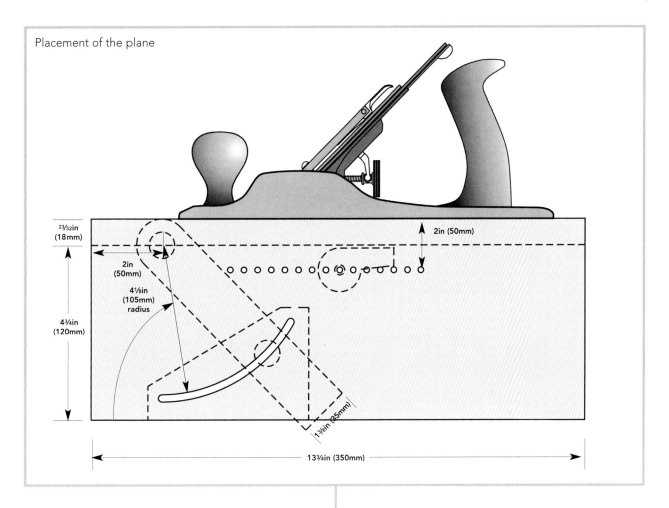

Placement of the plane

2³⁄₃₂in (18mm)

2in (50mm)

2in (50mm)

4¹⁄₈in (105mm) radius

4³⁄₄in (120mm)

1³⁄₈in (35mm)

13³⁄₄in (350mm)

The curved slot is best made with a router and trammel arm. If you don't possess a trammel arm you'll need to improvise. Screw a secondary base plate made from ¼in (6mm) MDF to the base plate of your router. The secondary base plate needs to extend beyond the router base plate long enough to accept a ¼in (6mm) diameter hole which will form the pivot around which the curved slot will be cut, as shown by the dimensions in the drawing. You'll need to use a carbide router cutter, but avoid plunging through in one cut as this will strain it.

Plunge through at the beginning and end of the curved slot and then swing between the two holes with a series of shallow cuts until you have routed all the way through. Decide on the sweep of the curved slot according to your own needs. My own shooting board goes from 90 to 45°. Much less than 45° and the cam clamp is not so efficient. It's also an advantage to drill the cam clamp pivot holes in the vertical section before jointing it to the horizontal platform. The same use of biscuits or a spline ensures good alignment, as recommended with the previous shooting boards. The procedure for gluing up and clamping is also similar.

◆ The adjustable stock

CONSIDERABLE FORCE IS TRANSMITTED TO THE stock from the cam clamp, which in turn has to be firmly held in place so the setting does not change when components are being planed (hence the reason for the simple but sturdy mechanism I have incorporated into the construction). Because the pivot hole at the top of the stock is close to the end, it's essential to use a stable hardwood like maple. After accurately preparing the stock to size, drill a ¼in (6mm) hole for the pivot. Assemble the stock with a temporary ¼in (6mm) screw, and punch through the curved slot from the reverse side to position the centre for the stock locking screw hole, which is also drilled to ¼in (6mm). I used screw heads that are flush and tighten with an Allen key. It's not necessary to recess the heads but if you wish to do so here's an easy way to drill concentric holes of different diameters. Clamp a piece of ²³⁄₃₂in (18mm) MDF to the table of your drill press and drill a ¼in (6mm) diameter hole. Insert a piece of ¼in (6mm) metal rod into the hole to project a few millimetres from the surface. This forms the register for a succession of larger diameter holes when the component is

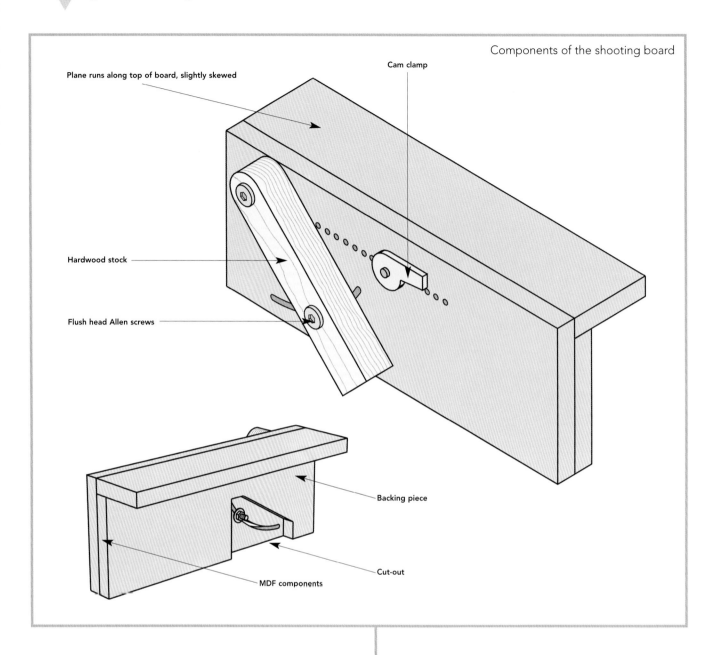

Components of the shooting board

Plane runs along top of board, slightly skewed

Cam clamp

Hardwood stock

Flush head Allen screws

Backing piece

Cut-out

MDF components

positioned over the projecting pin. Care must be exercised as the drill enters to avoid tearing the wood and to control the depth. A lip and spur drill works very well, as do appropriately sized router cutters. Set the depth stop and, finally, although the centre is supported by the pin, make sure the work piece is firmly held as you drill the hole.

◆ The backing piece

THE STOCK LOCKING SCREW PROJECTS THROUGH the curved slot and locks into a hexagonal nut protected by a large washer, to prevent compression damage to the inside face. To accommodate the protrusion of the hexagonal nut, a backing piece, with provision for the pivoting movement of the stock, has to be glued on to the inside face of the vertical section This also reinforces the vertical section making the shooting board more rigid. The principles of use are the same as the other two boards. However, with this shooting board an accurate protractor will make setting up easier and it's advisable to plane a test piece to verify the accuracy of the angle.

MARKING TOOLS

Quality marking and measuring tools for engineers can be relied on for their accuracy and even though the initial cost is high their reliability pays in the long run. I personally own an extensive selection of marking tools but the set-up that I use most is the combination set made by Moore and Wright, also made by Starrett, Mitutoyo and Rabone Chesterman. The standard square and mitre stock of the combination set is essential to the accurate making of the shooting boards featured in this section.

USING THE SHOOTING BOARDS

It is worth spending a little time preparing components for shooting. Saw off any excess, leaving not more than a millimetre to be planed away. With the component that needs to be planed held against the stock and kept in place with the cam clamp the shooting board is positioned in the vice. The platform rests on the bench firmly enough to enable the vice to be closed. If the component is thinner than the width of the stock a packing piece will have to be inserted. The component and shooting board are now firmly held in place.

The act of planing requires some explanation. The plane I favour is a jackplane, as a smoothing plane is too short. Make sure your plane iron is sharpened with a slightly cambered cutting edge. If not you will certainly damage the surface of the platform. Place the plane on the platform and skew it so that the blade centres on the end-grain of the work piece. Try and maintain this orientation through the planing phase. Because you are working over the top of the component, the plane is used with a two-handed grip. However, because the plane has been skewed, the forward section of the sole will be overhanging the work piece and platform and then there is a risk of over-cutting the outer edge of the component.

Hold the plane with both hands gripping the rear handle – it's the large surface area of the rear section of the sole that provides the control. With this downward pressure continue to plane until the plane stops cutting and that's it! With a little practice the awkward two-handed grip is quite easy to master.

The main criticism of these shooting boards is the risk of damaging the surface of the platform. With practice this can be minimized. However, it is possible to glue a layer of clean-grained hardwood ¼in (6mm) thick to the platform, which could be resurfaced if it gets damaged. Better still, carefully glue on a piece of Formica, which should resist damage. Do not glue the Formica on using a contact adhesive. Instead, use a conventional wood glue such as Cascamite or aliphatic resin and apply clamp pressure until the bond has formed. Once again, should you decide to include this refinement, do so before assembling the platform and upright section.

Horizontal shooting boards

Horizontal shooting boards are the perfect answer for intricate pieces of work such as boxes with small components.

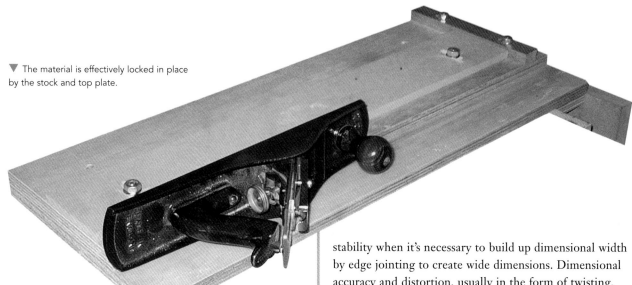

▼ The material is effectively locked in place by the stock and top plate.

SMALL-SCALE, BUT COMPLICATED PIECES ARE something I make quite a number of, usually in the form of boxes with trays and small drawers, where the components are small and thin in section. These are difficult to edge plane, a particular problem being planing edges square and parallel. Also, with small sections, the planing resistance is commensurately very low, so using a shooting board with the plane held on its side presents no problem. Another consideration that prompted my investigation of the horizontal board is the planing of the edges of veneers, which is best carried out with the plane held horizontally. My version of a veneer edging jig, which was instrumental in this exercise, is on page 29.

◆ Construction

I USED EXTERIOR GRADE PLY FOR MY SHOOTING board as it's much more stable than solid wood. The traditional use of beech for many bench-top devices requires careful selection to ensure orientation between radial and tangential growth. This is not a serious problem for narrow components, but seriously affects

stability when it's necessary to build up dimensional width by edge jointing to create wide dimensions. Dimensional accuracy and distortion, usually in the form of twisting, is quite commonly associated with beech and with most of the temperate hardwoods. All the components are best prepared on an accurately set-up table saw. The two layers that form the base of the shooting board can be glued and screwed together. I also used biscuits to ensure good edge alignment and parallel orientation. Two features give this shooting board high levels of control: the adjustable stock and top plate.

◆ Adjustable stock

THE END OF SHOOTING BOARD STOCKS THAT ARE permanently fixed in place get damaged when shavings are removed, resulting in poor end-grain control. I overcame this problem by letting the stock into a groove routed into the upper surface and held in place by bolts that run in slots. ⅜in (10mm) bolts are inserted through the bottom and the heads are recessed into hexagonal slots to hold the bolts captive, enabling the nuts to be tightened from above (using the same method described for drilling variable diameter concentric holes). The stock is best made from a stable hardwood with a chamfer cut on the trailing corner to prevent breakout. Determine which end to place the stock to suit left- or right-handed use, and make sure the stock is square to the edge.

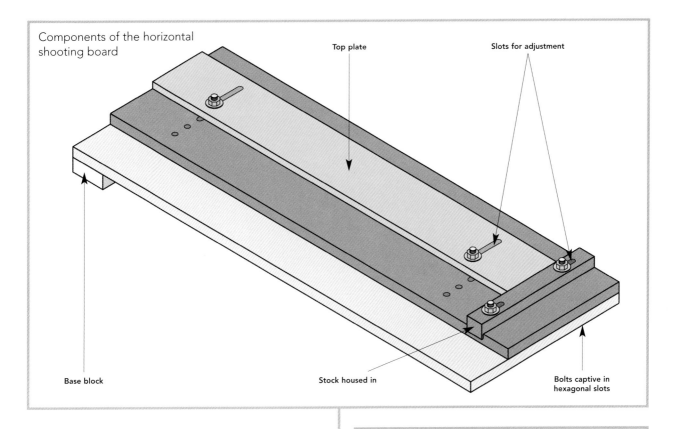

Components of the horizontal shooting board

Top plate

Slots for adjustment

Base block

Stock housed in

Bolts captive in hexagonal slots

◆ Top plate

THE TOP PLATE IS ANOTHER ELEMENT THAT GIVES you more control, particularly if you need to prepare several components of the same width, obviating the need for marking lines with a marking gauge before planing. Again, it consists of a strip of board material held in place with ⅜in (10mm) nuts and bolts running in slots, and ½in (12mm) thick MDF is ideal. To set the width, I use the ruler sliding facility on my engineers' combination square. Set the dimension in two positions along the edge and lock the top plate in place, and do double-check the setting.

◆ The base block

THE LAST ASPECT OF THE CONSTRUCTION OF THE shooting board is the base block which hooks on to the edge of your bench, or can be trapped in the vice to hold the board securely. Finally, glue and secure the block in place at the opposite end to the stock.

USING THE SHOOTING BOARD

The work piece is effectively trapped by the stock and top plate, requiring a little downward pressure to hold it in place. Although it can be used to shoot end-grain, this board is intended for planing long grain. Long components present no problems in planing, as the transference of pressure from the toe to the heel of the plane is distributed easily along the length. This is true for short pieces but a little practice is worthwhile to develop the necessary dexterity for the transference of pressure when planing shorter lengths. Continue until the plane stops cutting and the component will be accurately planed to width and the edge will be square. The only possible limitation to the process could be the squareness of the plane sole to the sides, or a blade cutting edge that is not parallel to the sole. Modern planes are quite accurately machined but if you discover the sole-side relationship is not square, try adjusting the cutting edge with the lateral adjusting lever to correct the problem. The alternative is to have the sides milled square by an engineer.

Veneer edging jig

This veneer edging jig eases the difficulty of edge jointing veneers by using a conventional shooting board.

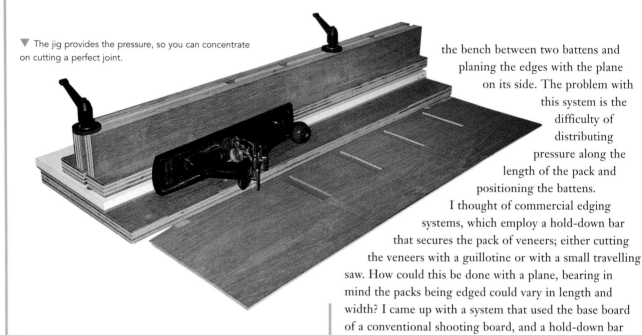

▼ The jig provides the pressure, so you can concentrate on cutting a perfect joint.

For many decades, veneering has been associated with the large-scale commercial manufacture of furniture. When I first started making one-of-a-kind pieces back in the late 1960s the thought of doing my own veneering seemed to be out of the question. The cost of equipment was formidable. I used to take my veneering needs to a specialist company in London who supplied the substrates, lipped the components, and supplied, laid and sanded the veneers. It was a total service, but there were problems. Quality left a lot to be desired, the edge jointing was not very good and the sanding of the surfaces varied a great deal.

Self-sufficiency

Now I have a comprehensive set-up, which includes a two-platen veneer press. With the affordability of vacuum bag presses, and the increasing use of veneering amongst small-scale woodworkers, the question of edge jointing veneer poses problems. Most of us improvise by clamping a pack of veneer down onto the bench between two battens and planing the edges with the plane on its side. The problem with this system is the difficulty of distributing pressure along the length of the pack and positioning the battens.

I thought of commercial edging systems, which employ a hold-down bar that secures the pack of veneers; either cutting the veneers with a guillotine or with a small travelling saw. How could this be done with a plane, bearing in mind the packs being edged could vary in length and width? I came up with a system that used the base board of a conventional shooting board, and a hold-down bar with two projections of threaded rod going through it at adjustable intervals along the length of the base board. The pack of veneers being edged is held together temporarily with a couple of pieces of masking tape so it behaves as a 'pack' rather than as separate sheets of veneer that are difficult to manipulate into position. The feature that makes insertion of the pack extremely controllable is the introduction of pairs of springs at each end between the base board and the hold-down bar. This creates a horizontal window into which the pack is easily inserted and positioned.

Construction

The base board is constructed in exactly the same way as the horizontal shooting board described above. When I made mine I had a length of white melamine-coated board which I used for the upper layer, but good quality exterior grade ply would work equally well. Accurate preparation is paramount and this is best done on a table saw. If you do decide to use

The jig components

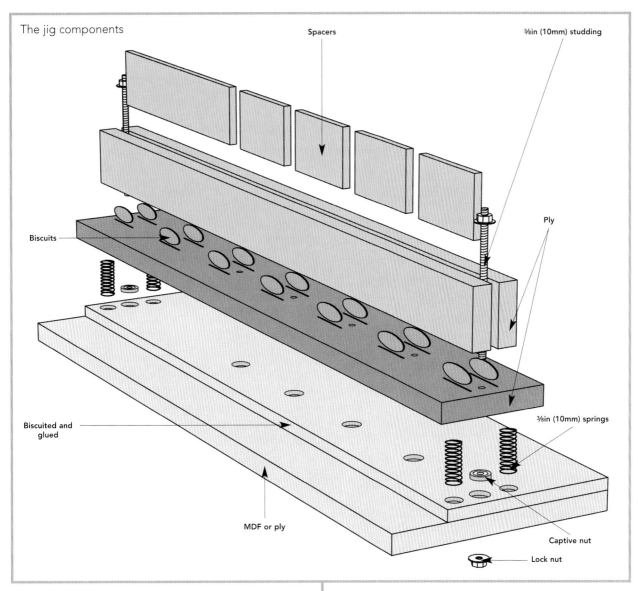

Spacers

⅜in (10mm) studding

Ply

Biscuits

⅜in (10mm) springs

Biscuited and glued

MDF or ply

Captive nut

Lock nut

melamine board it's still a good idea to glue and screw the two layers together. The added control of edge alignment, with the inclusion of biscuits, makes assembly that much easier. Next, drill the holes for the threaded rod. ⅜in (10mm) threaded rod – or 'studding' as it's often called – is readily available from any supplier of ironmongery. The holes are counter-bored from above and below to accept nuts and washers. To avoid having to reposition the upper nuts when changing the positions of the threaded posts, I put a drop of Superglue into the thread and this holds them in place. I also use a box spanner to tighten up the holding nuts from below.

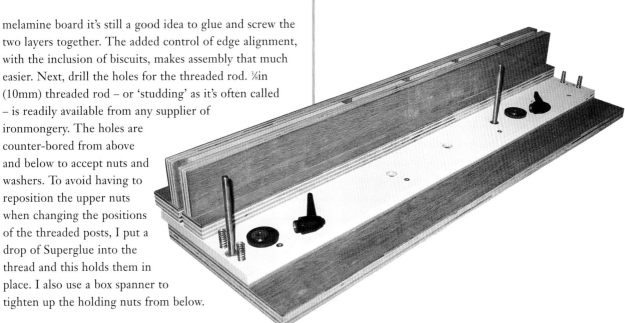

◆ The hold-down bar

THE HOLD-DOWN BAR IS A KEY COMPONENT IN the eventual success of the jig. It needs to be sturdy enough to withstand the loads applied at the ends so that pressure is distributed along the entire length of the pack being held down. To achieve this without excessive bulk I utilized the engineering principle of a 'T' cross-section. The slots going through to accommodate the vertical rods are created by sandwiching sections of ½in (12mm) MDF between the vertical sections of the 'T'. I use biscuits for the alignment of components for the hold-down bar, but routed splines would be just as effective. Once again, accuracy of alignment and ease of assembly ensure good distribution of load and an effective partnership between the base board and the hold-down bar.

◆ Hold-apart springs

I BUY SPRINGS FROM A SPECIALIST SUPPLIER FOR a variety of my adventures in design. From the Lee Spring Ltd catalogue it's possible to select the right springs for the job via their easy-to-use specification, and they're quite prepared to supply small quantities. I chose stainless steel springs 2in (50mm) long with a diameter of ⅜in (10mm).

Drill holes in the base board first and then, using dowel transfer points, position the hold-down bar in place to mark the centres for the upper holes. If you do not have dowel transfer points mark the centres carefully by measurement and drill ½in (12mm) diameter holes to allow for drill drift. In fact, it's advisable to drill the upper holes bigger than the diameter of the springs to facilitate easy assembly. In the drawing I've shown hexagonal nuts to secure the hold-down bar. These work quite well, but you'll see from the photograph my own jig uses Bristol locking levers, which obviate the need for a spanner.

▼ A more sophisticated 6ft (2m) version.

◆ Using the jig

I'VE NOT SHOWN A BASE BLOCK WITH WHICH TO hook the jig onto the edge of your workbench. The overall length is such that it's better to clamp the jig down onto a convenient part of the bench. Once you are happy with this position, the jig can be screwed down and the screws removed when it's not in use. Position the jig in such a way that you can stand at the end and plane with the plane on its side. For long pieces of veneer it may be necessary to stand with the plane on the far side of the jig. I find in practice that it's not necessary to plane the edge of a pack until the plane stops cutting. Quite often it's only necessary to remove a few shavings to true up the edges of a pack and when this is done I check for accuracy with a straight edge.

▼ Trimming edge of laminated form made up of edge-jointed veneers.

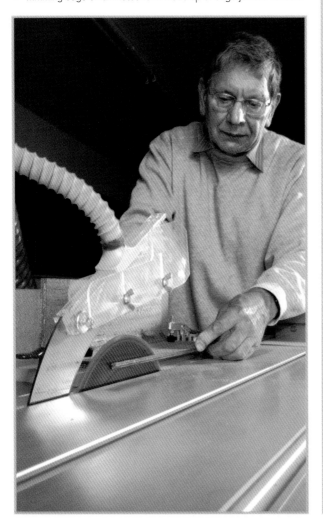

TAPELESS JOINTS

Once you're satisfied with the straightness of the planed edges, the leaves of veneer can be taped together for laying. Standard practice is to use a thin, gummed strip, which is removed by sanding after the veneer has been laid. If an effective power sanding system is not available the tape can be removed by dampening it with water and then peeling it off.

I've developed a system that glues the edges of the veneers together resulting in tapeless joints for laying. On the show surface of the veneers I hold the joint together with short strips of $^{23}\!/_{32}$in (18mm) wide masking tape. Slightly stretch the tape and its elastic quality brings the edges together. Space these strips to hold the edges together firmly at approximately 6in (150mm) to 8in (200mm) apart. Then run a length of tape over these strips along the length of the joint. Now turn the veneers over and let one leaf hang down over the edge of your bench. This opens up the joint. With a small glue bottle, on which the spout has been cut to produce a 'bird's mouth' effect, run a line of glue into the edges and then close the fold.

Carefully scrape off the excess glue and cross-tape to hold the joint together. When the glue has dried, peel off the tape from both sides and you have a tapeless joint. I use a small plastic bottle with a spout and the glue I favour is aliphatic resin, the same glue I use for laying the veneers.

Introduction to joints

Generations of craftsmen will have been introduced to the craft by learning how to make a mortice-and-tenon joint. This chapter explores the basic principles of joint-making.

FOR MANY WOODWORKERS, AN INTEREST IN JOINTS forms the bedrock of their pursuit. In this section I intend to address the fundamentals of making joints with the amazing variety of tools that are available to craftsmen today. I also want to strongly question the notion of the 'right' and 'wrong' way of doing things, preferring the word 'appropriate' and all that it represents.

The way my own attitude to woodworking has evolved, I now feel that with the benefit of experience I can question the established body of knowledge and make judgements that produce workable results. I am quite sure that this attitude was part of the rationale in the evolution of the craft through the centuries. However, it was probably supressed by the authoritarian attitude to passing on knowledge that was prevalent, for example, during the period of the Craft Guild System. For the apprentice, the master knew it all and the learner was not encouraged to question. This works well in the formative period of education but can easily lead to a mindset that excludes experimentation and evolution. I prefer to address the questions of the how, and the why, of making and using joints in the construction of wooden objects. In this regard, it is worth considering the development of joints and their evolution through history.

◆ Joints through history

THE HISTORY OF WOODWORKING HAS BEEN ONE of constant evolution, prompted by breakthroughs in man's understanding of materials and construction, progress that would not have occurred without a constant questioning of accepted practice.

Stone Age craftspeople used wood mainly for the construction of shelters and the weapons with which they defended themselves and hunted for food. There is little evidence of the inventiveness with which they wrought materials, even though the skill with which they worked stone was awesome. The only joint that they used in constructing things from wood was the post and hole, the forerunner of the mortice-and-tenon joint. The hole could be bored with a stone auger and the tapered post that fitted into it could be shaped with an axe or a scraper.

Egyptian craftsmen used a simple dovetail joint for the construction of sarcophagus linings. One large tail held by two half pins utilized the interlocking principle of the dovetail and rawhide thongs laced through a series of holes made the joint permanent. They also used mortice and tenons and halving joints to construct the complex stools and chairs that have been excavated from tombs. Egyptian woodworkers also had access to metal, for example using bronze to fashion chisels and saws. When you see examples of their saws it is amazing to think that they achieved such incredible results with these primitive tools.

Dovetail joint on Egyptian sarcophagus linings.

Rawhide thongs

By the time that cabinetmaking had become an established profession in the 17th century, metallurgical technology was very advanced. The development of making and heat-treating steel for military purposes led to the production of a variety of refined tools for all crafts, not least for woodworking. Introducing drawers into storage chests brought about the dovetail joint as we know it today and this was only possible because of the skills available to make fine-bladed saws. In more recent times the development of rotating cutters, such as those associated with shaping metal in engineering, have been adapted to the needs of mass production and once again the dovetail joint has been influenced by this technology. Some of the earliest containers had no joints at all. Dugout chests, used by the clergy to keep ceremonial valuables safe, were made from a log with a hollow carved out, and a simple lid strapped on for security. Such chests can still be found in early churches, often built into some part of the structure for security and permanence.

▼ This oak chest was made in the 1340s and belonged to the then Bishop of Durham.

A HISTORY OF CABINETMAKING

Man's longstanding fascination with containers, particularly boxes, is well documented and archaeologists have unearthed considerable evidence of it in recent times. Many ancient examples of baked clay pots, which can survive the rigours of time when buried under layers of soil, have been discovered over the years. Other materials, such as metal, leather and wood, were also commonly used to make drinking vessels and food containers; however, leather and wood tend to decay and few examples from early times exist. Nevertheless, in terms of wooden domestic artefacts, it is safe to say that boxes and containers were some of the earliest possessions made by man. For these people, the chest or coffer was long given pride of place, providing a safe haven for the small valuable items which represented their wealth.

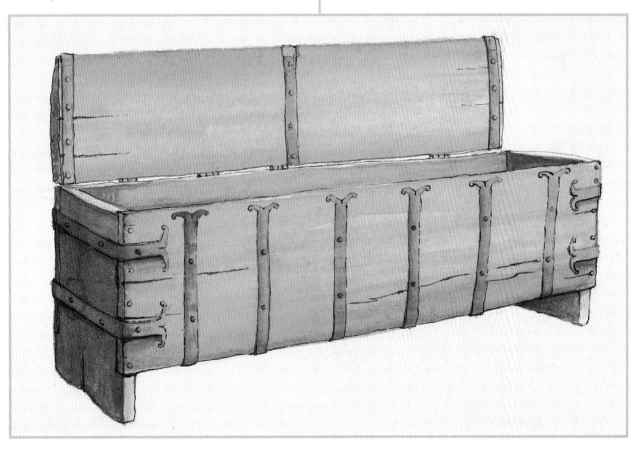

THE BIRTH OF A NEW PROFESSION

Progress made by craftsmen through the ages has led to improved technology and a better understanding of materials. When wood was first fashioned into planks, the simplest technique was to hold four pieces together at the corners with pegs or iron nails.

Over time, the mortice-and-tenon joint became the most widely used joint for fashioning containers. In turn, this eventually led to the frame and panelled chests of medieval times. These evolved into the typical chair style of those early times, as it was not unusual for the chest to be used as a seat. The technique of using four corner posts and horizontal rails as enclosing panels was adapted to make storage furniture for household items.

This method continued well into the 16th century as it suited oak, the most popular timber of the time. A hundred years later other timbers were being introduced into furniture-making, with walnut taking pride of place. It was a timber which had to be sawn to produce planks, and could not be as effectively riven as oak. The planks were wide enough to produce carcasses that did not rely on frames and panels, so a new method of construction was employed. The dovetail joint came into widespread use, and with it came the birth of a new profession. Prior to this period, carpentry and joinery were the main woodworking trades, but with the more involved construction of furniture came the specialized cabinetmaker. Through the centuries, these craftsmen continued to ply their trade until demand for their products, through an increase in wealth and home ownership, led to mass production and the inevitable development of man-made boards such as plywood and chipboard.

◆ The nature of wood

MOST WOODWORKING JOINTS ARE WAYS OF combining pieces of wood to form constructions that benefit from the strength of the material. They are also limited by the complexities of the material, the most challenging of which is the orientation of cell distribution. The main issue that influences the way a joint is made is grain direction, which is the result of the way a tree grows and has a considerable effect on the removal of material. In most joints, the removal of material to create 'location' often breaks the continuity of wood fibres, which affects the linear strength of the component. The resultant weakness can be accommodated structurally if the joint is part of a series of joints, such as those joining the corners of a frame. You can also overcome constructional weaknesses if you think about the amount of wood that is removed and how much is left.

Expansion and contraction of wood also has consequences for joints. Gaps can open up and joints can fail completely if this factor is ignored. Sometimes you have to accept a small amount of movement as part of the overall character of a piece. After all, the ambient conditions in which a piece exists will vary and the wood will respond accordingly. However, disregarding timber movement altogether will undoubtedly have consequences during the life of the piece.

The nature of wood also affects aesthetics. Being a natural material, with all that the growing conditions and particular features of the species bestow on each individual board, the aesthetic effect of combining different woods can often be stunning. The patterns and juxtaposition of joints in a piece can also contribute to the appearance. In particular the punctuation of end-grain, as is evident in through-dovetails and mortice-and-tenon joints, can give a piece a strong individual signature. This was a prominent feature of furniture from the Arts and Crafts period, when honesty of construction and truth to materials was a major statement in the movement's philosophy.

◆ Proportional ratios

AS A GENERAL RULE, WHEN DETERMINING HOW much wood to remove and how much to leave, I try to apportion half the strength of the joint to each component. At school my woodwork teacher said that a mortice-and-tenon joint should be divided into thirds, the tenon being a third of the thickness of the component. During a session investigating the structure of furniture

I tested the strength of mortice-and-tenon joints and was surprised to discover that the one-third tenon failed very easily. Of the ten different proportions that my students and I tested, the strongest combination was a 50:50 sharing of material thickness between the two parts of the joint. The tenon was half the thickness of the rail. In a situation where a construction requires joints with which you are not familiar, consider the proportions and if still in doubt make a test joint and subject it to the kind of loads that would be present when the piece is in use.

Many years ago I made a sedilia (group of three seats) for a small chapel. The central bishop's chair had to have arms and I was concerned that the front legs supporting the ends of the arms would restrict the priest's robes. My sketch designs showed arms that projected as cantilevers from the chair back. Knowing that the sitter would push down on the arms to get out of the chair, I found it necessary to make a prototype of the joint and test it rigorously. I am happy to say that it worked.

▼ This sedilia was designed and made so that robes would not catch on the arms, yet the arms would bear the weight of someone pushing down on them in order to stand.

Front elevation

Side elevation

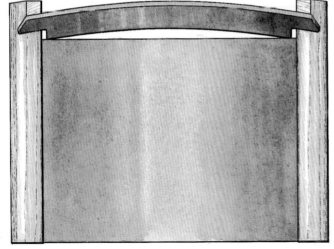

Plan (motif not shown)

Specification. Show-wood in Oak, to be finished in nitro-cellulose lacquer. Seat and back in pre-formed plywood covered in dark green leather. Motif inlaid in contrasting yellow leather.

Scale: 3 inches to a foot

designed by	R.D. Ingham
drawn by	

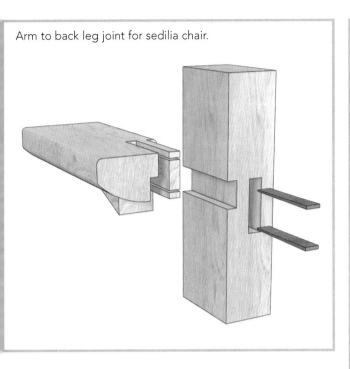

Arm to back leg joint for sedilia chair.

Glue penetrates wood fibres and forms a matrix that bonds surfaces together. The most absorbent surface is end-grain but, paradoxically, it provides the weakest bond. If possible, when designing a joint try to avoid end-grain to end-grain contact. Face-grain to face-grain contact is stronger, especially if the two surfaces have the grain running in the same direction. This factor is used to great effect in butt joints. Face-grain contact that is of contra-direction is subject to movement in opposite directions and in situations where the surfaces are large the bond can shear. Of course, whenever a basic premise is stated, there is usually an example that contradicts it. Plywood, for example, is made up of contra-directional layers and as such a face-grain bond will not fail, but this is due to the proportions of thin layers involved in the construction. Bearing these principles in mind, the strength of a joint can be improved if the internal surface area that can be glued is maximized.

This is the thinking behind twin or multiple tenons. If one large tenon is used, the resultant weakness of the component that carries the mortice is evident. Dividing the tenon into smaller sections spreads the load between both parts of the joint and maintains the continuity of linear fibres in the mortice component.

◆ Location

I MENTIONED EARLIER THAT THE EGYPTIANS USED a single dovetail to join the corners of sarcophagus linings. This interlocking junction between two boards held them together effectively while holes were drilled to accept the rawhide thongs. The other important factor was the positive location of one part of the joint into the other part. Some joints need to be located in one direction so that one component can be manipulated into position for final alignment. A typical example is a sliding dovetail, as used for a cabinet shelf that is slipped into place after the main carcass has been assembled. A mortice and tenon, on the other hand, has positive location in two directions and benefits from this feature when it is assembled.

◆ Joints and glue

T HERE IS NO DOUBT THAT MODERN ADHESIVES have made a major contribution to the effectiveness of woodworking joints (see page 112). Longer open-assembly times and very good adhesion result in ease of use and almost permanent bonds. This has its advantages but it will make restoration more difficult in future, as – unlike the heat-reversible animal glues of previous times – most modern adhesives cannot be reversed to enable a piece to be dismantled.

◆ Tightness of joints

A NOTHER IMPORTANT CONSIDERATION AFFECTED by glue is the tightness of joints. I remember from my early involvement with woodwork, the challenge of making joints where the fit had to be tight. Gaps, especially in through joints, were unacceptable! I prided myself on the tightness of my joints until I made a piece that was almost impossible to glue up. In fact I had to take the construction apart, clean the glue off the joints and ease the fit. It was a complex piece and the open assembly time was quite long. The wood had absorbed so much moisture from the glue that the resultant expansion of fibres made the joints even tighter. The shoulders would not go together, the result: gaps! Try and aim for a fit that can be assembled by hand, with a little assistance from a mallet or cramp to completely close the joint. A single mortice and tenon should be easy enough to assemble by hand and as long as there is no lateral movement the joint will be perfect when glued. A more complex joint such as a dovetail, with the number of internal surfaces that make contact, will be tighter due to the friction that needs to be overcome.

Examples of carcass joints

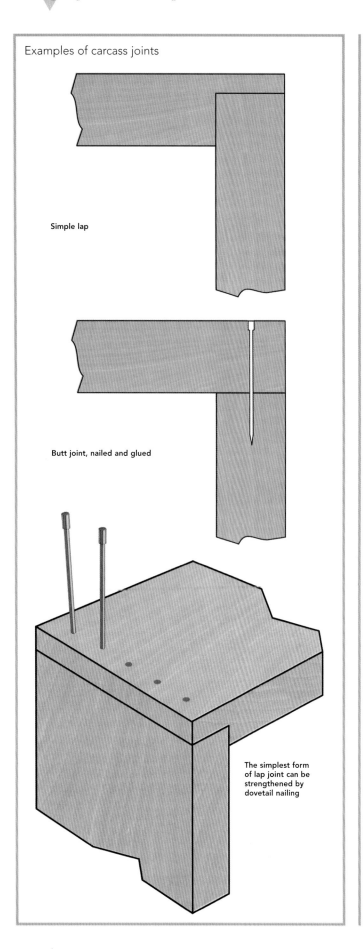

Simple lap

Butt joint, nailed and glued

The simplest form of lap joint can be strengthened by dovetail nailing

Corner butt joint

THIS, AS ITS NAME IMPLIES, IS A SURFACE -to-surface joint, which, if made from solid wood, suffers from the weakness of an end-grain to face-grain junction. It is bound to fail if it relies only on a glue bond to hold it together. It is also difficult to align the surfaces of the joint, even if nails are used to form the initial hold. Nails are perfectly suitable for a simple container.

Once the two pieces forming the corner are lined up, and a couple of nails have been driven in, the joint will hold until the remaining nails have been inserted. Although the joint can be strengthened by the addition of glue, further strength can be imparted if the nails or panel pins are driven in at a slight angle to replicate the configuration of dovetails. These days it is likely that containers such as this will be made from man-made boards. The same approach is suitable as for solid wood.

Whichever way the joint is held together, the most important factor before assembly is to make sure that the contacting surfaces are well prepared and square. This is a challenge if the material has to be trued up by hand. End-grain is difficult to plane, as breakout is always a problem, unless a shooting board is used. A table saw, if available, is the most appropriate machine with which to square up the components. The problem of poor location is the main weakness with the corner butt joint. There are various ways this can be improved, such as an increase in glue area, which adds to the strength of the joint.

The most convenient method of jointing for a corner butt joint is to use a biscuit jointer. In general, when I employ biscuits in a construction I consider them primarily as locations, so I don't make a real effort to put glue in the slots. For a corner butt joint, the major strength comes from the glue in the biscuit slots.

Lap joint

THE NEXT OPTION IS A SIMPLE LAP JOINT, WHERE one component has a rebate which locates the other. This can easily be carried out by machine, as it is quite demanding to produce a rebate across grain with hand tools. The router makes this joint simple as does a table saw, but, with either machine, care must be taken to avoid breakout at the end of the cut. This type of joint is strong enough to be held together by glue, but it is difficult to assemble as it needs to be cramped in two directions to close the joint completely. The location is most effective in one direction only. The effort required and the problems of assembly virtually rule out this joint.

More examples of carcass joints

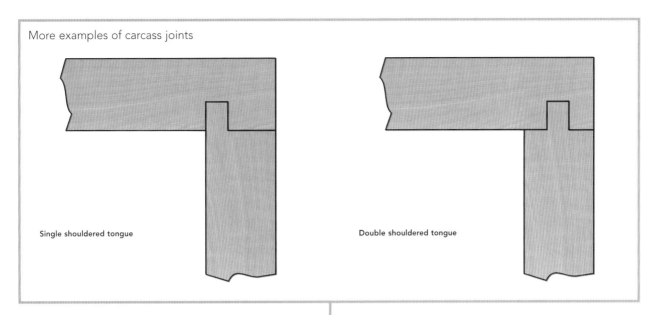

Single shouldered tongue

Double shouldered tongue

The introduction of a spline or tongue takes away the need for a rebate, and the ideal tool for the job is a router. It's even easier if a router table is available, as it can be difficult to control a hand-held router and fence on end-grain components. The tongue can be made from the material of the end-grain component by cutting a rebate on either side, which will leave a projection.

▼ A hall cabinet with bird's eye maple and walnut inlay.

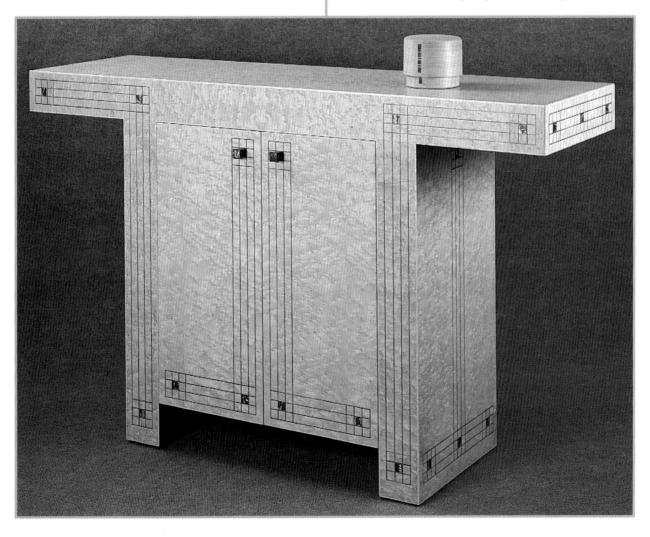

Examples of carcass joints

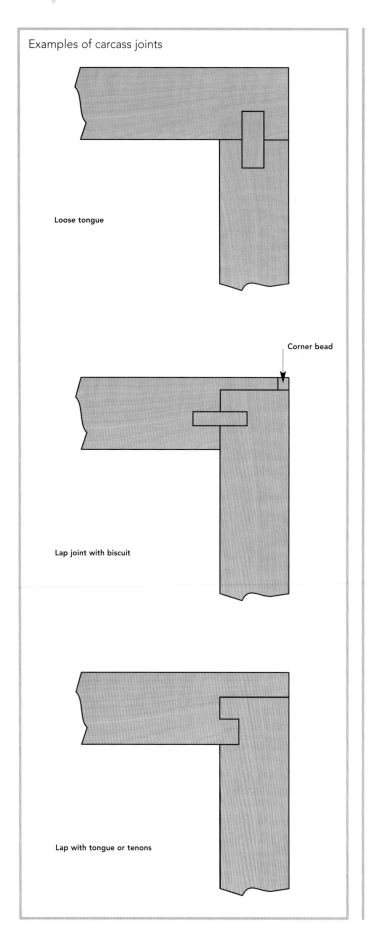

Loose tongue

Corner bead

Lap joint with biscuit

Lap with tongue or tenons

▲ A lap joint with mortice-and-tenon location for the hall cabinet.

GROOVES

A groove cut in the face of the corresponding component will complete the location. It's also possible to achieve a similar result with one rebate, cut from the outer face. Cutting a groove in the joining faces of both components, and inserting a loose tongue enables one cutter setting to be used for both grooves.

To address the question of subsequent movement resulting from expansion and contraction, the loose tongue should be cross-grained. However, as this method of construction is unlikely to be used for a sophisticated piece of furniture, the ideal material for the tongue is plywood.

More examples of carcass joints

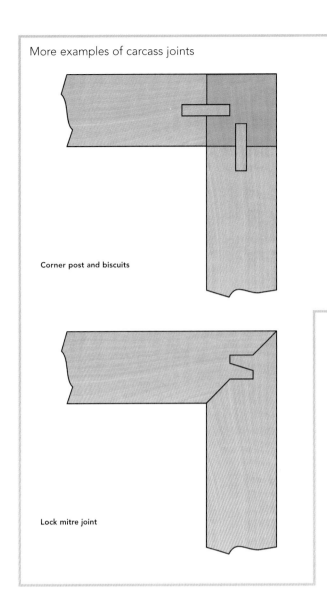

Corner post and biscuits

Mitre with loose tongue or biscuit

Lock mitre joint

▼ Poor equipment can let you down no matter how much planning and preparation you have done. Using well-maintained tools that you can trust will help make sure your joints are perfect first time.

◆ Equipment

My introductory thoughts would not be complete if I did not say something about equipment. Very often, even though a process is carried out with care and application, the results fall below expectations. In such cases, rather than abandoning the job we usually resort to adjustments and tweak the joint to make it fit.

The aim should be to get it right first time. If all the planning and knowledge of the processes were in place there are two possibilities that could influence the outcome: lack of skill and poor equipment. The lack of skill can be addressed through practice and diligence. But poor equipment will continue to let you down.

Edge joints

In terms of a progression from simple to complex – it is appropriate to consider edge joints first, then mortice and tenons and then finally look at dovetails.

Edge joints are associated today with the creation of wide surfaces from narrower boards. This has not always been the case. The main limitation that earlier generations of woodworkers experienced was that of converting trees into planks, which did not come about until the development of suitable conversion systems, such as pit saws. In fact, this inability to saw planks had a marked effect on construction and in turn on what we interpret as design, an effect that is clear when we look at pieces of work from bygone times.

One reason why oak (*Quercus robur*) was favoured for furniture-making from the Dark Ages to the end of the Middle Ages was the fact that it could be split or 'riven' to make planks. Although these planks were tapered in cross-section due to the fact that the splitting action exploits the weakness of oak's medullary rays, they could be made parallel in thickness with an adze or side axe and then scraped to an acceptable surface.

Tapered cross-sections were used where appropriate, for instance as the strips that make up a clinker-built boat, and this was an early example of an edge joint – although it would be more correct to refer to it as a surface-to-surface joint. The joint was made watertight with the addition of caulking and pitch.

Edge jointing as we know it today became a reality when reliable planes with long soles became available. Before this time, although they existed, planes were not really suitable for reliable surface and edge treatments. It was not until walnut (*Juglans* sp) became fashionable in the 17th century that edge jointing became necessary. This is because walnut cannot be riven and has to be sawn to produce planks, which were often too narrow for case furniture.

◆ Preparation

Boards must be planed to thickness before edge jointing can be attempted. Even if you do not possess a planer-thicknesser it is possible to buy pre-planed boards or go to someone who offers a planing service.

I do, however, remember preparing all the timber for a sideboard and a dressing table entirely by hand and it was a salutary and beneficial experience that taught me a great deal about preparation processes and the complex nature of timber.

▶ Planing an edge joint.

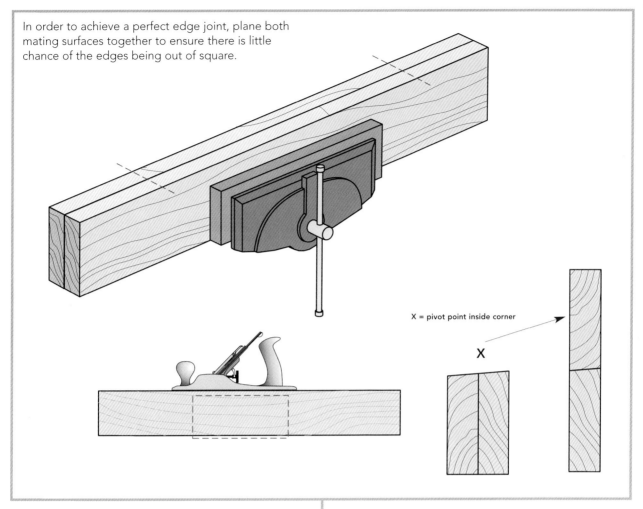

In order to achieve a perfect edge joint, plane both mating surfaces together to ensure there is little chance of the edges being out of square.

X = pivot point inside corner

X

While the long beds of a jointer are not necessary for planing edge joints on small-scale work, the beds of a machine planer must be parallel as any drop will cause the edges planed to run out. Although it is possible to glue the edge joints straight from the planer, I often shoot the edges again with a hand plane to 'open' the surfaces to glue penetration. The rotating cutting action of planer blades is powerful enough to compress the fibres being cut, particularly in dense woods such as oak. Skimming the edges with a hand plane overcomes this problem. The best tool is a long-sole trying plane or jointer, but a well-tuned jackplane will also produce good results.

It is possible to plane each edge separately but there is a risk that the edges will go out of square to the faces, causing poor surface alignment. It is easier to plane two edges at the same time by holding two boards together in a vice and planing both edges at once. So long as the inside corners form the pivot, any angularity that might result will be cancelled out when the boards are opened out. Try to avoid affecting the linear straightness when shooting the edges, although a slight hollow can be cramped out when gluing up.

◆ Gluing up

In the past, edge joints or butt joints to give them their period name – were glued together without cramps, cramps being fairly recent additions to the cabinetmaker's arsenal. The edges were planed accurately to produce a good edge-to-edge contact and the quick-gel property and suction of animal glue was used to hold the joint together.

This method of assembling an edge joint was known as a 'rub joint'. In addition to the gelling of the glue the excess was forced out by moving the components forward and back with a rubbing action until resistance was felt and the bond had been formed. It was then left leaning against battens until the glue set. The considerable time this took was a significant factor in the development of faster-setting glues.

With sash cramps, the job is so much easier, resulting in glue-line-free joints. In theory, if the joint has been planed slightly hollow, one cramp in the middle should be sufficient. In practice, this usually is not the case, particularly with boards over a metre in length.

▲ The flexibility of the tape allows the joint to be opened for spreading glue.

▲ Edge jointing cedar drawer bottoms using masking tape.

▲ Taped up boards.

My preference is to allocate one cramp to about 12in (300mm) of board length. It is also a good idea to place cramps above and below the boards being glued. In this way the contacting cramp bars cancel out the tendency for distortion that occurs if all the cramps are placed below the boards. This is particularly relevant when thin sections are being glued.

When gluing up edge joints in thinner boards such as drawer bottoms or drawer sides I prefer not to use cramps at all. I prepare the timber as described earlier and shoot pairs of edges to eliminate the out-of-squareness of the mating edges. Then I hold the edges together with masking tape at intervals along the joint. Another strip of tape is applied along the length of the joint. Slightly stretch the tape and the elasticity brings the edges together with amazing force. The joint can then be opened and one component hung over the edge of the bench while glue is applied.

Close the joint and tape the opposite side, once again stretching the masking tape. In addition to providing sufficient force to hold the edges together the tape also aligns surfaces and all of this is achieved without any distortion from cramps. I even edge joint veneers using this technique.

After removing the tape the veneers can be pressed. With care, the alignment of surfaces can be so good as to require no planing at all after the glue has cured. Even the little excess glue that oozes out when the joint is closed can be scraped off before the second set of tape strips is applied.

After the tape is removed a light sanding with a random orbit sander is all that is necessary for components such as drawer bottoms. Drawer sides can be thicknessed or skimmed with a hand plane to ensure accuracy of surfaces and thickness. If several boards are involved to make up a wide section, break up

the assembly into shorter sessions responding to the open assembly time. To avoid damage from cramp shoes, protect exposed edges with cramping blocks.

◆ Surface location

THE EDGE JOINTS I HAVE REFERRED TO SO FAR do not incorporate any form of location, surface alignment being achieved only by careful assembly. Sophisticated cramping systems, such as Plano clamps, that apply pressure both to the edges and faces of boards, are expensive but justified if a lot of solid-wood edge jointing is required, but the joint can be located with other effective systems.

▲ Biscuits are the most common of location joints – note the registration board which keeps the jointer flat.

◆ Biscuit joints

Probably the most appropriate is the use of biscuits, the main function of which is to provide positive location that makes assembly and gluing up much easier. The small increase in glue area that the indentation for the biscuit creates adds only marginally to the strength of the joint, so I do not make a special effort to put glue in the slots.

◆ Tongue-and-grooved joints

Tongue-and-grooved edge joints have been around for many decades and are usually associated with match-boarding where the joint is assembled dry. Even with matched sets of cutters, either with a router or a spindle moulder, it is quite difficult to get glue-line-free results.

◆ Loose tongue or spline joint

A loose tongue or spline overcomes this problem of visible glue lines. In addition to the very obvious advantage of good location, the increase in gluing area produces a stronger joint. This would be my choice if the result of using a combination of narrow boards to construct one wide section was going to be subjected to high structural loads. The ideal material for the loose tongues is plywood, although MDF is in many situations a suitable alternative.

Be prepared when cutting the groove to respond to variations in plywood thicknesses. It is better to make two cuts with a cutter that is narrower than the thickness of the ply than to play around adjusting the loose tongue to fit the groove.

Be sure that all grooves are cut with the fence against the face side. Recently I invested in a MicroFence edge guide for my router that gives me precise control over this kind of problem. The router is the ideal tool for stopped grooves if the appearance of the loose tongue is to be avoided on the end-grain.

Single tongue up to 1¼in (30mm) and double tongue for joints of 1¼in (30mm) plus

Router bit joint, used mainly in industry

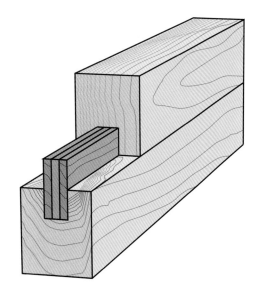 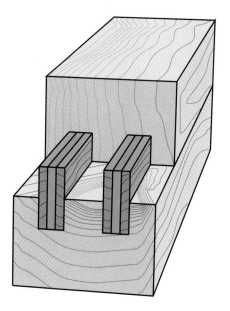 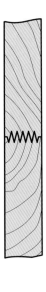

Through grooves can also be cut effectively using a table saw. Remember also that the loose tongue needs to be an easy fit in the grooves as it will expand when glue is applied. The joint could then become too tight, resulting in obvious glue lines. A single loose tongue, which is not more than a third of the thickness of the boards being edge jointed, is sufficient for timber up to 1¼in (30mm) thick. The depth of the groove in each piece should be equal to the thickness of the tongue. At more than 1¼in (30mm) in thickness a strength advantage is gained if two tongues are inserted because the glue area is increased.

◆ Dowels

DOWELS CAN ALSO BE USED TO PROVIDE assembly location, but to a large extent this method has been replaced by biscuits. It is quite difficult to mark out and drill holes accurately in the edges of boards using conventional drilling techniques. A good dowel jig would overcome this problem. Sized, chamfered and ribbed dowels would make the job easier.

◆ Self-locating edge joints

SELF-LOCATING EDGE JOINTS CAN BE PRODUCED with profiled router cutters. The manufacturers claim that the results are glue-line-free, but I have not used them so I can't say. With good machines, care in preparation and use of a router table, these cutters work well. Spindle moulder cutters are also available for this type of located edge joint, but the effectiveness of this approach would depend on the quantity of work being produced and the size of components being handled.

DERIVATION

The term 'to and fro' comes from this process of splitting or riving oak to make planks. The tool used to rive oak board was called a fro and the splitting action was made more efficient by moving the fro forwards and backwards.

COMB SPREADER

Glue can be applied quickly and easily on all edge joints by using a comb spreader. The spreader leaves just the right amount of glue, making cleaning up a task to enjoy later on.

STAINING SOLUTION

Staining can result from the cramp bars that have to touch the faces of boards coming into contact with glue. While these rust stains can sometimes be planed out later, with timbers that contain tannic acid the blue stain can penetrate quite deeply. Protect the cramp bar with masking tape or place a strip of plastic sheet in between the contacting surfaces.

▼ Edge-jointed veneers for laminated components.

Coopered edge joints

Coopering has largely been replaced by laminating, but coopered edge joints are the perfect solution if you need to create the impression of solid timber.

Careful selection and orientation of grain is an important consideration in both the aesthetic composition and the future stability of a piece of furniture. It is disturbing, to say the least, if the stiles of a framed door show the grain leaning to one side, causing the piece to look unstable.

Equally important is the potential for distortion if edge-jointed boards that comprise the width of a tabletop are not assembled with the end-grain arranged to cancel out the combined effect of timber movement. Simply put, the boards need to be flipped so that the annual rings alternate from one board to the next. Any diagram illustrating this arrangement usually shows the end-grain with the annual rings centred in each board. In practice, it is likely that this will not be the case but the principle of alternating the crown side up on one board and down on the next should not be ignored.

◆ Imported timber

This problem is further accentuated by the fact that most square-edged, kiln-dried timber that is available today, particularly if it is imported form overseas, is converted by a sequential cutting system. The result is that each board is a crown-cut board. This is not a problem with through or quarter-sawn boards. When these sequentially sawn boards are assembled with the crown appearing on all boards on one surface, the combined movement will result in an emphasis of the curve of each board. What is happening is the result of the wrap-around force that holds the annual rings together when the log is released after sawing. While the boards are drying the annual rings try to straighten out, resulting in a hollowing of the crown or outer curve of the annual rings.

Crown-cut boards

Sequential sawing of logs produces square edges but crown-cut boards

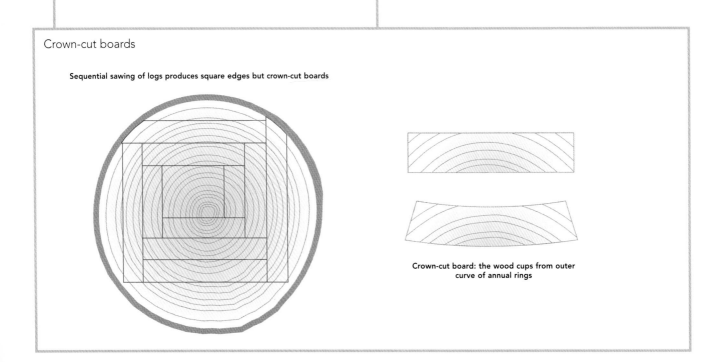

Crown-cut board: the wood cups from outer curve of annual rings

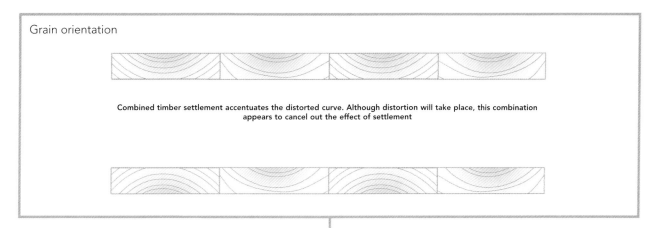

Grain orientation

Combined timber settlement accentuates the distorted curve. Although distortion will take place, this combination appears to cancel out the effect of settlement

Use narrow boards

THE PROBLEM OF DISTORTION CAN BE LESSENED IF crown-cut boards are reduced in width so the effects of movement are shared between narrower pieces. A good example of this is the stability that is achieved from the narrow core strips of block board or that of solid wood kitchen worktops. Unfortunately, the visual result is that of a busy surface of many strips and many edge joints and this could compromise the aesthetic effect that wider boards and the more recognized character of timber grain.

Drawers

WHILE ON THE SUBJECT OF STABILITY AND creating wider boards, as I mentioned earlier, I apply this principle to drawer sides, backs and fronts. It seems very difficult to source commercially prepared timber that is thin enough for drawer sides in a material that is both stable and has good wear-resisting properties. I prefer to use hard maple for making drawers and the

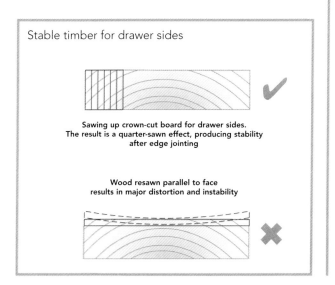

Stable timber for drawer sides

Sawing up crown-cut board for drawer sides. The result is a quarter-sawn effect, producing stability after edge jointing

Wood resawn parallel to face results in major distortion and instability

thinnest boards available are 1in (25mm) thick. Resawing these into appropriate thicknesses for making drawers results in so much distortion, both in the cross-section and the length, that there is so much waste and loss of dimensions as to render the exercise a failure. I use 2 or 3in (50 or 75mm) thick boards and saw them up into strips parallel to the edge of the board and glue them together using edge joints. I use the masking tape method I described earlier to hold the strips together while the glue sets, with the assembly held for a few minutes in cramps to squeeze out any excess glue. The resultant board is the equivalent of quarter-sawn timber with all the stability that this implies.

Coopered edge joints

COOPERING REQUIRES CURVED CROSS-SECTIONS – a particularly challenging application of edge joints. The most obvious example is that of barrel-making and it is from this trade that the joint gets its name. In barrel-making, however, the strips have both an angled cross-section and a curved taper in the length, resulting in the characteristic form of a barrel when assembled.

Coopering lends itself very well to the formation of a variety of curved forms – from gentle curves for chair seats to cylinders for columns. In general, this type of curved work has largely been replaced by laminating, particularly if strength is coupled with a thin section that needs to resist twisting. If, however, the result needs to give the impression of solid timber, then coopered joints are the answer.

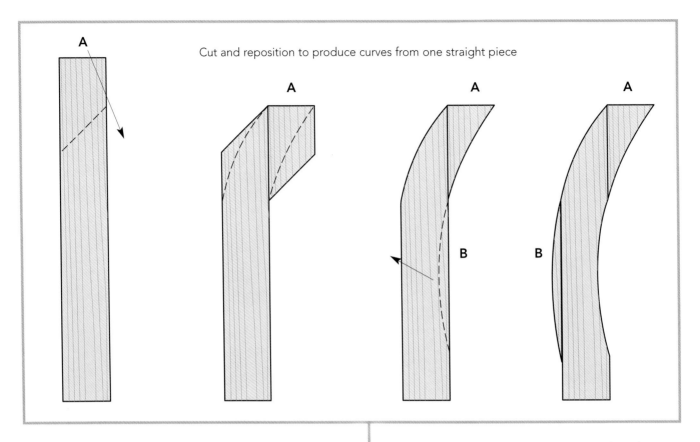

Cut and reposition to produce curves from one straight piece

◆ Coopered curves

To DETERMINE THE WIDTH OF THE STRIPS necessary, first draw the cross-section of the curve. Narrow strips need less final shaping if a smooth curve is necessary and in some circumstances can actually be left as flat facets that add to the character of the piece. Wide strips need fewer joints but may require extra thickness to produce a satisfactory curve. A drawing will help to sort out this question. It will also enable you to work out the angle of the mating surfaces of the joints. Once this has been established, consider the method of cutting the angle. Without doubt, the tilting arbor facility of a

▼ Profiled components sawn and awaiting a skim with a plane.

circular saw is the ideal way to cut these angles. The surfaces produced should be true enough to require little more than a couple of shavings from a well-set plane to produce a good edge joint. If the work involves a large number of components the edges could be planed by machine with the fence set over to accommodate the angle. My preference is to do this with a hand plane, for the reasons I mentioned earlier – that of opening up the grain that could be compressed by machining.

◆ Gluing up

IF YOUR COMBINATION OF COMPONENTS TO BE glued together has surfaces that will respond to cramp pressure that are not at 90° to the cramp shoes, you will need supplementary cramping blocks, fixed in position to resist sliding due to the ramped effect. The most effective way to achieve this is to temporarily glue the blocks onto the component so that the pressure face is parallel to the cramp shoe. If the angled force is not too great then a layer of newspaper glued in between will enable the block to be sheared away quite easily after the glue has set. All this requires a lot of extra work but in some circumstances it is the only way. I use masking tape to hold coopered sections together for gluing up. As with square-edge joints, masking tape can be amazingly strong when used

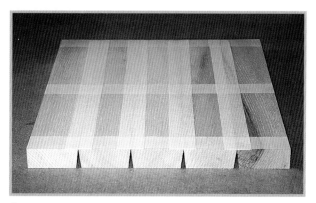

▲ Joints assembled and taped on the outer surface of the curve.

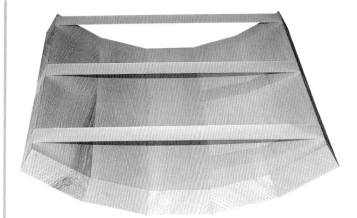

▲ Joints glued and pulled together and held from the inside of the curve with masking tape.

for coopered joints. Lay the components on a flat surface with the outside of the coopered curve uppermost and apply strips of masking tape at intervals across the pieces.

For small sections 1in (25mm) tape is strong enough but for larger sections scale up to 2in (50mm) wide. Then run a strip of tape along the joint to prevent any excess glue being squeezed out from this side. Carefully turn the assembly over and let one piece at a time hang over the edge of your bench and apply a line of glue to one face of each joint. Spread the glue with a comb spreader and move on to the next joint. The open assembly time of the glue determines the number of joints that can be glued before the faces can be closed and strips of masking tape are stretched across the inside curved void that is created by this action. If you were making coopered joints to produce a container or tube it would be best to glue up half the sections at a time and then assemble these two to produce the enclosed assembly.

There are router cutters available for coopering; the angles are carefully machined to provide combinations for hexagonal and octagonal sections. As with the self-location cutters for straight edge joints they are expensive and the joint quality varies according to the condition of the cutters.

Leg joints

SOME TIME AGO I DESIGNED AND MADE A CHAIR that had a side elevation profile of the back leg with a curve in the upper part. The option for laminating, which would have excluded short grain, was inappropriate as the curve was too tight for the laminations to be formed round it. I weighed up the risk of failure from short grain, which is the bane of using solid wood for curves, and decided that it would not be a serious problem, so I decided to use solid wood and cut out the profile. I looked at the drawing and realized that for a set

of six dining chairs I would be discarding a lot of timber. To prevent this I used the inner cut-away portion of the curve and glued it on to the outer face. I achieved this from a straight piece of wood with little or no significant loss of grain match. Again, the glue-up was done with masking tape and a few minutes in a bench vice.

Summary

EDGE JOINTS, OR FACE-TO-FACE JOINTS, WITH the grain of each piece running in the same direction, are strong as they are assembled in such a way that there is no stress from differential movement. With modern glues and good preparation of surfaces there should not be any loss of strength and the two pieces on either side of the joint can be expected to behave as one.

▼ Cooper-jointed seat on a stool.

Cutting mortice-and-tenon joints by hand

The ability to perform craft skills by hand can give you a unique understanding of the underlying principles of the task.

FROM THE EARLIEST TIMES, CRAFTSMEN USED sections of wood that were not planks and boards converted from large trees. They often worked with pieces of wood in the round, taken from branch stock and worked directly. There is evidence to support the fact that even in those early days, load-bearing constructions consisted of components set at right angles to each other. The simplest and strongest way to achieve this was to bore a hole in one piece and insert the end of the other piece into it. We still use this method of jointing today,

in the form of turned rails inserted into holes for the construction of seating, such as the Windsor chair. But for some reason this type of joint is not referred to as a 'mortice and tenon'.

▼ Coffee table in ripple sycamore and bird's eye maple. The legs are morticed through the top, using a similar joint to the turned rails in Windsor chairs or turned stool legs and rail joints. The through joint in the table becomes a major design feature. All other joints are also mortice and tenons, but with shoulders. Shaping is carried out after the glue-up.

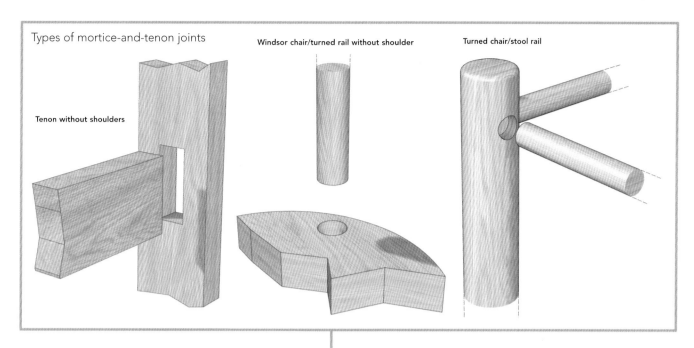

Types of mortice-and-tenon joints

Windsor chair/turned rail without shoulder

Turned chair/stool rail

Tenon without shoulders

Control issues

IN ITS SIMPLEST FORM THE TENON, OR MALE component, is a rectangular section inserted into a rectangular hole, and is commonly used for fencing. The problem with this method is the disproportionate strength of the rail to the stile. Also it is difficult to control the depth of the mortice slot accurately if you are cutting it by hand. A construction often needs several components to be structurally successful and it needs to have stiles that are parallel and dimensionally accurate. It is impossible to rely on tenons fitting to the bottom of mortices.

This would not be a problem today if cutting mortices by machine; however, before the advent of machined mortices the method employed was to cut the tenon so that it had shoulders. The distance between shoulders could be controlled, which was essential for the construction of early pieces of furniture such as the wall panelling with which stylish houses were lined. The introduction of shoulders must have marked a major step forward in terms of technique and this would only have been possible with the parallel development of metallurgy to produce the tools to control the sawing process.

Simple mortice and tenon

MY GUESS IS THAT MOST WOODWORKERS TODAY would not make a simple mortice-and-tenon joint by hand. This is probably true of all the constructional joints we use to make wooden objects and it is a sign of the times that even the home handyman will go straight

to his local hardware supermarket and buy a machine or jig to do the job. Having said that, it is still possible to buy all the original hand tools associated with this joint.

Technology is of its time and we cannot ignore it, but the downside to it is that if you stop performing many craft skills by hand, you risk losing the understanding of the underlying principles of those skills. So, for the benefit of a more complete understanding, I will outline how to make a mortice and tenon by hand.

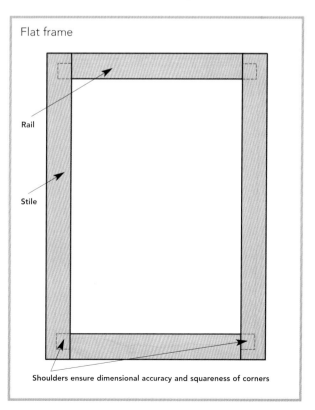

Flat frame

Rail

Stile

Shoulders ensure dimensional accuracy and squareness of corners

◆ Marking out

THIS METHOD IS UNIVERSAL TO ALL MORTICE AND tenons that you would need to produce a flat frame. This was probably the construction used most historically, and is still very popular today. The two parts of the joint have a lot in common dimensionally so it is a matter of choice whether you start with the mortice or the tenon. However, because the mortice is the first in the title it is usually first to be made. I was taught to mark out the location of the mortice using a pencil. This makes sense if you plan to cut the mortice through the component, as you can remove the material from both edges effectively and project the dimensions easily from one edge to the other with a try-square. It is easy to remove the pencil line later, with little loss of the thickness of the component. Be sure you consider the pencil as a precise marking tool. The mark it makes is not just a line but also an important definition of position. I use a click type of propelling pencil with an 'HB' lead for consistency of line width.

If you sharpen a wooden pencil, do it with a chisel and create the effect of a blade, so that the line is thin and the drawing action is consistent. For a stopped mortice I prefer to mark out the position with a knife line. Make sure your marking knife is sharpened with only one bevel and the bevel is orientated to be on the waste side of the line. A tool such as a Stanley knife is inappropriate, as it has two bevels that produce the cutting edge, so one will always compress the defined corner, producing a small chamfer. If several mortices are involved it is better to mark out all the positions on one stile and then clamp all the other stiles together with the first and square all the lines across from the master component.

The next step is to mark out the shoulders of the tenons. Here, a single bevelled marking knife is absolutely essential to ensure crisp, square corners to the shoulders. It also makes it easier to pare cleanly to the shoulder line after removing the cheeks of the tenon.

◆ Uniform thickness

NOW TO MARK OUT THE THICKNESS OF BOTH the mortice and the tenon. You can carry out this task most effectively with a mortice gauge. Select a mortice chisel that is proportionally suitable to the thickness of the components. If the construction is to be a frame with two rails and two stiles, the tenon should not be less than a third of the thickness.

The choice of chisel has a direct bearing on the mortice gauge setting – it is easier to cut a slot for the mortice and fit the tenon into it than the other way round. This is a common engineering principle – it is more difficult to adjust the inside of a hole than it is to remove material from the inserted piece.

Having selected the appropriate chisel size, set the mortice gauge to its width. Bear in mind that the spurs of the gauge are tapered so it is necessary to adjust the setting to the points. Centre the two spurs in the thickness of the components. Centring first by eye and pressing the spurs into the edge surface can do this well.

Repeat this from the corresponding face. If the two sets of marks coincide, the spurs are centred. If not, gently lock the gauge stock in position and tap one end or the other of the stem to move the spurs until they are centred. Once you are satisfied, lock the stock firmly in place.

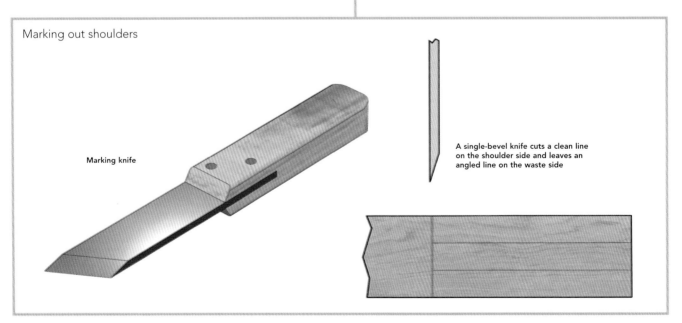

Marking out shoulders

Marking knife

A single-bevel knife cuts a clean line on the shoulder side and leaves an angled line on the waste side

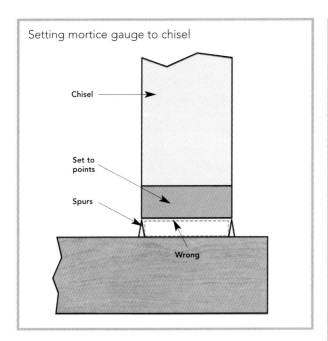

Setting mortice gauge to chisel

Chisel

Set to points

Spurs

Wrong

Using a gauge

MORTICE GAUGES AND MARKING GAUGES should, in principle, be easy tools to use. In practice, however, it takes some time to master them. There are three points of contact to carry out in sequence. Firstly, place the inside face of the stock against the face side of the component. Then do the same with the corner of the stem and finally the spurs so that they trail in the direction that the gauge is pushed. I have tuned my gauges for smoothness of action and this includes the removal of the sharp corner that makes contact with the stem. In fact I have rounded this corner so that the stem rolls smoothly to make contact with the spurs easy to control, both visually and mechanically.

To mark the lines, always work from the face side so that any variations in the thickness of components will only be evident in the assembled joint on one side. Face surfaces are bound to align, provided you have cut the two parts of the joint competently. Here is a little tip to prevent over-shooting the limits of the mortice position. Press the spurs into the far line of the mortice to make a pair of indentations. The spurs will click into these when they reach this position while marking the lines. You can also use this for marking out a tenon on the end-grain and both corresponding edges.

Working from the face side and face edge is regarded as general good practice and is essential when preparing timber by hand. If you are using machines for timber preparation there should be no variations, unless you have changed thickness settings and then reset them. The final

act of marking out is to identify the waste with a visual mark to minimize the risk of cutting on the wrong side of the line, particularly when sawing the tenon.

Chopping the mortice

MORTICE CHISELS ARE STURDY TOOLS THAT HAVE to be strong enough to withstand a power blow from a mallet and the levering forces used to remove the waste. Nowadays most manufacturers produce the registered pattern with ferrules at both ends of the handle. The blade is quite thick and the surface area of the sides resists twisting when removing the waste, keeping the sides of the mortice clean.

Support the component on the surface of the bench and hold it down with a clamp. Position it, so that you can stand square to it and try to avoid standing to one side. This will enable you to hold the chisel upright – the only check that can be applied to vertical accuracy is visual.

The fact that mortices have always been chopped with a chisel, starting the first cut in the centre with the cutting edge across the grain, shows a significant realization of the natural structure of wood. This first cut produces a V-shaped indentation that creates a void into which all subsequent cuts displace the material being removed. I am sure that this was clearly understood by craftsmen from very early times as the mortice and tenon has been around for many centuries.

▼ Cutting a mortice.

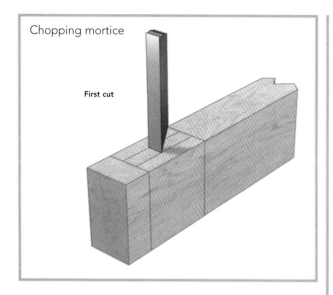

Chopping mortice

First cut

◆ Use two hands

I LIKE TO HOLD THE CHISEL WITH BOTH HANDS TO carefully guide the cutting edge into position between the gauge lines. Then I hold the handle before picking up the mallet to strike the end of the handle. By doing this I can use the entire length of the blade as a visual marker to ensure that the cut is upright and parallel to the eventual sides of the mortice. Some craftsmen hold the blade only and position the cutting edge between the gauge lines with one hand. It saves time, as the chisel is held in one hand and the mallet in the other. However the length of the blade is obscured, so you lose a valuable sighting tool.

After the first cut continue with a series of cuts and stop a few millimetres away from the end lines. This will leave enough material to provide a fulcrum for levering

out the waste. When removing the chisel after each cut do not move it from side to side or the mortice will be too wide. Hold the flat face of the chisel towards the end lines until the series of downward cuts are made. Then turn the chisel round and lever out the displaced fibres and repeat in the opposite direction. The depth of cuts will depend on the density of wood and the ease with which the fibres shear between cuts. Practice and experience will enable you to judge the effective depth but if it is too deep the levering action to remove the chips will require a lot of force. Be prepared to chop a mortice in stages. If it goes through, turn the component over and repeat from the other edge. Finally, cut back to the end lines to square up and accurately dimension the mortice. I use a marking knife for these end lines as a chisel's cutting edge can be firmly trapped while being struck with a mallet. For small mortices I pare back to the lines using hand force and a vertical paring action. There should be no need to clean up the sides of the mortice unless tearing occurs. Rough sides improve the glue bond.

◆ Cutting tenons

I T IS NOW TIME TO LOOK AT CUTTING TENONS by hand with the same degree of precision. Marking out of tenons should be done at the same time as that of the mortice. After the marking out of the shoulders with a try-square and marking knife, set out the tenon with the mortice gauge, working as before from the face side. The gauge lines should be marked on both edges and the end-grain. For right-handed users, hold the component in your left hand and guide the gauge with your right hand.

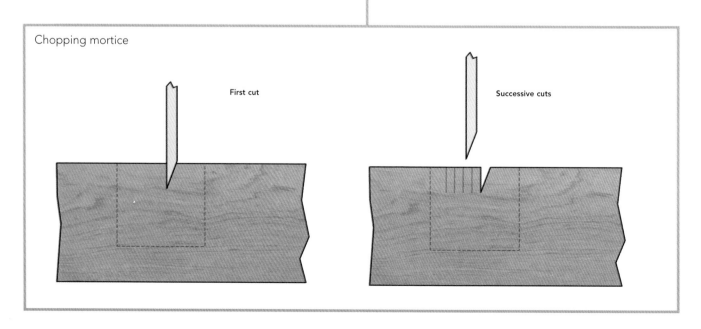

Chopping mortice

First cut

Successive cuts

To prevent slipping off the end, with the possible risk of injury, I use the thumb of my left hand to push the gauge to the end of the component and repeat this process on the end-grain. Spur indentations on the shoulder line can be used to prevent over-shooting this line with the gauge. For difficult to handle components, it's best to hold the pieces in a vice, but once again you should use both hands to control movement of the gauge.

◆ Sawing tenons

I T IS BEST TO SAW TENONS IN STAGES. HOLD THE component in a vice sloping away from the direction of sawing at approximately 45°. Saw down with the saw kerf on the waste side of the line so that the inside face of the saw cut just touches the gauge line. Continue to saw until you reach the far corner and the shoulder line. Then turn the component round and repeat this process from the opposite edge. Finally, hold the piece upright in the vice and complete the third saw cut down to the shoulder line. This is how tenons have been cut by generations of craftsmen and we take it for granted that it is how it is.

It works, but it was not until I began to apply my own powers of observation to woodworking processes that I realized why it was necessary to go through these stages. The principle of sawing to lines that you can see is the reason for this sequence of three stages. If the work piece is held upright and the saw cut is made from one edge, you can only see the line on the nearest edge and the end of the tenon. The line on the far edge is obscured.

In most cases the tenon should be cut in material proportions, and where the rail is quite wide any likelihood of the saw drifting is accentuated by this extra width. By sawing from corner to corner from both edges, you are always working to lines you can see clearly, so you can achieve a greater level of control.

▲ There are high standards of precision in the workshop.

◆ Sighting the saw

F ROM MY EXPERIENCE AND OBSERVATION OF people in the early stages of mastering woodworking tools, the problem often encountered in sawing is that of sighting the blade. Particularly with the accurate use of backsaws, I'd like to explain the principle of positioning your head so that you can see both sides of the blade. If you only look at and concentrate on the waste side of the line it is very difficult to keep the blade upright and parallel to the eventual saw cut. The fact that we have binocular vision means that we can position the cone of vision so that the vertical plane that represents the blade of the saw can be aligned to bisect the cone. By doing

Sawing a tenon

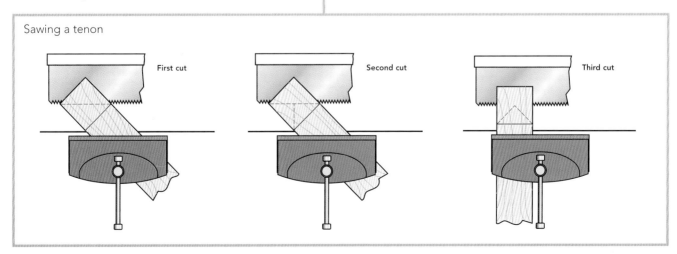

First cut

Second cut

Third cut

this, it is possible to see both sides of the blade and the wood on both sides as well, thus keeping the saw upright and parallel to the saw cut.

It is surprising how few woodworkers are prepared to take the time to practise and master this technique effectively. You should practise starting by positioning the saw carefully in relation to the line, using the thumb as a guide, then try to make the first cut on the push stroke. When starting on the corner of end-grain it is surprising how often the saw bounces, if the first cut is made on the pull stroke. The expectation of sawing to a line should be such that the inside edge of the teeth just touches the middle of the V-section of the gauge line. There should be no need to clean up or adjust the surfaces after the saw cut has been made. It should be left straight from the saw.

◆ Tuning a tenon saw

Having said that, the expectation that it can be left straight from the saw will depend on the condition of the teeth of the saw. Many years ago I made myself a dining table and six chairs. The set was made from teak, which was the popular design choice of the time. I marked out all the joints for the six chairs and chopped the mortices quite quickly, because teak cuts well when chiselled. Sawing the tenons was a different matter and I stopped after cutting the tenons for the first set of joints and wondered how I could speed up the process.

I realized that, apart from sawing the shoulders, all the cutting action was *with* the grain. In other words, I needed a ripsaw. Tenon saws are general-purpose saws that are designed to crosscut and rip. I had access to a second tenon saw so I converted it to a specific ripsaw action and I sped through the tenons of the other five chairs.

It is not difficult to convert the saw, as you can carry out all the profiling from one side. It does, however, require discipline and a sense of purpose. If the saw is a new one you will not need to reset the teeth as very little metal is lost to create the new profile. Rip teeth have a more upright leading edge and, being filed square across, the actual cutting edge is like a series of chisels set in line, producing a groove that runs parallel to the grain. In contrast, a crosscut saw is similar to a series of marking knives cutting across the fibres.

After reshaping the teeth, run a fine diamond slip stone along the outer points to even up any variation in the set. When doing this, support the blade on its side and move the slip stone from the heel to the toe, making sure that it contacts both the apex of the points and the side of the blade, while keeping the pressure constant. In this way you can be certain that the contact is consistent. Two stokes on each side should be sufficient. Test the saw and you will be amazed at the improvement in cutting action. If, by any chance the saw tends to drift to one side, make one more pass on that side of the saw with the slip stone. If you still enjoy cutting joints by hand I am sure this approach will enhance your skill and satisfaction.

Eyes focus on either side of blade where the cutting edge touches the wood

Saw bisects cone in vertical plane

Cone of vision

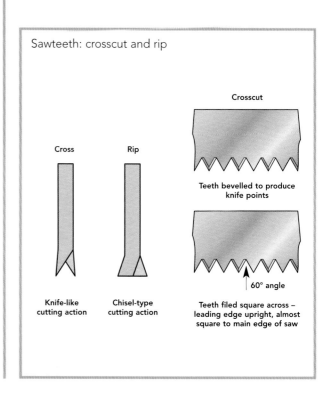

Sawteeth: crosscut and rip

Cross

Rip

Knife-like cutting action

Chisel-type cutting action

Crosscut

Teeth bevelled to produce knife points

60° angle

Teeth filed square across – leading edge upright, almost square to main edge of saw

The shoulders

AFTER SAWING THE MAIN PART OF THE TENON, you need to remove the cheeks to create the shoulders. It is best to do this with a conventionally sharpened tenon saw as the direction of cut is across the grain. For this purpose, a bench hook is the ideal accessory to support the component, as it not only helps to hold the piece securely but also protects the surface of your bench. For cutting wide rails, or in situations where two wide and two narrow shoulders are needed, you also need to hold the component in a vice. I was taught to saw right to the line when cutting shoulders. It is very difficult to be consistently accurate when sawing across the grain so I took the well-established approach to crosscut sawing and paring for dovetails and applied the thinking to tenon shoulders. I saw as close to the line as possible, leaving a small amount to be removed with a paring chisel. I was taught to use a paring chisel with a vertical hold. But nowadays, I do most of my cutting with the work held in a vice, using a horizontal action.

With the component held in the vice, the chisel can get trapped in the knife line as you apply pressure to produce the cut. A series of narrow overlapping cuts is better than fewer wide cuts, which will require more force. Remember – force often cancels out control! But narrow cuts do not necessarily mean you have to use a narrow chisel. For paring shoulders I favour an approx ¾in (19mm) wide, bevelled-edge chisel. I also use a paring jig for wide shoulders. The positive alignment with the shoulder line eliminates any chance of error. This jig, developed for paring dovetail shoulders is shown on page 79.

Fitting the joint

BEFORE TRYING THE FIT OF THE TENON INTO the mortice, I chamfer the corners of the end of the tenon. In addition to making the assembly of individual joints easier to control, it also contributes to the overall efficiency of the final glue-up, where several joints may be involved and time is in short supply. I mentioned earlier that the expectation is for the joint to fit first time, and this is certainly the long-term objective once you have mastered the technique. But, bearing in mind the variables of carrying out any skill by hand, there will be times when you need to make adjustments to achieve an optimum fit.

Ideally, you should assemble the joint without undue force. Small joints with relatively little internal surface areas of contact should go together with hand pressure. Larger joints may need a little assistance from a mallet or

hammer blow and a block of wood to prevent damage to the components. If the joint is too tight, the wood will expand when you apply glue and the joint will become even tighter, resulting in possible glue starvation due to the piston effect of the tenon. This is a common fault with mortice and tenons that fail eventually, something you may see with old chairs. If the joint is too tight, check both parts to determine what is causing the tightness and avoid guesswork. Generally, I find that it is the mortice that needs adjustment, and this is quite easy to do with a chisel. If, however, the tenon is too thick, the ideal way to remove any excess is with a shoulder plane and block plane rather than a chisel.

Japanese saws

A DISCUSSION OF SAWING TENONS WOULD NOT BE complete without reference to Japanese saws. I have these much-recommended saws, which have become so popular over the last decade, and I am very impressed with their cutting action. They cut on the pull stroke and are available with both rip and crosscut actions. However, I prefer the action of the conventional tenon saw, which cuts on the push stroke. I am sure that the final choice will depend on personal preferences but both types of saw respond well to the principles that I have outlined above.

▼ Interior of chest of drawers, showing drawer frames using mortice- and-tenon joints.

Cutting mortice-and-tenon joints by machine

Speed, accuracy and continuity are major advantages of cutting joints with machines but don't forget your hand tool techniques.

I AM A GREAT BELIEVER IN EMBRACING ANYTHING that can make a job easier, as long as it is appropriate to the task. However, I do feel strongly that, wherever possible, it is a good thing to start exploring techniques using hand tools and then progressing on to machines. In this way, the complexity of the material, and the sensitivity that develops from working it, is enhanced and reinforced.

◆ Machine morticer

FROM A MODEST BENCH-TOP VERSION TO A sophisticated floor-standing model, the morticer that most of us will come across will undoubtedly be fitted with a hollow chisel and drilling bit. This simple but effective principle is a combination of techniques that existed in mechanical form quite some time ago. Drilling out the waste with a brace and bit and then cleaning up the inner faces with a chisel was common

▼ Traditional hollow chisel morticer found in many workshops.

practice early in the last century, particularly for large mortices. A large chisel blade, held in a clamp, being driven down by a powerful hand-operated lever and counterweight, was the forerunner of the combination of the hollow chisel and bit that we know today.

It was the engineering knowledge that came about when rotating power was effectively harnessed that brought about this combination. The method of holding the work piece and the ability to move it both forward and back for position and from side to side to traverse along the mortice had already been exploited in the chisel-type morticer, which in every other respect replicated the action of hand-morticing.

The hollow chisel and bit was the final stage in the combination that we take for granted today, and is probably the type of machine that most small-scale operators would acquire.

The cutting system is also available and can be fitted to a vertical pillar drill, which has both rotating and plunging facilities. Some kind of fence needs to be clamped to the drill table and in general the work is held firmly by hand. It would be suitable for small-scale, occasional use, as the amount of plunge force that is necessary would strain the rise-and-fall mechanism, resulting in serious wear quite quickly.

◆ Chain morticer

THIS MACHINE USES A CUTTING ACTION AKIN TO that of a chainsaw. The chain is mounted vertically and is plunged in, end first into the work piece, being driven downwards with the same type of lowering device as that of a hollow chisel morticer. The main limitation of this method of material removal is the rounded corners of the bottom of stopped mortices. The machines are large and complex in their engineering, and although they are still available they have not enjoyed the popularity of the more affordable and simpler hollow chisel counterparts.

Slot morticer

THIS TYPE OF MORTICER USES A CUTTING BIT that is similar to a router cutter. The system clamps the work piece horizontally. The work piece is then moved forward until the depth of cut has been achieved. It is then traversed from side to side to complete the width of the mortice.

This method is popular in Europe and is an option that is often available on combination woodworking machines. The resultant mortice has rounded ends, which can be squared up with a chisel. When used as a production machine, slot morticers are teamed up with tenoners that produce matching rounded tenons.

Swing chisel morticer

THIS TYPE OF MORTICER USES A VERY sophisticated engineered system that is almost impossible to describe in words. It consists of a chisel that is roughly 'T' shaped in profile. The inverted 'T' swings like a pendulum, which is driven downwards into the wood. While swinging from side to side in the line of the mortice, the chisel also oscillates in the thickness of the mortice to make the removal of the chips more efficient.

It is without doubt a production tool. Once the depth and width of swing have been set, the mortice is cut with one plunge without the need to traverse from side to side. Another distinct advantage is that mortices, or slots as small as ⅟₁₆in (1.5mm) thick, can be cut. It goes without saying that the cost of such a machine reflects the complexity of its design and is therefore outside the scope of anyone other than the serious manufacturer.

Morticing with a router

MY OWN PERSONAL PREFERENCE IS TO CUT mortices with a router. This choice reflects the scale of work that I design and make and the fact that the mortice and tenon does not play a significant part in the strength of construction that is necessary. As such I do not need a hollow chisel morticer for large numbers of frame-and-panel doors or chairs with many horizontal rails. This is a personal decision based on the aesthetic forms that have evolved over the years in my design ethos. In short, I do not have a hollow chisel morticer.

What I particularly like about the router is the precise control I can exercise both for the centring or positioning of the mortice relative to an edge, and the accurate depth of plunge that the adjustable stop affords. This is particularly important for frame construction, such as would be applied to horizontal drawer frames for a chest of drawers. Both the mortice and the tenon are centred in the thickness of the components. Because the material is thicknessed accurately, I know that I can work from both sides.

I mark out the position of the mortice with a knife line so that I can chisel back to this when cleaning up the rounded ends that result from a router cutter. I then select a router cutter, preferably with a down-cut spiral flute that is slightly narrower than the final thickness of the tenon.

▼ Two-fence routing of mortices for the Placet chest's drawer frames.

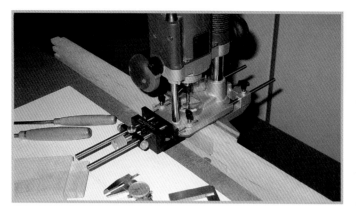

▲ Close-up of the two-fence routing system using a MicroFence.

The cut is positioned slightly off centre, away from the router fence. The first series of plunges removes the bulk of the waste and then a final traverse cleans up the walls of the slot. This process is then repeated from the opposite face. Once again, the off-centred cut removes material from the inner surface furthest away from the fence, permitting a forward traverse. The result is a mortice slot perfectly centred in the component.

A problem that is often encountered when working on a narrow edge with a router is that of insufficient control during plunge strokes. The router can very easily tip sideways. I overcome this with the addition of a second fence. Once I have set the position of the cutter with the micro-adjustable fence and locked it into place, I slide the second fence onto the projecting fence rods in order to accommodate the thickness of the component. When this is locked in place the router cannot tip over and the cutter can be plunged down with confidence.

I bought a spare fence specifically for this purpose in the days when my collection of tools included only one router. The 8mm-diameter guide rods of my Elu and DeWalt routers are not always long enough to carry the second fence, so I have made a set of longer rods to the same diameter, in stainless steel.

Tenoning machines

UNLIKE THE AFFORDABILITY OF A HOLLOW CHISEL morticer, a dedicated tenoner – even a single-ended version – will set you back quite a few thousand pounds, while a double-ended version will require you to take out a second mortgage.

The machines are extremely complicated pieces of engineering with an over-and-under set of cutter blocks that can be adjusted to accommodate the space between them to change the thickness of the tenon. To withstand the considerable amount of power distributed by the

▲ A single-ended tenoner is one option, but it's expensive if your work only has a few tenons!

cutters as they rotate, the work piece is held in a clamp, and the whole assembly moves in a slide to form the tenon. The set-up time for any tenon is quite long due to the complications involved in adjusting the settings. Once again, these machines are really suitable only for production workshops.

Sawing tenons

IT IS POSSIBLE TO PRODUCE VERY GOOD TENONS with more modest equipment, and this is particularly relevant if the work requires an assortment of different sizes of joints. In America, the table saw is a popular machine for tenoning. Using a simple jig, the component is held vertically and passed over the blade. The biggest problem that I have experienced with this method is that of setting the fence accurately. It helps to have a spare piece of material prepared to the size of the finished component, so that it can be used for the set-up; otherwise, one has to risk setting up using the intended component with the possible risk of the tenon being too loose. It is also necessary to remove the riving knife and saw guard, which also gives me cause for concern.

A well set-up bandsaw is also very useful for cutting tenons, but again, adjusting the fence requires a lot of care. A screw adjuster makes the job much easier and it is worth tuning the movement so that there is little angular play when the fence is locked in position.

If a bandsaw is the preferred option, fit the widest blade that the machine will take and, to avoid any drifting of the saw cut, make sure the blade is truly sharp. I use my band resaw for large, or multiple, tenons. With its 3in (75mm) wide, stellite-tipped blade, the problem of drifting never occurs.

◆ Using a spindle moulder

ALTHOUGH MY FELDER COMBINATION MACHINE is fitted with a spindle moulder, I have never used this facility for cutting tenons. In principle, the set-up time and the cost of tooling make this approach more suitable for production runs. Also, the maximum length of tenons is confined to the safety limitation of cutter projection determined by the manufacturers.

◆ Tenoning with a router

IN CONJUNCTION WITH MY METHOD OF CUTTING mortices with a router I also use my router table to size the thickness of tenons accurately, particularly for flat frames, where the materials of rails and stiles is constant, and the joint is centred in the thickness.

I remove the bulk of the waste on the bandsaw, leaving about half a millimetre to be skimmed with a router cutter, then install the largest-diameter parallel cutter with an end cut that will suit the length of the tenon. The fence is then set so that the cutter reaches the tenon shoulders with the end running up against it. Then the depth of cut is set to skim the faces of the tenon.

It is often necessary to make a few passes over the cutter as the length of the tenon may be greater than the diameter of the cutter. Where possible, the setting up is carried out on a spare piece of wood prepared to the right dimensions.

MORTICE-AND-TENON JIG

I have not tried the latest mortice-and-tenon jigs that have appeared recently, which use a router to remove the wood when forming both parts of the joint. However, the demonstration that I witnessed at a trade show looked very promising and the results were quite impressive. Maybe sometime in the future I will investigate the potential of these jigs.

I installed a cross-cut slide into the surface of my router table and this is how I pass the component over the cutter with safe control. The adjustable wooden fence can be moved to prevent breakout as the cutter passes the end of the shoulder. The same result could be achieved by using a block of wood to push the component. Be sure that the end is perfectly square and that it has sufficient contact with the near edge of the component and the fence.

With this method I know that the tenon is perfectly centred and will be compatible with the mortice. It also gives me the degree of control I need to achieve the right tightness of fit. I always aim for a fit where the joint can be assembled by hand, safe in the knowledge that any expansion from the application of glue will not make the joint too tight.

MILLING MACHINE

When cutting small mortices my precision milling machine displays a versatility that knows few limitations, having precise manipulation of movement in all the three axes needed to cut a mortice with a rotating cutter.

▼ Routing tenons to final thickness on a router table with sliding fence.

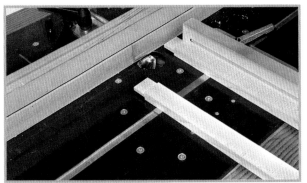

▼ Bandsawing excess for tenons on the same frames.

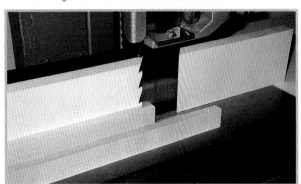

Some variations on the mortice-and-tenon joint

Mortice and tenons are versatile joints and it is worth exploring some of these less common variations that can be found.

◆ Haunched tenons

THE MOST COMMON FORM OF ADDITION TO a tenon is the square haunch, which came about entirely as a result of necessity. Primarily associated with frames and panels, it dominated joinery until cabinetmaking established itself as the progressive woodworking skill of the 17th century. The groove that holds the panel was cut with a plough plane. A stopped groove that did not show at the end of the mortice component was difficult and time consuming to produce, whereas a groove, run through with a plough plane, left its profile.

The practical answer was to extend the tenon with an additional projection to fill the gap. The tenon, in turn, could be made narrower to avoid the groove.

Today, we can cut stopped grooves quite easily with a router, so in principle there is no need to incorporate a square haunch. The argument that the extra surface area of a haunch strengthens the joint with increased gluing area is negated by the efficiency of modern glues. In fact, the slot that is cut to accept the haunch actually weakens the mortice, which is near the end-grain of the component.

The justification for a tapered haunch is based on the weakness of end-grain to face-grain gluing. This refers to the region beyond the mortice where the outer shoulder of the tenon makes contact. This problem is accentuated if the rail bearing the tenon is very wide. Any lateral distortion of the rail could cause the end-grain to face-grain bond to shear and fail. The penetration and extra gluing area of a tapered haunch will overcome this problem and is commonly applied to situations where the appearance of a square haunch would be unacceptable. Luckily this type of technique is no longer necessary; timber is better dried today and is therefore more stable.

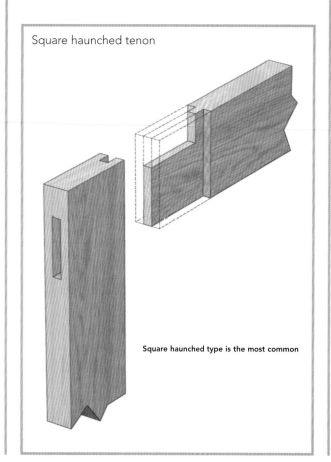

Square haunched tenon

Square haunched type is the most common

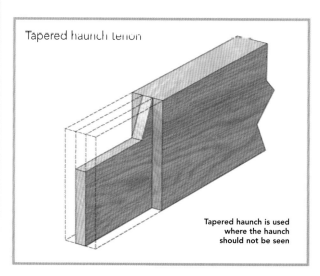

Tapered haunch tenon

Tapered haunch is used where the haunch should not be seen

◆ Long- and short-shouldered tenon joints

Long- and short- shouldered tenons are another example of the manipulation of tools affecting the configuration of joints. Long- and short-shouldered tenons are associated with flat frames where the panel or insert is dropped in after the frame has been glued up. A typical example is a mirror or window frame. The through rebate that accepts the mirror was cut with a rebate plane and the long shoulder on the tenon was proportioned to fill the gap. Although the assembled result looks good, the extended shoulder is no longer necessary as stopped rebates can be cut effectively with a router or spindle moulder before or after assembly of the frame.

It is not my intention to diminish the practicality of these types of joint, but to draw attention to the fact that technology has rendered them unnecessary in this day and age.

Long- and short-shouldered tenon

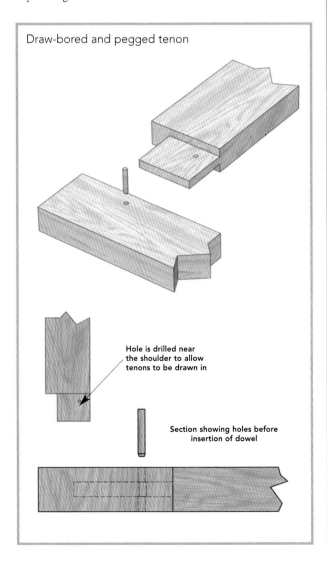

Draw-bored and pegged tenon

Hole is drilled near the shoulder to allow tenons to be drawn in

Section showing holes before insertion of dowel

◆ Pegged tenons

Today, we take it for granted that joints will be assembled, glued and held in place with cramps until the glue has set. This has not always been the case and in the past the most common way to close the shoulders of mortice and tenons was with a peg or dowel, which became a feature of the joint. In some cases the peg was driven in dry so that the construction could be dismantled, a technique used in building construction.

The holes are deliberately offset by drilling through the mortice component first. The joint is then assembled and the shoulder of the tenon driven home as far as it will go. The drill is then inserted into the previously formed hole and the spur centre point is transferred to the tenon. The joint is then taken apart and a hole drilled through the tenon a little closer to the shoulder. The difference between the centre mark and the second hole will depend on the density of the wood and the size of the joint being pegged – ¹⁄₁₆in (1.5mm) of offset is usually sufficient.

The peg, which is best made from a piece of dowel rod with a strongly chamfered end, will try to align the two holes when it is driven into place and in turn will close the shoulders of the tenon. To reduce the effect of future movement that results from expansion and contraction of the wood, place the hole quite close to the shoulder line. As a general guide, the centre of the hole through the mortice should not be more than ⁵⁄₁₆in (8mm) from the shoulder line with a ¼in (6mm) dowel being strong enough to close the joint.

This method of assembly was known in the past as 'draw boring', the two holes being drawn together by the peg. For joints that may be taken apart in the future, square-sectioned, tapered pegs were used that were left projecting so that they could be driven out of the holes with a hammer. Glued and pegged joints are ideal where a lack of cramps would make assembly a problem.

◆ Wedged through tenons

THROUGH TENONS BENEFIT GREATLY FROM THE extra strength of wedges. The mortice is widened to accommodate the wedges, which, when driven into sawcuts in the tenon, creates the effect of an internal dovetail. The extra strength can be exploited in many situations and is well suited to the flat frame, particularly for large doors that are subjected to heavy diagonal loads.

The mortice is cut through from both sides, either by hand or machine. An internal taper is then formed with a chisel, being cut from the outer face. Very little taper is required, and for most cabinet-sized flat frames, ³⁄₃₂in (2mm) at each end should be enough. The taper stops short of the inner edge of the mortice component.

This constriction at the base of the tenon prevents the action of the wedges from splitting the rail. The sawcuts that accept the wedges should also end at the same depth as the constriction. Be sure that the sawcut is orientated so that the compressive force of the wedge impacts onto end-grain. Never insert a wedge into a tenon so that it runs parallel to the grain of the mortice as this could split the mortice component.

These sawcuts should be set in from the outer edges of the tenon such that the material being displaced requires little force from the wedges. This dimension should be slightly more than the taper on the inside of the mortice. The dimensions of the wedges can then be calculated by measuring the depth of the sawcut and adding a few millimetres for the length and the thickest part is the sum of the taper, plus the sawcut, plus a little more for compression of the wood. If only a small number are required they are best cut from a piece of wood prepared to the thickness of the tenon, and the profiles cut with a tenon saw. Mark out the profiles to ensure continuity of size and taper. For large numbers, I make up a simple jig and cut them sequentially on the bandsaw.

Wedged through tenon

Slotted cramping block for gluing up wedged tenons

Bandsaw blade

Grain direction

Bandsaw jig for sawing wedges

Multiple tenons

To prevent any weakening of the mortice component and benefiting from the increased gluing area, large tenons can be split up to form multiple tenons. A typical example can be seen in large framed doors where the bottom rail is deeper than the top and intermediate rails. A single tenon would be much stronger than the accompanying mortice.

It is therefore better to cut double tenons, dividing up the space occupied by the mortice into thirds. The material left between the mortices then maintains the continuity of the wood, providing strength to compensate for the tenons. In the case of thick components, twin tenons positioned side by side produce the same result.

▲ Dining table and chairs (detail). Indian rosewood, pigskin suede and glass. Showing through, wedged and multiple tenons on the table and chairs.

Rail to leg mortice and tenons

The top joint at the front of a chair or the four top joints of a stool, where two rails come into a vertical post, need to be strong enough to withstand the range of variably directed loads. As is often the case, the rails are usually the same depth so the two mortices are of the same dimensions. A lot of material is removed to form the mortices and the extra strength that long tenons can contribute is a factor that needs to be exploited. This can result in the mortices meeting at the internal corner.

Mitring the ends instead of having one long and one short tenon can overcome the problem of maximum length. Alternatively, a step can be cut on the end of each tenon to create an overlap. It is not unusual to see some examples of old chairs where a haunch is also incorporated into this joint. However, this may lead to some dire consequences if too much material has been removed from the leg and the leverage that the tenons impart to the corner is greater than the pressure the surrounding material is able to bear.

In making this joint, I would avoid using a haunch and, if it was absolutely necessary, I would employ a tapered haunch. For added strength and long-term security a corner block can be added.

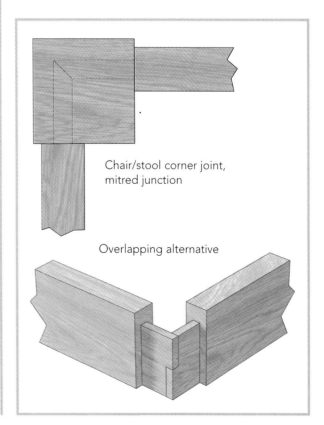

Chair/stool corner joint, mitred junction

Overlapping alternative

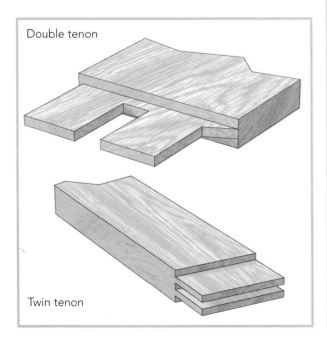

Double tenon

Twin tenon

◆ Knock-down mortice and tenons

Flat-pack furniture is associated with knock-down or take-apart joints that are assembled dry. I am trying to think of an occasion when I have actually dismantled a piece of knock-down furniture and the only time when this has been an advantage has been when moving house. If it is necessary to include this option into a mortice and tenon then there are two ways that spring to mind.

The first method is strongly associated with refectory tables where the tenons of the rails project through, long enough to accept a tapered peg that is driven through a square hole. This technique can even be used to add a decorative statement to the piece. A more recent method is to use a cross dowel and bolt, which holds the joint very firmly and is less obtrusive. It is the method frequently employed in flat-pack bed construction to join the headboard and tailboard to the mattress frame. The bolts can be acquired from specialist suppliers such as Woodfit.

In situations where the appearance of knock-down fittings is not so critical, a wooden dowel can be glued in place instead of the metal dowel, and a wood screw inserted to hold the joint together. The cross grain of the dowel overcomes the problem of weakness associated with screwing into end-grain, although modern wood screws have largely overcome this limitation.

◆ Tenons with scribed shoulders

This type of joint involves a rectangular-section rail, which is tenoned into a cylindrical component. It is best to cut the mortice while the component has a square section and then either turn or rout away the excess material to make it into a cylinder.

Knock-down wedged joint

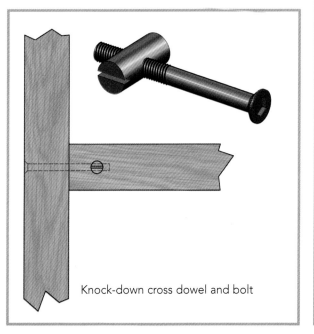

Knock-down cross dowel and bolt

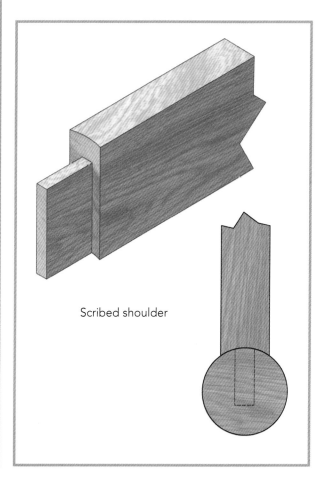

Scribed shoulder

Make the piece a little longer than is necessary so that a template can be formed by cutting off a small cross-section. This template can then be used in conjunction with a scalpel, to mark the profile of the rounded or scribed shoulders of the tenon.

The ideal tool for cutting the shoulders is an in-cannel or scribing gouge which, unlike a carving gouge, is bevelled and sharpened on the inside of the curved blade. The first time you make such a joint it is well worth practising the paring of the scribed shoulders on an offcut before committing yourself to cutting the joint.

Gluing up a scribed joint also requires a different approach from conventional mortice and tenons. A hollow cramping block with a cork lining is ideal but requires a lot of effort to make. I have glued up this type of joint successfully using a cam clamp. I have also pulled a joint together with a woodscrew inserted from the opposite side of the mortice and then into the tenon, bringing the shoulders up perfectly. The head of the screw was sunk into a counter-bored hole that was finally filled with a plug. On one occasion I made a feature of the plug using a contrasting timber colour.

◆ Angled mortice and tenons

THE PRINCIPLES FOR CUTTING ANGLED MORTICE and tenons are essentially the same as the 90° configuration. The main difference lies in marking out and gluing up. If the two parts of the joint lie on the same plane then the shoulder angle can be worked out from a drawing or workshop rod. The angle can then be transferred to a sliding bevel and marked out with a marking knife. Very often, angled components are load-bearing members that take the strain in compression. For this reason, the tenons do not need to be very long, as their main function is to create location. Gluing up requires cramping blocks where the pressure face is parallel to the tenon shoulders, and the most effective way is to glue the block onto the tenon component (as described above). A layer of paper between the glued surfaces will make the removal of the block easier after the cramps are taken off.

NOTE

This section on mortice-and-tenon joints is intended to form a referential starting point rather than a step-by-step, 'how to do it' manual.

My hope is that it will provide a springboard for investigation and the application of these intriguing joints in your involvement in designing and making challenging pieces of furniture.

▼ Dining table in mahogany. Showing single and double, through and wedged tenons.

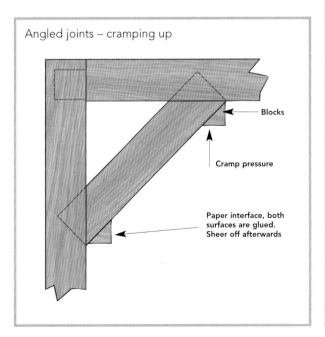

Angled joints – cramping up

Blocks

Cramp pressure

Paper interface, both surfaces are glued. Sheer off afterwards

Dovetail joints and jigs

Many woodworkers avoid using dovetail joints because they appear too difficult, but I believe that with a clear understanding of the principles, right tools and practice, the joint is quite easy to make.

▲ Swivel-stack jewellery box in pearwood and ripple sycamore

▲ Fitting a pivot into one of the boxes.

PROBABLY MORE HAS BEEN WRITTEN ABOUT THE through dovetail than about any of the other joints associated with woodworking. There is no doubt that it attracts much interest from members of the fraternity of wood enthusiasts judging by the response that one sees at exhibitions, particularly when a drawer is opened and scrutinized. Its popularity as a way of creating a container from solid wood has resulted in the availability of an assortment of commercially available jigs, from the very sophisticated to the surprisingly simple.

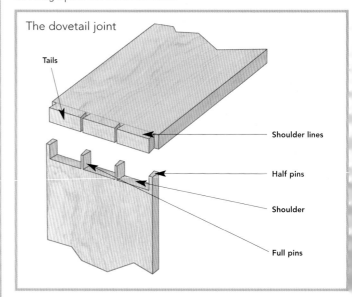

The dovetail joint

Tails

Shoulder lines

Half pins

Shoulder

Full pins

◆ Timber preparation

MY EXPECTATION IS THAT THE COMPONENTS will be prepared by machine. The timber needs to be accurately surfaced and planed to thickness. If the final thickness of the components is critical, add a small amount to this dimension; it will eventually be removed after the joints have been glued and the outer surface cleaned up.

Because of the control that I can exercise over the setting of my thicknesser, I prepare my material two tenths of a millimetre oversize. The significance of the setting will become clear when I look at the final assembly of the joint. As most of the marking out is done from the inside surfaces of the components it is useful to identify them with face marks. This is also true of reference edges, so I put a face edge mark on the edge that is most important to the subsequent control of accurate alignment.

After thicknessing and planing a face edge, I saw the components to width, using a sharp circular saw blade with a trapezoidal tooth pattern which will rip and cross-cut very cleanly. I dimension the components accurately to width, knowing that the sawn edge will be skimmed with a plane after the joint has been glued up. With the same blade the components are dimensioned to length using the sliding table facility on my saw to ensure dimensional accuracy and squareness of the ends.

Before I had access to machines, preparation was all done by hand planing, working with hand-held measuring and testing tools. If an accurate cross-cutting facility is not available, the next best way to square up the ends is with a shooting board, preferably one that holds the components firmly while the end-grain is being planed. I must stress the importance of accurate timber preparation, as this stage in the making of dovetails is critical to subsequent processes.

◆ Marking out shoulders

THE NEXT STAGE IN THE SEQUENCE IS TO MARK out the shoulders. I was taught to do this using a try-square and marking knife. This works quite well but is limited to the size of try-square available. The first time I made a cabinet that was wider than the blade of my try-square I improvised and used a cutting gauge and this is the method I now use for marking out shoulders irrespective of the width of the components. A cutting gauge is easy to control, producing a consistent line from the squared ends of the components. However, straight

off the shelf of a tool shop, the gauge will produce disappointing results. It is ground with two bevels and the line or cut that it produces is crude and ill defined, so I regrind the blade to produce an elliptical profile and then hone it to a sharp cutting edge on my water stones.

This shape allows the cutting edge to be rolled into contact with the surfaces being marked until the gauge can be smoothly pushed forward to produce a clean cut. The rolling action can be made even smoother if the corners of the cutting gauge stem are rounded off. This is because the sharp corners produced by the manufacturer cause an awkward rocking movement. I have found that many tools benefit from tuning to improve their performance and this is certainly true of all the family of marking gauges.

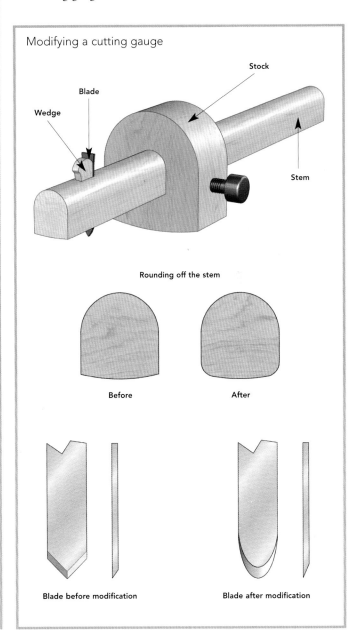

Modifying a cutting gauge

Stock

Blade

Wedge

Stem

Rounding off the stem

Before

After

Blade before modification

Blade after modification

◆ Pins or tails first?

I USED TO MAKE MY DOVETAILS BY MARKING OUT the pins first and using them to transfer the profile to the tails. This was the method I was taught and I justified it further by stating that this approach was also suitable for lap dovetails and secret mitre dovetails. In fact it is the only way that the latter joint can be marked out. Through dovetails can be marked out by using either the pins or the tails for the transfer of the profile.

Nowadays I usually mark out and cut the tails first. This change of approach came about when I was making a chest with 18 drawers and realized that I could speed up the process by cutting pairs of tails together, needing only to mark out the profile on one component. Despite the economy of time and effort gained when cutting pairs of tails together, it is worth noting that this method requires more care when sawing the profiles.

Pins or tails first: the choice is personal. I use either method depending on the convenience it contributes to the end result. The one thing that is common to both methods is that the second part of the joint is generated by the first. The first stage forms the template for the second stage. This is done by holding the first stage over the position of the second stage and transferring the profile to the second. In the early stages of my interest in woodworking I simply held the pins over the tails as best I could and transferred the profile with a pencil. I got acceptable results from this method.

◆ Developing a transfer jig

ON ONE OCCASION WHEN WORKING IN A VERY dark timber – bog oak to be specific – I had great difficulty seeing the pencil lines. I used a scalpel instead and overcame the problem! Because the scalpel line is an indentation in the surface of the wood, it catches the light in such a way as to create two edges, making it easier to see the line. I now use a scalpel for marking out all my dovetails. Even with a scalpel I noticed that the occasional gap appeared which affected the fit of the joint. Was it caused by inaccurate sawing? I took great care to limit this, but gaps continued to appear. After analyzing the problem I realized that during the transference stage it was possible for the components to move slightly sideways and this was the cause of the odd gap. To overcome this problem I tried clamping the pieces together from side to side but this was too fussy and slow. I held the two pieces together against a block clamped down onto the bench but this registered the two components in one direction only and movement could not be completely prevented.

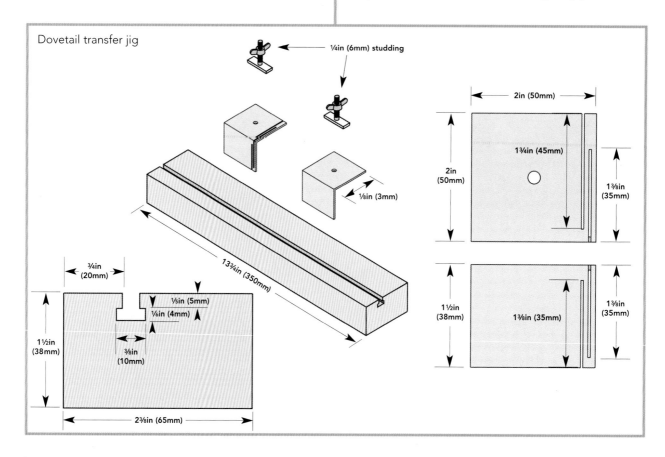

Dovetail transfer jig

¼in (6mm) studding

2in (50mm)

1¾in (45mm)

2in (50mm)

1⅜in (35mm)

⅛in (3mm)

13¾in (350mm)

¾in (20mm)

⅕in (5mm)

⅙in (4mm)

1½in (38mm)

⅜in (10mm)

2⅜in (65mm)

1½in (38mm)

1⅜in (35mm)

1⅜in (35mm)

THE DOVETAIL TRANSFER JIG

The mark two version of my dovetail transfer jig is simplicity itself. It is universally suitable for making either pins or tails first. It consists of a backing block and two sliding clamps, one of which has the two-way sliding spring system I also employ in my dovetail paring jig (see page 79). The backing block or body is made from 1½in (38mm) thick MDF with a T-slot to accommodate the slides that hold the sliding clamps in place. Build up the thickness with two layers of ¾in

(19mm) MDF if 1½in (38mm) thick is not available. I used a keyhole slot cutter to rout the T-slot. However, the waist of the keyhole slot cutter is too narrow so it is necessary to enlarge it to accommodate a ¼in (6mm) diameter screw. I found it easier and safer to rout a ¼in (6mm) groove first and then open it up to form the T-slot. Both operations were carried out on my router table so the fence setting was common to both cuts.

SLIDING CLAMPS

The sliding clamps are made from 2in x 2in x ¼in (50mm x 50mm x 6mm) extruded aluminium section. As I make a variety of workshop jigs and devices I had a length of this section in stock. It will be necessary to source this material but if you can buy it from an engineering material stockist it is likely that you will have to buy a 13ft (4m) length.

I would recommend locating a local engineering company and begging for an offcut! The sliding clamps need to be cut and the edges faced accurately. Being an engineer as well as a woodworker I was able to carry this out on my milling machine. However, it is possible to cut aluminium on a table saw using the crosscut slide. For safety and to ensure squareness, clamp the aluminium to the crosscut slide and feed it through slowly. Also make sure you are wearing eye protection, as the lightweight swarf can be a problem.

A triple chip or crosscut blade will do the job, leaving a little cleaning up to be done with a sheet of fine abrasive paper held down on a flat surface. You can cut the sliding spring slots on a bandsaw, but unless you are prepared to make a jig to hold the aluminium section it is safer to cut these slots with a hacksaw, while holding the component in a vice.

I tried to source off-the-shelf sliding screws and actually found some in a plumbers' supplies shop in downtown Aspen! Unfortunately they were not the right size. Instead I used strip brass, which is very easy to work and is also likely to be available from your friendly neighbourhood engineer. Insert ¼in (6mm) threaded rod (studding) into a drilled and tapped hole in the brass slide, with a drop of Superglue to hold the two together. The sliding clamps and screw slides are finally locked in place with wing nuts on washers.

USING THE TRANSFER JIG

▲ Mark two jig in use.

After cutting the tails of the dovetail joint, insert the components for the pins into the jig between the sliding clamps against the narrow face of the backing block after locking the non-sprung sliding clamp in place. Then tension the sprung sliding clamp with a little pressure against the edge of the component and lock it into place. The component will be held firmly but you can slide it between the clamps to align the end onto which the pins are to be marked with the upper face of the jig.

Next, hold this assembly in a vice and slide the component with the tails into position between the sliding clamps. Take into consideration any overhang – the projection of pins and tails – that is planed off after gluing up. I do this with a small engineers' adjustable try-square, used as a depth gauge, but you could cut a step into a small block of wood to achieve the same control. It is also possible to align the inner face of the shoulders, between the tails, with the corresponding inner face of the pins, by eye.

Once you have achieved this alignment, you can carry out the transference with a pencil or a scalpel. If you cut the pins first reverse the process – but with this method it is better to position the jig and components on the bench rather than in the vice.

I analyzed the problem and narrowed down the requirements to alignment of the edges and inside faces of the components. As with all my jigs my first dovetail transference jig was assembled temporarily from readily available workshop offcuts held together with double-sided tape. In those days I was a strictly 'pins-first' dovetailer so I developed the mark one version and produced it in Perspex. It worked quite well but was limited in capacity and was still tedious to use. After further analysis and some in-depth thinking. I came up with the mark two version. Mark one is now regarded as a piece of sculpture and resides on a display shelf in my showroom.

◆ Gradient angle

THE ANGLE OR SLOPE OF DOVETAILS CAN VARY according to the density of the wood being used. A gradient of one in seven is regarded as being suitable for softwoods and one in eight for hardwoods.

The angle is produced by using a dovetail template and commercially manufactured examples use the angles to which I have referred. Angles of more than one in seven run the risk of the corners being too fragile, and in open-grained timbers like oak these corners will break off easily. Angles less than one in eight work very well and can produce a strong interlocking effect even down to just less than parallel. If you decide to experiment with dovetail angles, use a sliding bevel to mark out the profile, and make your own template when you are satisfied with the result. In my opinion the final choice is essentially aesthetic and the angle chosen is a design statement.

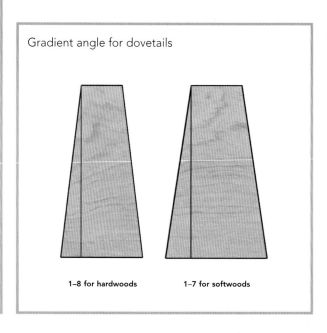

Gradient angle for dovetails

1–8 for hardwoods   1–7 for softwoods

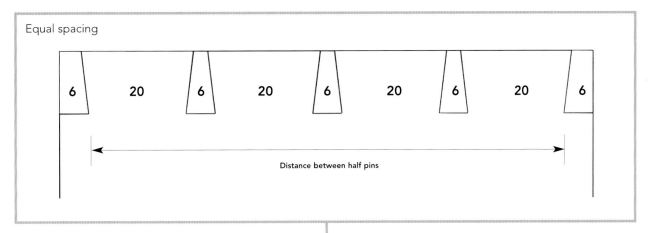

Equal spacing

Distance between half pins

Spacing

AS WITH THE GRADIENT ANGLE, THE SPACING of pins and tails can also be regarded as a personal statement. Examples of Victorian cabinet pieces show that just one pin in the middle of a drawer front joint is strong enough to withstand the pulling action required to open it. The considerable glue area and the stiffness of the pins contributes to the overall strength. Once again the choice of numbers of pins and the spacing is open to personal choice. More often than not the use of equal spacing seems to be most popular.

I have come across two methods of working out equal spacing. The first relies on the geometric construction – dividing a line into a number of equal spaces – and the second relies on simple calculation. I favour the latter method, which is even easier now that calculators are commonplace.

I start the process by looking at the width of the components and deciding how many pins the space requires. There is no magic formula to aid this decision, but once it has been made the next task is to choose the width of the pins. I favour narrow pins but the choice has to be based on the width of the chisel that will be used to pare the shoulder of the space left between the tails.

I measure the width with dial callipers and increase it by half a millimetre. This will be the final size of the full pins. I use this measurement to mark out the two half pins and then measure the distance left between them. They are known as half pins because they only have half the profile rather than being half the width of the full pins.

I then subtract the sum of the pins from this measurement and divide the balance by the number of tails. There will always be one more tail than the number of full pins. The resultant figures are easily transferred with dial callipers to the components and marked out with a dovetail template. In the past I marked out with

a pencil until I experienced problems seeing the lines on dark timbers such as wenge. There was also the problem of varying line thickness due to the rapid wear of the pencil lead. To overcome this I marked out the joint with a scalpel. The fact that the line is an indentation makes it easier to see due to the way light falls on the surface. A thick blade such as a Stanley knife is not suitable as the indentation is quite wide and the compression of the cut will result in damage to the corners of both the pins and the tails. A Swann Morton scalpel with a 10A blade is the ideal tool for this type of marking out.

The profile of the tails is marked out on the inside face of the component as this is the direction from which the joint will be cut and this is also the direction of assembly. The profile scalpel lines can then be transferred to the end-grain with a scalpel and try-square. Finally, before the pins are cut, it is advisable to identify the waste with pencil marks to avoid cutting on the wrong side of the line. As you gain confidence this can be left.

Sawing tails – theory

MAKING DOVETAILS BY HAND IS OFTEN regarded as an extreme test of craftsmanship. The fit of the joint should be achieved straight from the saw, and the only aspect that relies on a paring chisel should be the end-grain of the shoulders between the pins and tails. Many beginners saw away from the lines and try to pare back to them in case their sawing is not accurate enough. Apart from taking more time, it is difficult to clean back to the profile lines with a chisel as the cutting action tends to follow the grain. The key to successful sawing lies in the cutting action of the dovetail saw. The profiles of both pins and tails are sawn parallel to the grain, and even though the cuts are quite small the saw needs to be sharpened to produce a ripsawing action. I converted a dovetail saw from a crosscut to a rip, with a triangular

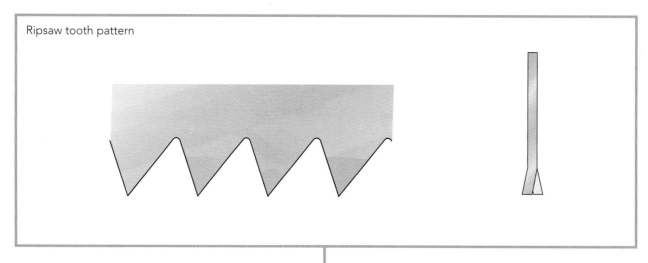

Ripsaw tooth pattern

needle file. When I started teaching, I found that this exercise was a useful introduction to cutting dovetails. More recently, I have noticed that some of the leading saw manufacturers have reintroduced ripcut dovetail saws, so if you are buying a new saw this is a good choice.

◆ Sawing tails – practice

Now we can enjoy sawing the tails in the knowledge that the cut will be clean and should not require any further adjustment. Hold the component in a vice with sufficient wood projecting above the jaws so that it is rigid and will not vibrate or flex. Good lighting is essential but avoid using a lamp as it is quite likely that at some stage you will be working in the shadow of the directional light source. I fix a strip of white masking tape to the top edge of the vice jaw and this reflects enough light onto the face of the component.

The most critical aspect of sawing dovetails is the start of the cut. Sight the saw to the waste side so that the inner set of teeth actually touches the scalpel line. Use your thumb as a guide and start the cut with a forward push of the blade, parallel to the line on the end-grain.

Starting with a backwards cut will cause the blade to bounce, producing indentations, which will trap the saw on the forward cut. Because the teeth are pressing down on end-grain, a light forward stroke will start the cut cleanly without digging in. Once the cut has been started the focus of attention should be on the angled line of the tail slope. Using the cone of vision technique that I explained in detail for sawing tenons, see page 58, saw with a light action, avoiding too much pressure on the forward stroke as the teeth could dig in. Stop the cut just short of the cutting gauge shoulder line. To get into a rhythm that will reinforce the practice and control, saw all

the cuts with a right-hand slope first and then go on to left-hand slopes. Some craftsmen hold the component at an angle in the vice so that the sloping lines are upright. In principle, this should produce better control but in practice I find it better to tilt the saw and position my head over at an angle to look at both sides of the saw blade.

▼ Sawing a joint.

CONVERTING A DOVETAIL SAW

If you already have a dovetail saw it is not difficult to convert it to a ripcut yourself. Using the existing profile, file square across with a needle file. Four strokes of the file per tooth should be sufficient to create a rip tooth and all the teeth can be filed from one side of the saw blade. Use a couple of strips of wood to support the blade when it is held in the vice. Although the process of re-cutting the teeth is quite straightforward it needs to be done with a real sense of purpose.

I have also found that the amount of set, particularly of a new saw, is more than is necessary. The set is there to provide clearance so that the saw can be brought back to the line if it tends to drift. I have reduced the set to the absolute minimum on my dovetail saw and the cut is very clean with no loss of directional control.

To reduce the set, run a fine diamond slip stone down the sides of the blade in such a way that the abrasive surface makes contact with the extreme outer point of the teeth and the side of the blade. Two or three passes should be enough, but make sure that the pressure is constant along the entire length of each pass and that the number of passes is the same on each side. Also make sure that the direction of each pass is made from the heel to the toe, from the handle to the front of the saw.

Finally, to check that the saw will not drift off line, make a sawcut from the end of a straight-grained piece of wood. Saw parallel to the grain and use as light a grip as possible so as not to influence the direction of the cut. Saw down to about 1in (25mm) and examine the cut. If it is curved then the saw has too much set on the hollow side of the cut. This indicates that there is more set on this side so another pass with the slip stone is necessary. More often than not, one pass with the stone should be sufficient.

Adjusting set with a slip stone

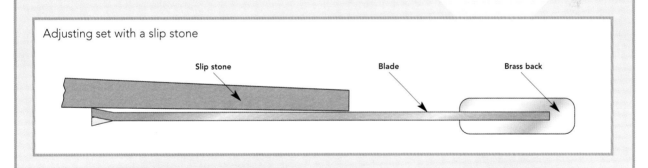

Slip stone   Blade   Brass back

SPACING

Formula for calculating equal spacing

Distance between half pins – sum of full pins
Divided by number of tails = width of base of tails

Example:
Distance between between half pins = 98
Sum of full pins =18
Number of tails = 4
98 – 18 = 80 ÷ 4 = 20
Width at base of tails = 20

◆ Removing the waste between tails

REMOVING THE WASTE BETWEEN THE TAILS IS best done with a coping saw or modified piercing saw. Chopping out the waste with a chisel and working from both sides inevitably results in breakout where the two directions cross over. If a standard coping saw blade has a set that is too wide to slide down the cut made by your dovetail saw, a fretsaw blade held in a piercing saw does the job.

Unfortunately, the frame will not be deep enough for wide components, although it can be bent upwards to provide clearance. Hold the frame in a vice and bend the blade clamps over using a piece of wood driven by a hammer to carry out the modification. Make sure the bend allows you to saw in the direction that suits your eye – I saw out the waste with the piercing saw held horizontally, moving from right to left.

◆ Shoulder lines

I USED TO PARE DOWN TO THE SHOULDER LINES, holding the chisel vertically and cutting alternatively from both sides. However, when lower back problems began to make this practice painful, I decided to sit, working with the components held vertically in the vice against a back board. My preferred seat is an adjustable stool, which allows me to carry out most techniques, from paring dovetail shoulders to involved and repetitive marking out.

Coping saw

Bent upwards to clear end of pins and tails when removing waste

Once again, it was the prospect of making a large number of drawers, which encouraged me to develop my horizontal paring jig, featured below. In principle, a block of wood held against the shoulder line is used as a guide. Adding a spring clamp enables the block to be held firmly in place while the assembly is mounted in the vice.

Not only does the jig ensure that the shoulders are cut square to the face of the component, it also enables the cut to be made from one side only. As this is the inside surface, it's only necessary to mark out this shoulder line on the inside. This results in a clean contrast between the end-grain of the pins and the face-grain of the tails after the joint has been assembled and cleaned up.

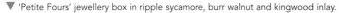

▼ 'Petite Fours' jewellery box in ripple sycamore, burr walnut and kingwood inlay.

Dovetail paring jig

Back and front of the different-sized jigs

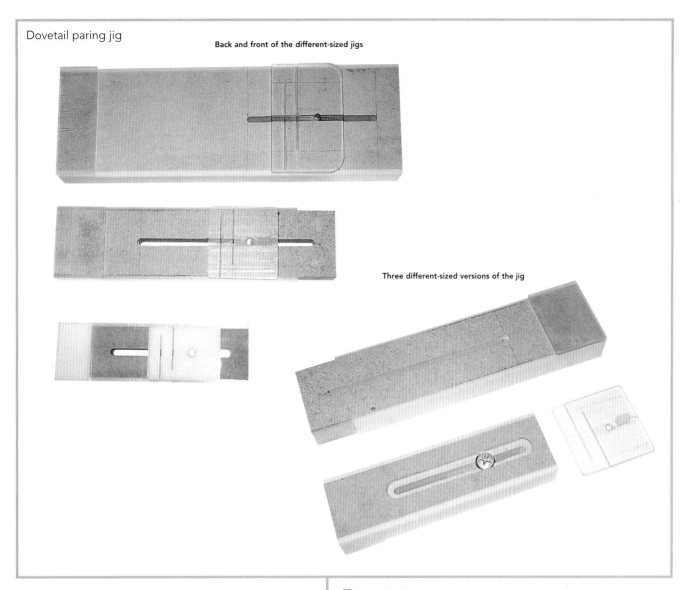

Three different-sized versions of the jig

◆ Making a dovetail paring jig

ALTHOUGH I USE MACHINES WIDELY IN MY WORK
for their speed, economy and accuracy, I still get
a great deal of satisfaction from using hand tools – in
particular, cutting dovetails by hand. I pride myself in the
knowledge I can cut dovetails quickly and accurately, and
have resisted the urge to investigate dovetailing machines.

Many people mention 'the uniform sterility of a
machine-cut dovetail' as an argument against using such
machinery. Arguments like this can usually be supported
from several standpoints but equally they can be destroyed
again from others. I have nothing against a mechanized
approach, apart from my stated personal preference for
cutting dovetails by hand – but I must add that I have
investigated ways of speeding up the hand-cut approach.

▼ The paring jig in use.

◆ Breakthrough

Some time ago I designed a chest of drawers that contained 18 drawers. After preparing the materials for the drawers l looked at the stack of components on my bench and didn't relish the thought of the length of time it would take to cut the joints. This prompted me to investigate the development of a paring jig to remove the waste between the pins and tails accurately.

I favour removing the bulk of the waste with a coping saw and then paring down horizontally to the shoulder lines. I hold the work in the vice and support the back with a piece of MDF to prevent breakout, working from both sides. I am not in favour of undercutting the shoulders, so care has to be exercised when paring from the second side to get the shoulder square. I have, on occasions, used a piece of carefully prepared wood clamped in place to assist in paring accurately to a knife line. It works but is difficult to position and takes more time than is justifiable. A second piece of wood fixed at 90° to the first makes alignment easier but it is still difficult to clamp it in place without the jig moving, resulting in misalignment.

My design breakthrough came about when I noticed how much pressure could be exerted with a two-way feather board – the type that can be made from a piece of MDF with two alternating sawcuts. It's a system I've used on my router table for many years and I certainly cannot claim to have developed it. However, I've adapted it and used it to great effect to hold my dovetail paring jig in place when aligning the paring surface with the shoulder line of both components of a dovetail joint.

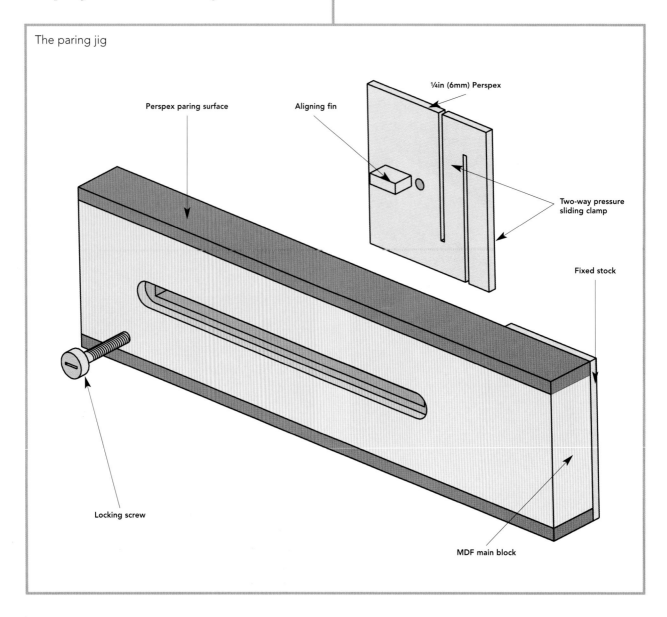

The paring jig

Perspex paring surface

Aligning fin

¼in (6mm) Perspex

Two-way pressure sliding clamp

Fixed stock

Locking screw

MDF main block

◆ Construction

IT IS USUALLY BEST TO MAKE THE MAIN BODY FROM MDF. The minimum thickness I'd recommend is 1in (25mm) but as I pointed out in other chapters it's not an easy size to source. You could build up the thickness with two ½in (12mm) layers but if building up the thickness is your option it would be better to use two ⅝in (15mm) layers resulting in a wider, more effective paring surface. The two paring surfaces must be parallel and absolutely square to the wide surfaces. The paring surfaces are subject to a great deal of wear, which can be effectively reduced by skinning them with a layer of Perspex. The fixed stock and sliding clamp are also ¼in (6mm) Perspex.

While the use of this jig will undoubtedly give you more consistent results, speeding up work, I must stress that it's not, in my opinion, a de-skilling process. It will be necessary to practise until you feel comfortable, and be prepared to vary the depth of cut so as not to force the chisel. The final bonus is that it can be done sitting down paring horizontally – which must be good for the back!

◆ How to make the dovetail paring jig

THE MAIN BODY CAN BE CUT EFFECTIVELY ON A table saw with a fine-toothed blade. I use a blade with a trapezoidal tooth pattern, known in the trade as a triple-chip blade. It's also possible to plane the edges of Perspex either by hand or with a machine planer. I fix everything in place with double-sided tape. I have to sing the praises of this amazing instant adhesive system. I use about five rolls of double-sided tape every year. Try and get hold of 3M's pressure sensitive tape. It's a thin tape with a powerful bond that can be used in a wide variety of situations. Virtually all my jigs – including those of a one-off nature – benefit from the immediacy of use and sufficient strength of double-sided tape. Fix the Perspex paring surfaces, which need to be cut slightly oversize, in place and apply pressure with your vice. Carefully remove the overhang with a sharp plane. Incidentally, offcuts of Perspex can be obtained from advertising signmakers.

Groove

A ¼in (6mm) groove needs to be routed through the main body to accept the sliding clamp locking screw. This is best done on a router table with a series of shallow cuts to avoid straining the cutter. My shop-made router table has sliding stops fitted to the fence so I can start and stop the length of the cut accurately. When you have penetrated all the way through, turn the main body over and rout a wider groove deep enough to accept the head of the clamp locking screw. The ideal screw for this job is a large-headed roofing screw available from builders' merchants. Next, the fixed stock. This and the sliding clamp are made from ¼in (6mm) thick Perspex. Accurately prepare the fixed stock and fix it in position with double-sided tape. The inner edge has to be perfectly square to the paring surfaces. This can be done by clamping an engineers' try-square on to the inner face of the main body and carefully offering the inner edge up to it before lowering the fixed stock in to position. Further reinforce the bond with pressure from your vice. A couple of small woodscrews through the fixed stock will prevent any sideways movement when the paring jig is in use.

The sliding clamp

Prepare the sliding clamp to size and then cut the two spring slots with a bandsaw. Drill a ³⁄₁₆in (5mm) hole, which is tapped to accept a ¼in (6mm) screw thread through the sliding clamp and temporarily align and screw it in place on the main body. If you are keen to get involved in jig-making it's worth investing in tools like taps and dies. I started by buying taps individually and gradually built up a comprehensive collection rather that spending a lot of money initially on a set. Such tools are available from any engineer suppliers.

Cut a piece of Perspex about 2in (50mm) longer than the projection of the aligning fin. Carefully apply a thin film of cyanoacrylate resin to one end and slip it into the groove until it contacts the inner face of the sliding clamp. Wait until it has bonded and then remove the sliding clamp and saw off the excess projection of the aligning fin. A wipe of candle wax on the inner surface of the groove will prevent the migration of glue that could bond the sliding clamp to the main body. I cannot stress the importance of the aligning fin to the success of the jig enough!

Using the paring jig

After removing the bulk of the waste from both the pins and tails, offer the component up to the inner edge of the fixed stock. Slide the sliding clamp up to the opposite edge, compressing the spring slots, and lock it in place. Slide the component down until the shoulder line aligns with the edge of the paring surface and clamp the entire assembly with a backing board into your vice. Keep the whole assembly as low in the vice as possible to avoid the

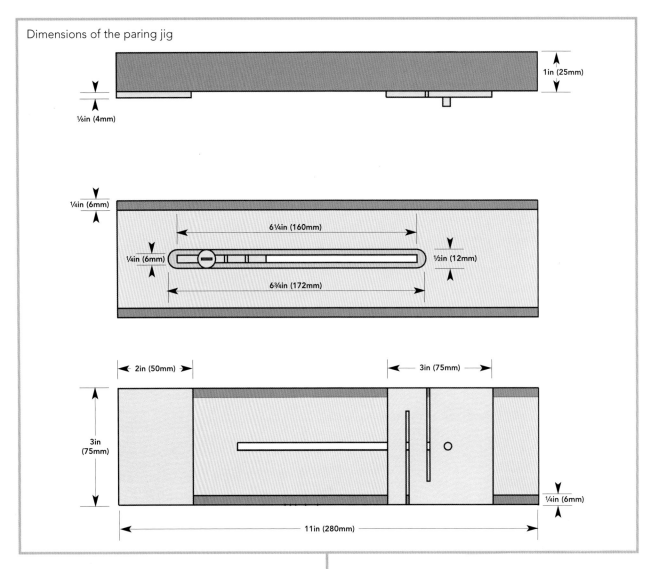

Dimensions of the paring jig

1in (25mm)

1⁄6in (4mm)

1⁄4in (6mm)

6¼in (160mm)

1⁄4in (6mm)

½in (12mm)

6¾in (172mm)

2in (50mm)

3in (75mm)

3in (75mm)

¼in (6mm)

11in (280mm)

component being pulled away from the jig. If this is a problem then it may be necessary to service the jaws of your vice to make sure they are parallel.

When removing the waste between pins and tail with a coping saw I try to leave as little as possible to be pared down to the line. I aim for not more than 1⁄32in (1mm). Using a narrow, bevelled-edge chisel I pare sequentially along from one side to the other until the chisel finally rests on the paring surface and can pare no further. All this can be done from the inner face of the component. Because the jig is double-faced the pins or tails at the opposite end can now be slid into position without removing the component. It's worth checking the flatness of you paring chisels. I have a few old chisels, which hold a sharp edge very well, but unfortunately the flat face is not flat enough, so they are not suitable. Modern chisels, even though the steel may not be as hard as older versions, are machine ground and are better suited to this application.

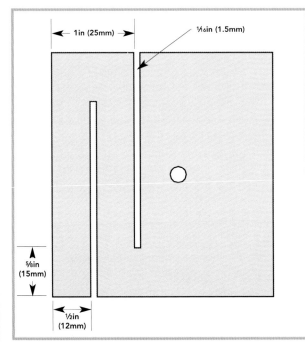

1in (25mm)

1⁄16in (1.5mm)

5⁄8in (15mm)

½in (12mm)

◆ Tails to pins

I
N PRINCIPLE TRANSFERRING TAILS TO PINS IS
quite easy. Hold the component with the tails over
the end-grain of the corresponding pins and transfer
the profile from one to the other with a scalpel. It's often
during this process that misalignments occur. In practice,
it's quite difficult to hold the two components together
so that the edges, and what will eventually be the inside
corner of the joint, align and don't move during the
transfer. It's possible to position the two components
and hold them in place with a cramp but this can be
inconvenient when a large number of joints are involved.

I developed my transfer jig to eradicate the problems
associated with this stage in cutting dovetails (see above
page 70). It enables the components to be moved into
position positively, and they stay in place, being held
firmly once the assembly is held in the vice.

The jig is versatile enough to be used for tails to
pins, or pins to tails transfer. After the profile has been
marked on the end-grain, the lines, square to the end-
grain, can be projected from the profile to the shoulder
lines with a scalpel and try-square.

◆ Sawing the pins

T
HIS PROCESS IS VERY SIMILAR TO THAT OF THE
tails. First concentrate on the angled line on the
end-grain and, once the cut has started, then focus on
the vertical. Making sure that the cut is on the waste side
of the line is important. For thick sections – anything over
⅝in (16mm) – start the cut on the near corner, with the

▼ The jig set-up with backing board clamped on.

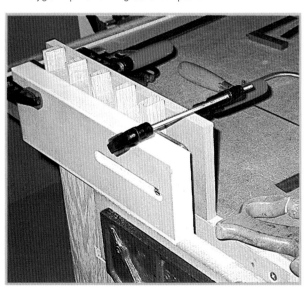

saw at about 45°, and progress down to the shoulder line,
alternating the concentration between the end-grain
and face-grain lines. Then finish the cut with the saw
held horizontally. This procedure is similar to the one
employed when sawing tenons, although here it is not
necessary to turn the wood round and finish the cut from
the other side. Once again, carry out all the left-hand
cuts first and then switch to those sloping to the right,
and benefit from the reinforcement of repetition.

◆ Waste

O
NCE ALL THE VERTICAL CUTS HAVE BEEN MADE,
the waste can be removed with a coping saw or
modified piercing saw. Identify the waste with a pencil
to prevent removing the wrong pieces. The shoulders can
now be cleaned up with the paring jig, but because of the
direction of slope it's necessary to pare from the outer face
of the component. I use a fairly narrow bevelled-edge
chisel, not more than ⅜in (10mm) wide, so that I don't
have to use excessive force for the first cut in each space.

Subsequent cuts can be narrower as they overlap
the previous cut. Try not to use too much force as force
cancels out control. Ensure the internal corners have been
cut cleanly: if they are not this could prevent the joint
being fully closed after assembly.

◆ Ready for gluing

I
CAN'T WAIT TO ASSEMBLE A JOINT ONCE IT HAS
been cut. This is particularly true with dovetails as
I want to reassure myself that theory and practice have
gone hand in hand. I challenge the old maxim that a joint
should only be assembled once (ie when it's being glued
up). If you don't test a joint before assembly you have no
chance to make any corrections to it. Moreover, the slight
compression that mating surfaces undergo when being
tested actually makes the finally assembly much easier.

I also finish the inside surfaces and seal them before
gluing up. If the initial preparation of the components was
done carefully, the surface quality should be good enough
to go straight to sanding, unless they have become so
dirty and covered in marks that they require skimming
with a smoothing plane.

The face marks can be removed with an eraser and
the surfaces then lightly sanded with 240 grit paper and
a cork block. Avoid sanding the actual area of the joint
itself. This is also true if you need to plane these surfaces.
I use a random orbit sander for the insides of cabinet-size

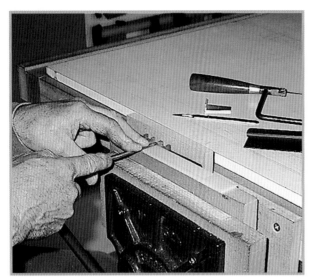

▲ Jig in use.

pieces, exercising extreme care near the joints. Apart from the advantages of its speed over large areas the sander can also be connected to a dust extraction system, which is always desirable both from the perspective of improving workshop hygiene and protecting personal health.

Spray finishing

I FAVOUR SPRAY FINISHING, WHICH IS PARTICULARLY appropriate for the insides of a dry-assembled piece with dovetails. Doing this overcomes the problem of removing excess glue from the inside corners. I let the glue set and pick it off with a chisel, as it does not adhere to the lacquered surface. This approach is not suitable for oiled finishes as oil will migrate into the dry-assembled joint. If there are other joints in the construction, such as housings, it's necessary to cover them with masking tape. However, grooves and rebates can often be cut after spraying the insides, and this is advantageous if glue is to be added into these cuts.

Sash cramps

BEFORE SASH CRAMPS WERE AVAILABLE TO cabinetmakers, the dovetail was assembled and glued using a heavy hammer and a block of wood. With its positive location and interlocking facility, sustained pressure was not really seen as important. But the process is quite straightforward with sash cramps, and the assembly can be squared up, should the corners require it.

Earlier I said the material should be prepared slightly over thickness, and that the shoulders should be marked out with the cutting gauge set to the final dimension of the thickness of the sides. This means that the outer faces of the tails will be proud of the ends of the pins. This surface will carry the pressure of the cramp blocks. After the glue has set and the outer surfaces are cleaned up, one simply has to plane down to the end-grain of the pins.

I use MDF for cramping blocks and cover the contact faces with parcel tape so that they don't adhere to the joints. Make sure that the surface area of contact of the blocks only covers the same area as the tails, or the cramp shoes will distort the unsupported areas of the assembly.

Square

CHECKING FOR SQUARE IS BEST DONE BY measuring the diagonals. If the assembly goes together square first time, the cramps can be removed sooner rather than later. This could release cramps for further assemblies if several containers have to be glued up. If the assembly is out of square, move the clamp bars in the direction of the longer diagonal until the two diagonals are equal. Leave them in place until the glue bond has formed. With aliphatic resin this need only be for about half an hour.

Cleaning up

THE MAIN PROBLEM WHEN CLEANING UP THE outer surfaces is how best to support the area between the internal corners. Even a small box is difficult to hold, as the downward weight of the smoothing plane will cause the wood to sag. I overcome this problem by hanging the assembled container on a base board made from a thick piece of board material, such as an offcut of kitchen counter top.

The base board has to be clamped down onto the bench and it's often possible to position it close to the vice so that some extra grip can be included in the set-up. If it's essential that the outer corners should be finished absolutely crisp and square, then it is necessary to plane in from each end. This could be tricky if one direction is against the grain. In most cases this can be overcome by tuning the plane to resist tearing. I prefer a small chamfer on the corners, which are often vulnerable to damage. This enables me to plane through in one direction, from corner to corner.

SAWING

For many craftsmen in the early stages of their careers, the skill of sawing is quite a difficult undertaking. Experience helps and the process can be speeded up with practice. Pianists or golfers practice their skills even when they have reached the pinnacle of their careers. We should take a leaf out of their books and apply their commitment to our craft.

It needs to be done with a true sense of purpose, and the effort will be fully justified. Prepare the material and mark out a series of left-hand profiles and practise sawing, then repeat the set-up for right-hand cuts. It's likely that the next time you make a piece containing dovetails will not be for some time, so do a practice run beforehand. This will add to your confidence.

RIGHT TOOLS

The most appropriate tool for paring down to the shoulder line is a bevelled-edge chisel, and I have heard that it was for just this purpose that bevelled-edge chisels evolved. You may find that the bevels have not been ground low enough to form a clean, angled corner, as some manufacturers seem to think of bevels as more of a cosmetic detail. If the bevel leaves a 90° angle, it won't cut cleanly into the corners of the tails. Be prepared to carry out a regrinding modification and make sure, if a vertical grindstone is used, that the metal is not overheated, otherwise it will draw the temper of the steel. Although it's slower, it's safer to use a coarse water stone or diamond stone.

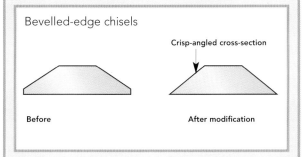

Bevelled-edge chisels

Crisp-angled cross-section

Before

After modification

GLUING UP

Now to the application of glue; I prefer aliphatic resin for most of my cabinetwork. Use a small, stiff-bristled paint brush and apply glue to the surfaces of the tails and the spaces between them of the first in the sequence, and assemble the joint driving it together with a hammer and block – it's not necessary to apply any glue to the pins. Repeat this for the adjacent corner. Three of the components have now been assembled leaving the remaining two joints to be glued up simultaneously. Now the joints can be fully closed using the sash cramps and blocks.

This method of assembly works well for small containers, such as boxes and drawers, as the amount of surface area from corner to corner is quite minimal. Little effort is required to clean up the outer surfaces, down to the end-grain of the pins and tails. For larger carcass construction, it's better to let the pins and tails project and to glue up the assembly with notched cramping blocks. Cleaning up the outer surfaces is then simply a matter of planing down the projections; and the surfaces can then be finished with abrasive paper.

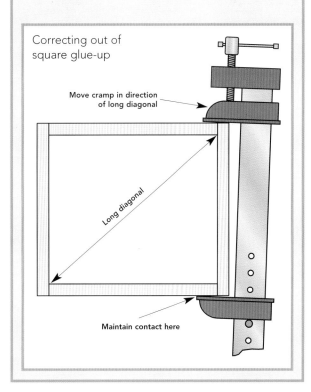

Correcting out of square glue-up

Move cramp in direction of long diagonal

Long diagonal

Maintain contact here

Miniature dovetails

In principle, there should be no difference between large and small dovetails. In practice, the difference in scale can affect the approach to cutting and to the sort of tools that should be used.

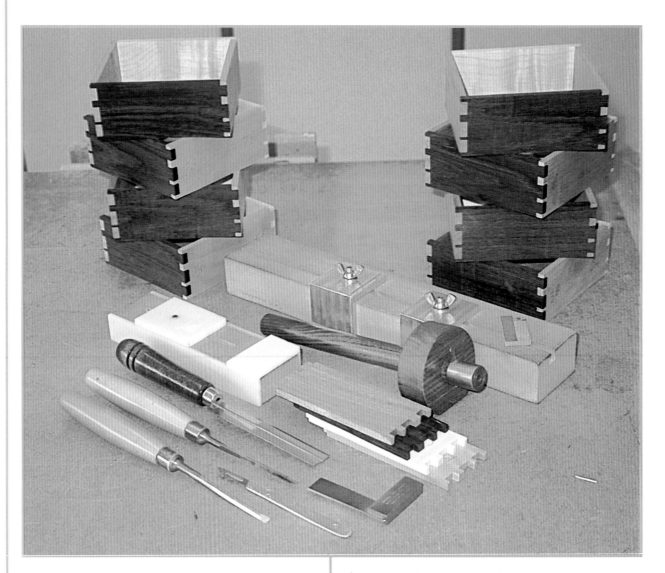

▲ Examples of dovetails and the tools required.

MANY YEARS AGO, I MADE A SCALE MODEL OF A desk, which I designed for my National Diploma in Design exam. I was given four weeks to make solid scale models, which could quite easily be made in a few days. With this in mind, I decided to make exact scale models in precise detail, with drawers that worked properly and lap dovetails for the solid wood carcass construction.

I had a small collection of hand tools similar to the kind that most students would have had at the time and my set included a Roberts and Lee 8in (200mm) dovetail saw. I still have the scale model. I looked at it recently and marvelled at the lap dovetail joints I cut in material ³⁄₁₆in (5mm) thick. Now I have a comprehensive collection

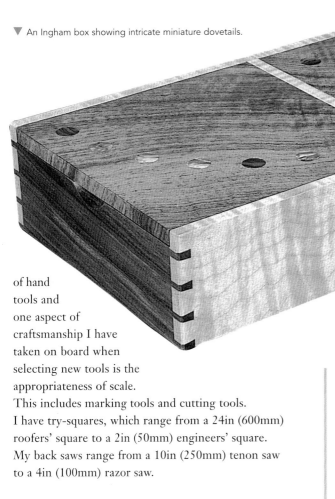

▼ An Ingham box showing intricate miniature dovetails.

of hand tools and one aspect of craftsmanship I have taken on board when selecting new tools is the appropriateness of scale. This includes marking tools and cutting tools. I have try-squares, which range from a 24in (600mm) roofers' square to a 2in (50mm) engineers' square. My back saws range from a 10in (250mm) tenon saw to a 4in (100mm) razor saw.

◆ Timber preparation

THERE IS MUCH IN COMMON BETWEEN THE preparation of timber for large or small containers that use dovetail joints. The material has to be planed, face side and face edge and to thickness and width. There are essentially two methods: working by hand or by machine. For me, the choice is quite simple. It has to be my Felder combination with its precise control of dimensional accuracy. I often make a batch of small boxes and this rules out the preparation of components by hand. The four-blade cutter block on my planer-thicknesser results in a surface quality that is never in question. My sequence of preparation of thin components, which are very often cut from thick stock, is to plane a face side and then remove a slice, slightly oversize, with my Hitachi resaw. The two machines then form the basis of a partnership where all the components can be cut in succession without any change of settings.

This stage produces an accurate face side on all the components. It would seem that, in terms of progression, the next stage would be to plane the face edges. Although it means having to change from surfacing to thicknessing, which needs resetting the tables, I find it better to thickness the components before planing the faces' edges. When returning to the surfacing aspect of the planer in conjunction with the fence to plane the face edges, I have a choice of two surfaces from which to determine the direction of feed which matches the grain direction. This choice is not always possible if the face edge is planed immediately after the face side. I can also put in an identification mark on the face side at this stage. I prefer to have the face sides on the inside surfaces of the box so if one surface is visually better than the other, the face side becomes the least attractive of the two. My thicknesser will plane down to a minimum of ⁵⁄₃₂in (4mm). When ordering the machine, I chose to omit dead rollers in the thicknessing table so that there was never any chance of a snipe at the end of the cut.

I spray a small wipe of lubricant on the table to overcome feed problems and this works well for material upwards of ³⁄₁₆in (5mm) in thickness. There is a risk of

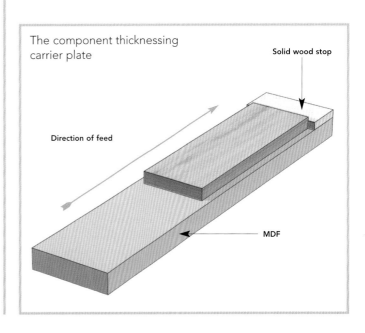

The component thicknessing carrier plate

Solid wood stop

Direction of feed

MDF

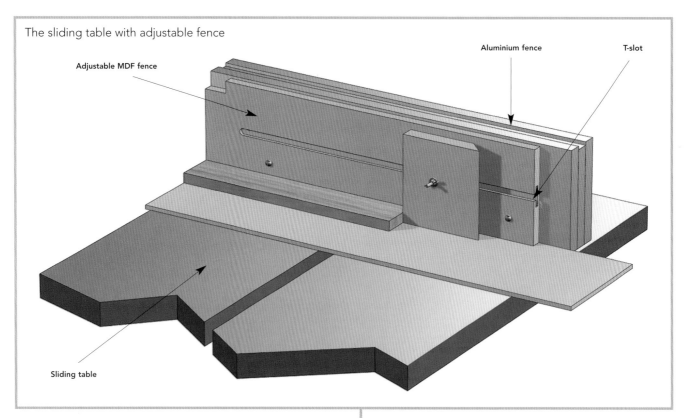

The sliding table with adjustable fence

Adjustable MDF fence

Aluminium fence

T-slot

Sliding table

chatter when planing thin stock, so to overcome this I use a carrier plate made from ⅝in (15mm) MDF. Ensuring that no lengths are shorter than the distance between the two feed rollers is an important thing to think about. Permutations of component lengths will overcome this problem as the final sizes can be dimensioned later. I also enjoy having the sophistication of a variable feed speed, so I ensure this is set on the slowest speed helping to eliminate breakout in difficult timbers.

◆ Length

THE CROSS-CUT FENCE FITTED TO THE SLIDING table is designed for handling large components and panels of board material, and the sliding stops and plastic spelch block are aimed at this approach. Unfortunately, the system is not quite fine enough for sawing small components, so I have installed a modification to the cross-cut fence in the form of a strip of MDF with a T-slot machined into the outer face. A sliding stop fits into this slot, which runs much closer to the end of the fence and, as such, much closer to the saw blade. The MDF fence is fixed to the extruded aluminium fence using sliding nuts so that the end of the fence can be trimmed periodically, giving an accurate measuring reference and perfect support for the end-grain of the component being cut.

The sliding table clears the saw blade, leaving a gap, meaning the underside of the component is unsupported, which can cause breakout. To overcome this problem I fix a ⅛in (3mm) thick strip of MDF onto the sliding table with small dabs of double-sided tape. It's positioned right up to the fence strip, and is slightly longer until it is sawn through by the first cut.

It not only provides support for the component, but is another useful reference for accurate measurement. For precise transfer of dimensions I use an engineers' combination square with a sliding stock. The stock is held up against the end of the MDF fence with the rule running towards the sliding stop, which, in turn, is moved and set against the end. Measurements are often very

▼ The sliding table fitting with adjustable MDF fence and sliding stop.

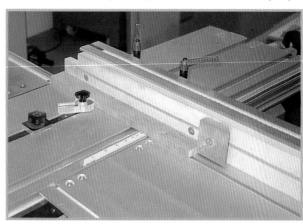

WIDTH

The next stage in timber preparation is to dimension the components to width. For this I use the ripping function of my dimension saw. I made a replacement mouth insert from MDF as the one supplied with the saw has a large clearance to facilitate tilting the blade for angled cuts. This extra clearance can lead to breakout even with a fine blade, particularly with cross-grained timbers. The insert was made by using the profile of the original as a template and the inside edge was cut by feeding the blade up through it, after it had been screwed into position. This in turn supports the wood being sawn and completely eliminates any breakout. I set the rip fence in the flat position when sawing narrow components to width, which is another useful alternative Felder has incorporated into its universal fence. This affords high levels of safe control over small components. My saw is fitted with a trapezoidal tooth blade, which rips and crosscuts perfectly, leaving the sawn edge almost as good as a planed edge. This edge will eventually be the bottom edge of the assembled box.

small. If the components are small enough to fit the capacity of dial callipers, it's more accurate to use this tool and transfer the setting to a combination square. With this set up for dimensioning components to length, I saw one end on each piece to establish an accurate end reference. This is done against the stop, which is set a few millimetres over length. The finished dimension is then set with the combination square setting and the stop slid into place and locked, and the components are sawn accurately to size.

◆ Marking and cutting out

THE APPROACH TO MARKING AND CUTTING OUT miniature dovetails is very similar to the method used for larger through dovetails. This is certainly true for a one-off box. Use a cutting gauge for marking out the shoulders and set the dimension so that it is a few shavings less than the thickness of the components. This means the box can be assembled and glued up without the need for slotted cramping blocks, as the ends of the pins will be below the outside faces of the box.

▼ The Perspex template with component in position.

▼ An assembled box on carrier ready to be cleaned up with a smoothing plane.

▼ The template and component held in vice with razor saw in position.

◆ Small boxes

I ALWAYS MARK OUT AND CUT THE TAILS FIRST ON small boxes. Mark out the profile of the tails on the inside face with a scalpel and dovetail template. If you plan to use my shoulder paring jig, remember that it is only necessary to mark out the shoulder line on the inside face.

I use a 4in (100mm) Zona razor saw for miniature dovetails. These model makers' saws are available in a variety of lengths, with a selection of tooth sizes and also a choice of pull or push cutting action. I prefer the pull cut for small dovetails because the cut is so fine that there is no ragged edge to obscure the scalpel cut marking out lines. Removing the bulk of the waste is carried out with a jewellers' piercing saw. However, because the cut produced by the razor saw is so narrow, it is necessary to fit the thinnest blade available. If that is still too thick for the razor saw cuts, don't be tempted to force it down to the shoulder line. Start a new cut and remove the waste with two cuts per space, and then pare down to the shoulder line with a bevelled-edge chisel.

▼ A Girandole swivel stack, made from bog oak and ripple sycamore – a good project for miniature dovetail-making.

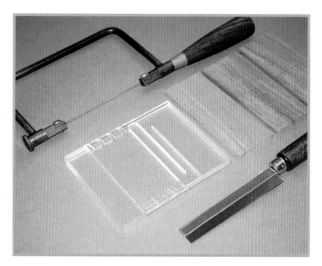

▲ Perspex marking/sawing template with a razor saw and piercing saw.

◆ Razor saw

NEXT I TRANSFER THE PROFILE OF THE TAILS TO the pins with my transfer jig and square them down to the shoulder line on the outside face with a small try-square and scalpel (although this can be done without the jig). I had the problem of starting the sawcut on the waste side of the line when I first used a razor saw for miniature dovetails. The blade is so fine that it kept slipping into the scalpel line of the profile on the end-grain, resulting in too loose a joint. I found that the joint was loose by the thickness of the saw blade as each cut actually removed half the thickness of the blade from the waste side and the finished side of the cut.

I overcame this by moving the profile of the tails away from the shoulder line; in effect making the pins slightly thicker. With a little experimentation I worked

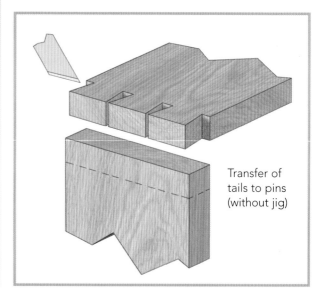

Transfer of tails to pins (without jig)

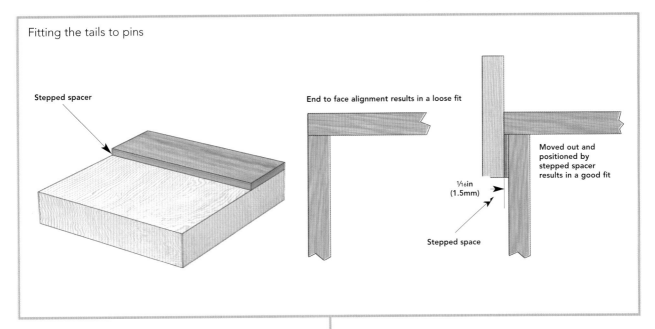

Fitting the tails to pins

Stepped spacer

End to face alignment results in a loose fit

Moved out and positioned by stepped spacer results in a good fit

¹⁄₁₆in (1.5mm)

Stepped space

out a shift of ¹⁄₁₆in (1.5mm) and made a small stepped spacer to control this measurement. Now I just drop the razor saw into the scalpel line with the assurance that the transfer of the profile from tails to pins will produce a good fit every time.

◆ Batch production

A LMOST ALL ASPECTS OF BATCH PRODUCTION involve the kind of repetition that can lead to boredom and frustration. This is certainly the case when marking out the tails. It's possible to mark out the spacing for one set, and then use this as a master from which the spacing can then be projected to a pack of components held together in the vice.

On one occasion I made a template from aluminium litho plate, but the material was so soft that it wore out too quickly. I then decided to make the template from ¼in (6mm) thick Perspex sheet. I marked out the profile and sawed down to the shoulder line with a razor saw. I was just going to remove the material between the tails, which would have produced a positive template, when I had a flash of inspiration. Why not use the sawcuts as guides for sawing the profile in the actual wooden components? This would eliminate marking out altogether.

I then spent some time developing the jig so that the depth of cut could be controlled by the distance of the cutting edge from the inner edge of the saw back. I fixed a rigid fence onto the Perspex with double-sided tape to form the face edge register, and a sliding clamp fence on the other edge allowing the component to be held and slid into position. This has sped up the cutting of miniature

dovetails to such an extent that I can now spend more time on the design and expression of my boxes. This also gives each batch sufficient individuality to be referred to as a limited edition.

◆ Gluing up

S OME BOXES ARE SMALL ENOUGH FOR THE JOINTS to be assembled and cramped up in a bench vice. Even the shortest sash cramps are very cumbersome for this scale of work, and it is difficult to distribute the pressure without distorting the thin box sides. In fact, they are more of a nuisance than a positive aid to assembly. I use pieces of MDF covered in parcel tape as cauls, and pop them and the assembled box in my bench vice. The parcel tape acts as a release agent.

You will need to measure the diagonals to check for square and then tap the corner of the long diagonal with a block of wood and a hammer if the box is out of shape. The lid and base of the box can be used to ensure squareness, if they are fitted into the construction as part of the assembly.

I have three bench vices in my workshop, so the assembly of a batch of boxes can be achieved without ruining continuity. With quick-setting glue, such as aliphatic resin, the assembled box can be taken out after 15 minutes. The interlocking feature of dovetails and the rapid grab of the glue will hold the box firmly together, as long as any correction to ensure squareness is not too extreme. Don't be tempted to clean up the outside of the box until the glue has set hard enough to resist distortion.

Lap dovetails

Pragmatism and evolution were the driving forces beind the development of the lap dovetail joint. It is an aesthetically pleasing and very strong joint, ideal for drawers and carcasses alike.

THE LAP DOVETAIL JOINT IS A FASCINATING combination of man's ingenuity in developing a practical and reliable means of forming a junction between two pieces of wood, and the aesthetic evolution woodworking has undergone since its beginnings. The first large-scale use of dovetails in carcass furniture was applied to drawer-making. These through joints

▼ Lap dovetailed drawer fronts.

were employed to resist the stress imparted to a fully loaded drawer, when the front pulled the sides out of the carcass. Many saw the pins as a distraction from the overall appearance of the piece, and some form of applied decoration was often used to disguise the joint. As the actual quality of craftsmanship in the construction of these early pieces was not very good, the application of an applied moulding or inlay was seen as an acceptable way of overcoming the problem.

◆ An emphasis on decoration

MANY OF THE FINER PIECES WERE VERY ORNATE, with the emphasis placed on decoration rather than construction. In fact, it was often the case that if some aspect of the piece did not show, then the quality of craftsmanship didn't really matter. With the increasing use of imported timbers and a realization that the colour and grain of the wood was an important contribution to the appearance of a piece, the problem of the through dovetail in drawer-making came under scrutiny. By this time in the evolution of design and construction, veneers were in use, and sawcut examples could be laid over the drawer front, thereby covering the front corner joints. It was not long before the economic advantages and the ingenuity of the observant craftsman, together with improvements in tool technology, resulted in the lap dovetail joint being cut from the solid. This meant the entire drawer front was made from one piece of wood. Very soon the joint was being used not only for drawers, but also for larger scale carcass construction. In principle, lap dovetails are very strong joints with good location and large gluing areas. They are best suited to situations where the appearance of the joint on show surfaces would compromise the aesthetic appearance of the piece.

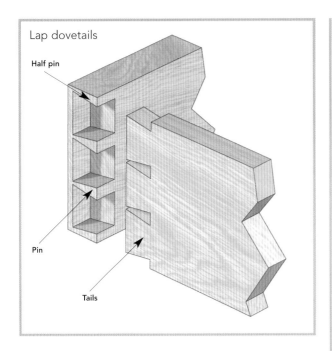

Lap dovetails

Half pin

Pin

Tails

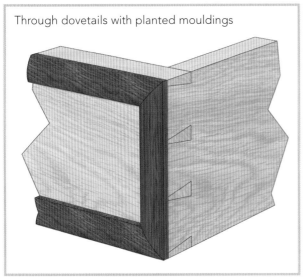

Through dovetails with planted mouldings

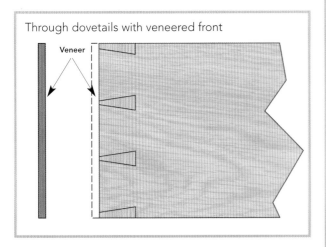

Through dovetails with veneered front

Veneer

▶ 'Ceres' chest of drawers with olive ash and dyed red sycamore inlay, 24in high x 8in deep x 8in wide (610mm x 200mm x 200mm).

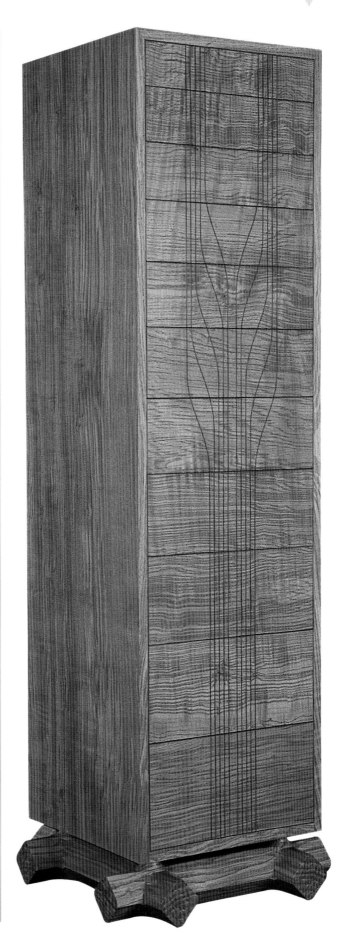

◆ Marking out

WHEN MAKING A LAP DOVETAIL, THE PREPARATION of components is essentially the same as that for any carcass construction employing dovetail joints. Once again, as most of the marking out is done from the ends of the components, it is essential to carry this out with care. A reliable dimension saw is the best tool to use.

The main difference between lap dovetails and through dovetails is in the cutting of the pins. Again the question of tails or pins first is a matter of personal choice. Whichever choice is made it is advantageous to work the marking out of both aspects of the joint in a harmonious sequence.

▼ Miniature chest of drawers. Olive ash and red inlay 7in high x 4in deep x 4in wide (180mm x 100mm x 100mm).

◆ The shoulder lines

AS WITH ALL THE DOVETAIL JOINTS I HAVE described, the shoulder lines are best marked out with a cutting gauge. In fact, it was as a result of the marking out of this aspect, on a very deep drawer I made many years ago, that I first decided to use a cutting gauge instead of a marking gauge, as the profile of the blade ensured a clean, square corner by getting the orientation of its faces right. Make sure that the flat face of the blade is away from the face of the cutting gauge stock and start by marking out the shoulder lines for the tails. There is a proportional consideration to be made here, which affects the thickness of the lap as it appears on the end-grain of the drawer front.

I used to employ a ratio of 1:4, but I now rely more on intuition and decide on the thickness of the lap very much by eye. This thickness contributes mainly to the appearance of the joint, so long as the lap does not get too thin, running the risk of being cut through when the waste is being removed later. Having marked out the shoulder lines for the tails, repeat the process from the inside face of the pins. If you have made one of my paring jigs remember that it's only necessary to mark shoulder

▼ Lap dovetailed drawer fronts of the miniature chest of drawers.

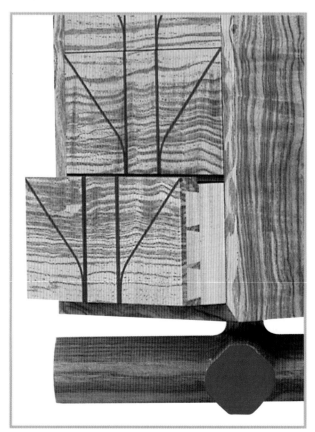

▲ Lap dovetailed drawer fronts.

▲ Carrying case for 2¾in x 2¾in (70mm x 70mm) slides. Olive ash and ebony inlay 14in x 9in x 3½in (355mm x 230mm x 90mm).

lines on the inside faces of components bearing tails, as all the paring is done from the inside! Next mark out the shoulder line for the depth of the pins. The cutting gauge needs to be reset to slightly less than the thickness of the tail-bearing components. This reduction in the dimension is absolutely necessary for small objects and for drawer-making. After the joint has been glued up, without the need for slotted cramping blocks, the extra thickness can be easily removed with a smoothing plane. This is not the case for a large carcass, so for these allow the pins to project slightly and clean them off later, without having to remove a lot of material from the larger surface areas of the carcass.

◆ Pin profile sawing

THIS IS PROBABLY THE MOST DEMANDING ASPECT of cutting lap dovetail joints. The first requirement is to emphasize the end-grain profile of the pins. This is best done with the same back saw used to cut the tails. As the pins are constrained by the lap, the only way to saw the profile is to start on the nearest corner and saw down at an angle of 45° until you reach the two cutting gauge lines defining their limits. Don't be tempted to saw away

from the line and pare back to it later. A well-sharpened and set saw, directed so that it halves the scalpel line, will produce a clean, accurate cut. If you put off this challenge, and rely on a chisel to cut back to the line, you run the risk of the chisel following the grain. Perhaps through a lack of confidence in your ability to saw accurately, the likelihood is that you will never attempt to use it directly. In general, if it's necessary to cut a profile with a chisel, avoid cutting into the end-grain as the wedge action can cause the chisel to follow the direction of least resistance, so drifting off line. This is less likely to happen if the cut is made across the grain.

Pin profile sawing

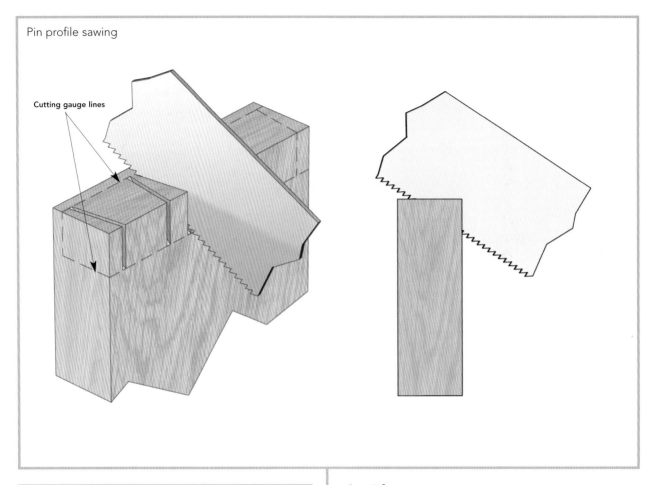

Cutting gauge lines

◆ Chopping out

BEFORE THE ROUTER WAS INTRODUCED THE WASTE between the pins had to be removed with a chisel and a mallet, a crude but effective technique. If this is your only option then the sequence will be dictated by the nature of the wood. Hold the component down with a cramp, on a part of the bench top that will withstand the impact of a mallet blow. The end-grain of the component needs to be level with the edge of the bench top.

Choose a chisel slightly narrower than the slot being produced and make the first cut across the grain a little way in from the end-grain. The depth of this first cut should be equal to the distance in from the end. It's likely that because this first cut is close to the end that the wedge shape of the chisel will cause the waste material to simply split off. If not, pare in freehand from the end-grain to remove the waste. Repeat this process until the slot being produced reaches the limits of the angled sawcuts that produced the profile of the pins. To proceed beyond this point you will need to cut down across the grain in the corners with a chisel narrow enough to be held at the angle of the pins.

Paring across the grain

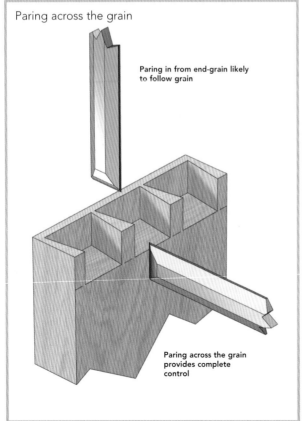

Paring in from end-grain likely to follow grain

Paring across the grain provides complete control

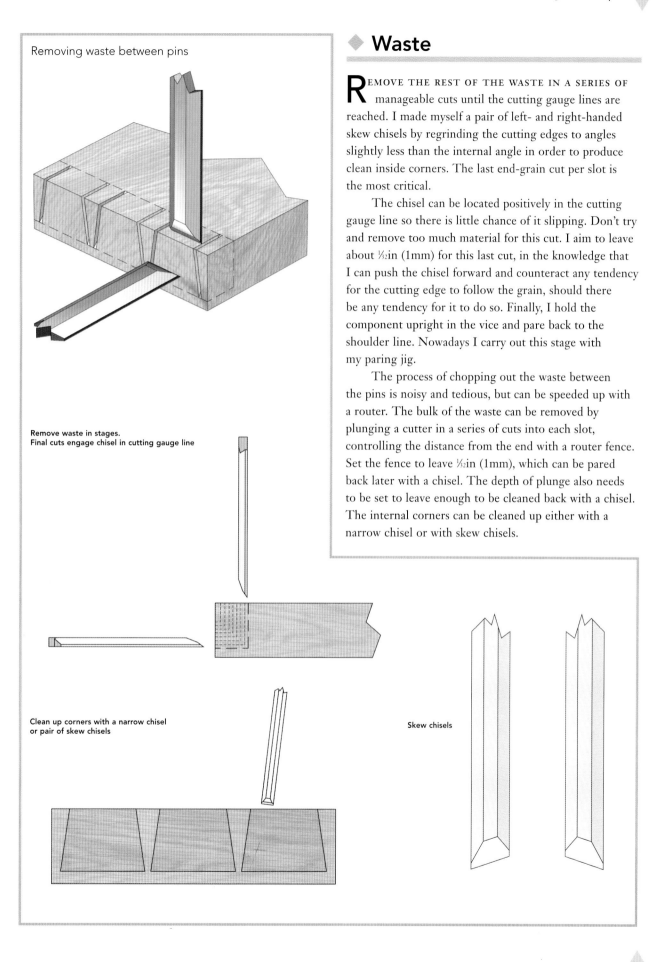

Removing waste between pins

Remove waste in stages.
Final cuts engage chisel in cutting gauge line

Clean up corners with a narrow chisel
or pair of skew chisels

Skew chisels

◆ Waste

REMOVE THE REST OF THE WASTE IN A SERIES OF manageable cuts until the cutting gauge lines are reached. I made myself a pair of left- and right-handed skew chisels by regrinding the cutting edges to angles slightly less than the internal angle in order to produce clean inside corners. The last end-grain cut per slot is the most critical.

The chisel can be located positively in the cutting gauge line so there is little chance of it slipping. Don't try and remove too much material for this cut. I aim to leave about $\frac{1}{32}$in (1mm) for this last cut, in the knowledge that I can push the chisel forward and counteract any tendency for the cutting edge to follow the grain, should there be any tendency for it to do so. Finally, I hold the component upright in the vice and pare back to the shoulder line. Nowadays I carry out this stage with my paring jig.

The process of chopping out the waste between the pins is noisy and tedious, but can be speeded up with a router. The bulk of the waste can be removed by plunging a cutter in a series of cuts into each slot, controlling the distance from the end with a router fence. Set the fence to leave $\frac{1}{32}$in (1mm), which can be pared back later with a chisel. The depth of plunge also needs to be set to leave enough to be cleaned back with a chisel. The internal corners can be cleaned up either with a narrow chisel or with skew chisels.

◆ Assembly

IF ALL THE CUTTING AND REMOVAL OF WASTE HAS been carried out by working carefully to the marked lines, the joint should fit together without any tweaking or fiddling. However, bearing in mind that at least four components will have to be assembled when gluing up – possibly more if the construction is a cabinet that may have partitions and shelves – anything that can be done to make this stage easier is worth considering. With mortice-and-tenon joints the ends of the tenons can be chamfered. Although it is not possible to do this to through dovetails, it is possible to chamfer the inside edges of the tails of lap dovetail joints as these will not show after assembly. Bear in mind that the inner surfaces need to be cleaned up and treated with a couple of coats of finish before the final assembly. As with through dovetails, I only apply glue to all the mating surfaces of the tails when gluing up to reduce the open assembly time of what is often a stressful stage in the construction of carcass pieces.

◆ Aesthetics and context

A FINAL WORD ON THE APPROPRIATE APPLICATION of the lap dovetail to a piece of furniture. When designing a piece, give some thought to the visual contribution that joints make to its aesthetics. In my opinion the lap dovetail joint is often used out of context. The very fact that it is available in the extensive arsenal of joints we have inherited and developed over the years encourages some craftsmen to use it to create an impact, often for the wrong reasons! The fact that the dovetails can only be seen from one face suggests that it is the other side that should be emphasized. This is perfectly demonstrated by its application, for example, to drawer fronts.

PINS AND TAILS

This aspect of the lap dovetail is probably the most contentious issue of the joint. It's always the lap dovetails, particularly in pieces containing drawers, which get the most scrutiny. The nod of approval from the uninvited judge will reveal whether you have got it right or wrong! Once again, as for through dovetails, there is no right or wrong permutation of gradient and spacing. Personal preference is the final factor as the joint, with all its excellent location and surface area for glue, is strong enough to do the job.

Having decided on the spacing, mark out the profile on the inside face of the tails. If the joint is going to show, and you have decided on delicate roots for the pins, make sure that the two half pins are not too thin as they are almost bound to split when the joint is assembled. The profile can now be cut with a back saw that suits the thickness of the material. The waste can be removed with a jewellers' saw, and the shoulders pared down to clean up the tails.

▶ The kind of joints you choose have a visual impact on the aesthetics of a piece as well as practical implications. Always make sure that your choice is appropriate to the style of the work.

Secret mitre dovetails

The secret mitre joint is often regarded as the most complex carcass joint in furniture-making. However, it is no more difficult to make than a lap dovetail, with which it has much in common.

▲ A secret mitre dovetail.

To START, IT HELPS TO APPRECIATE THE CONTEXT in which the secret mitre joint is best employed. There are many situations in which the appearance of a piece made from solid wood, with a complex grain, texture and colour, would be compromised if the corner joints were through dovetails. This is the main reason why the secret mitre dovetail came into being.

Through joints work in clean, straight-grained timbers, and were hailed for their honesty of construction by the exponents of the Arts and Crafts movement. But imagine the strain on the eye if through joints were used for a timber as visually complex as satinwood, with its multi-directional figure and strong colour.

Very often, such strongly figured woods were cut into veneers and laid onto less interesting and more affordable woods for economic reasons. The veneering was carried out after the carcass had been assembled using through dovetail joints for its construction. It's not unusual to find an antique cabinet where the dovetail joint underneath the veneer is apparent due to shrinkage. Like the lap dovetail joint, the secret mitre dovetail evolved from a through dovetail being covered with a veneer – the effect being achieved by cutting the joint from the solid.

▲ A miniature chest of drawers in yew (*Taxus baccata*) and madrona burr (*Arbutus menziesii*) using secret mitre dovetails. Carcass sides and top ⅟₄in (6mm) thick.

◆ Strength

ANOTHER DISTINCT ADVANTAGE OF THE SECRET mitre dovetail over a mitre held together with a loose tongue is the strong interlocking effect of the dovetails and the very large gluing surface area of the joint. I remember one of my students arguing against the secret mitre dovetail in favour of a mitre and spline. His piece included three drawers where the sides and ends showed, and the drawers were pulled out in three different directions. Although the timber was quite plain in appearance he did not want to use through joints. When it came to gluing up the drawers he was struggling, not only with the distortion in the components, but also with the problem of installing the necessary angled cramping blocks.

▲ The chest with the drawers revealed.

He glued up all three drawers in succession, using almost every cramp in the workshop. When he removed the cramps some of the joints sprung apart due to glue starvation, as there had been too much pressure on the end-grain surfaces of the mitres. Because of the large numbers of cramps involved it was very difficult to check the assembly for square, which was very evident once the cramps had been removed. Admitting he had chosen the wrong course of action, he then used secret mitre dovetails for the second attempt.

One well-known book on woodwork joints, which was the encyclopaedia of its time, stated that the secret mitre dovetail should only be used in high-class work. I have not included this story to compare one approach against another in terms of which one is 'best'. Instead, what I suggest is that the inclusion of a particular joint in a piece should be judged by the appropriateness of its contribution, allied to the considerations that fit the analysis of the construction of the piece.

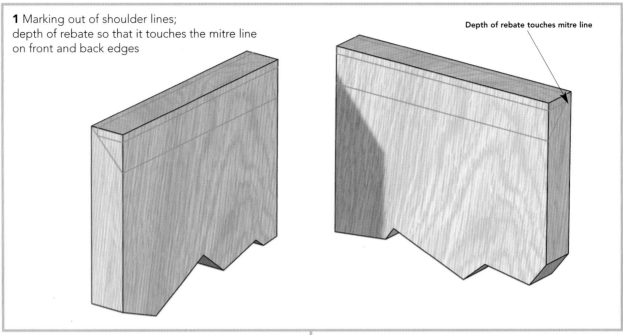

1 Marking out of shoulder lines; depth of rebate so that it touches the mitre line on front and back edges

Depth of rebate touches mitre line

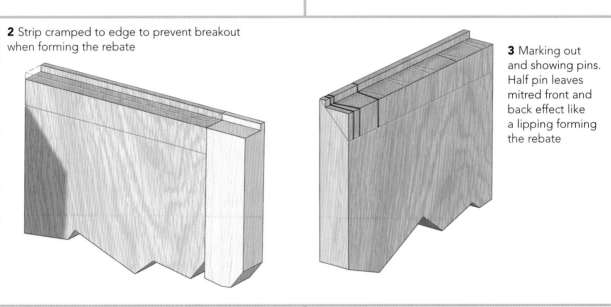

2 Strip cramped to edge to prevent breakout when forming the rebate

3 Marking out and showing pins. Half pin leaves mitred front and back effect like a lipping forming the rebate

◆ Timber preparation

TIMBER PREPARATION IS ESSENTIALLY THE SAME AS for lap dovetails. The only difference is that all the components that form the carcass will be the same thickness, so the components need to be surfaced and planed to thickness and face edges planed and dimensioned to width and length.

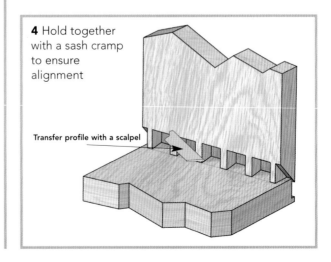

4 Hold together with a sash cramp to ensure alignment

Transfer profile with a scalpel

◆ The rebate

BEFORE THE ADVENT OF THE ROUTER, FORMING the rebates for the laps was a tedious and difficult task, as the bulk of the material had to be removed across the grain with a rebate plane. I carry out this stage using my router table, but there is no reason why it cannot be done with a hand-held router. Whichever method is chosen, bear in mind the potential risk of breakout at the end of the cut. The easiest way to avoid this problem is to cramp a prepared strip of wood against the breakout edge, which will support the grain.

Use the screw-adjusted depth and width settings of your router to control the dimensions of the rebates as these surfaces will form accurate references for the marking out of the dovetails later on. With care, it should be possible to adjust the settings on one of the components and obviate the need to produce a test sample.

◆ Dovetail marking

ALL THE OTHER DOVETAIL JOINTS I HAVE described so far can be made either by marking out the pins or tails first to establish the profiles of the joint. With the secret mitre dovetail there is only one option: you must start with the pins. During my period as a woodworking purist, I held the view that, because the secret mitre dovetail could only be marked out with the pins first, then this had to be the right way for through

and lap dovetails. Now, as a craftsman who is prepared to try out an approach that produces results irrespective of the dogma of 'right' and 'wrong', and thinking more in terms of appropriateness, I am much more flexible in my choice of starting point.

The proportions of pins and tails can be quite generous, as they make no aesthetic contribution to the appearance of the assembled joint. Because the internal details of the joint are completely concealed, the two half pins have to be set in from the edges, creating what, in effect, would be a lipping to be mitred later.

The remaining space can be divided up between the full pins and tails in the same way as that of a through joint and the profiles marked out on the end-grain of the rebate. Once the profiles have been marked out they can then be squared down to the shoulder line on the inside face, to provide visual control for the sawing stage.

◆ Removing waste

THIS PROCESS IS SIMILAR TO THAT OF THE LAP dovetail. Saw the profiles first, starting on the near corner and stopping just short of the shoulder line and the inside corner of the lap formed by the rebate. Don't worry about the sawcuts in the lap itself, as they will be removed when the mitre is formed. The waste between the pins can then be removed, either by chopping it out with a mallet and chisel or by plunging a router cutter down to remove the bulk of the waste and paring back to the limits of the slots with a chisel.

MARKING OUT

Even though the outsides of the carcass will be the show surfaces, I place the face marks on the insides as it is from these reference surfaces that all the marking out and cutting will take place. As with all the dovetail joints I have described in this section, start the marking out with the shoulder lines using a cutting gauge.

Set the gauge to a couple of shavings less than the thickness of the components and mark a line from the ends on the inside faces. When the mitres are eventually cut, this reduction in the setting will produce a small flat edge rather than a vulnerable feather edge.

Follow this by marking out the mitres on the front and back edges using a mitre square and marking knife. Next mark the depth of the rebate that will form the lap, which will eventually be the mitred overhang. The depth of this lap needs to be about a quarter of the thickness of the component. This is because its main function is to hide the dovetails. It is worth keeping the surface area of the end-grain of the mitre to a minimum, bearing in mind that it involves end-grain to end-grain gluing. It is also easier to form a narrow mitre, which will be easier to fit later on. The dimensions of the lap also need to be such that the inside corner touches the mitre knife lines on the front and back edges.

CUTTING TAILS

The transfer of profile from pins to tails can only be done from the inside corner as the projection of the rebated section prevents access from the outside. It also means that a transfer jig cannot be employed but the positive location of the rebates does enable one component to be held firmly in place over the other. To prevent any misalignment from side to side, a small sash cramp can be used to hold the two in place, and the profile can then be transferred from pins to tails using a scalpel. The profile can now be cut using a dovetail saw, taking care to cut on the waste side of the line such that the sawcut just touches the line. This can now be followed by the removal of the waste between the tails in the same way as that of the pins. It is now possible to partially assemble the joint to determine how tight it fits. Because the dovetails do not show when the joint is assembled, the corners on the ends of the pins can be removed by cutting small chamfers, which will make it easier to assemble the joint when it is finally glued up.

◆ Cutting the mitres

CUTTING THE MITRES IS THE MOST CRUCIAL aspect of the joint. It is critical to the appearance of the assembled joint, but it is not difficult to do. There are two stages involved and they must be carried out in the right sequence. Firstly, the front and back edge mitres need to be cut by removing the bulk of the waste with a dovetail saw and then paring back to the knife line with a chisel. This is best performed with the components held in a vice so that complete control can be exercised over the cutting action, particularly when paring back to the knife lines. Although it is possible to pare down vertically, I prefer to hold the components in the vice. This means the line can be pared horizontally in the same way that I pare back to any shoulder lines, be they those of tenons or dovetails.

Alternatively, you could make a mitre paring jig, which will ensure control over this important aspect of the joint. It consists of a strip of wood with a rebate cut along the length. The ends are then cut to an angle of 45° enabling the jig to be used for both right-hand and left-hand cuts.

▲ A mitre paring jig.

◆ Problems

THE MAIN PROBLEM WHEN USING THIS JIG IS TO hold it in place securely before it and the component are held in the vice. I made my jig from Perspex acrylic blocks, and machined the mitred surfaces on my milling machine to ensure absolute accuracy. I also built in a small clamping device, which enables careful alignment with the knife line and positive hold when the component is placed in the vice.

Once the front and back edge mitres have been cut, the mitre along the rebate can be removed. Before the advent of the hand-held router, this mitre would have been cut with a shoulder plane. With a router table this process is quite straightforward. Care in adjusting the cutter settings needs to be taken to remove the waste wood accurately. The mitre profile cutter needs to be set into the fence, which can be adjusted so that the cutting edge touches the pared mitre surfaces that have already been cut. This stage may well also require the cutter to be raised until contact is made. Both of these adjustments are best done using the screw adjusters fitted to the fence and the depth control. It's also possible to cut the rebate mitres with an overhead hand-held router, but extreme care needs to be exercised at the beginning and end of the cut. If the set-up is carefully carried out, the two mitres should fit when the joint is assembled. If, however, adjustment is needed, this can be done with a shoulder plane.

Assembling the joint

THE SECRET MITRE DOVETAIL, OUT OF ALL carcass joints, is by far the easiest to assemble and glue up, as the location is positive in all directions. There is no need to make any special cramping blocks. Because of the large surface area of glue contact in the joint and the time it takes to apply the glue, I reduce the open assembly time by applying glue only to the components with the tails. For large carcasses, glue up opposite corners of the construction, and assemble the other two corners dry. This will give you plenty of time to apply the cramps and test for square. Repeat this process for the two remaining corners when the glue in the first two has set. For small boxes, it should be possible to assemble and glue up all four corners in one continuous sequence.

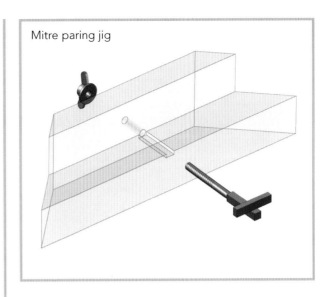

Mitre paring jig

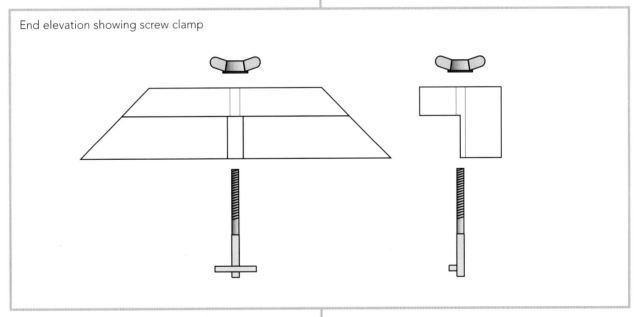

End elevation showing screw clamp

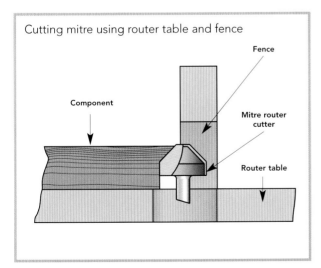

Cutting mitre using router table and fence

Component

Fence

Mitre router cutter

Router table

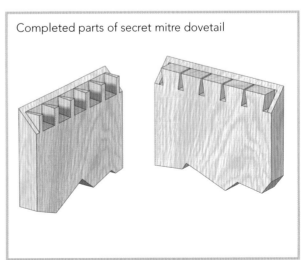

Completed parts of secret mitre dovetail

Cramps and cramping

Why is gluing up so stressful and fraught with problems? I have given a lot of thought to the question and the main consideration, as I see it, is that of planning, even at the design stage.

MANY ARTS AND CRAFTS PIECES, PARTICULARLY cabinets, had a logic of assembly that employed the simple strategy of assembling all components in one direction, with all cramp pressure being applied in one direction, too. When you consider the very short open assembly time of hot melt animal glue this simple logic makes a lot of sense. I sometimes shudder at the prospect of such an experience and remember asking a senior cabinetmaker how he tackled the problem. His answer was: teamwork… get as many pairs of hands to help as you can and then make sure that everyone knows what to do and when, as with gluing up you do not get a second chance.

▼ Glue-up using Kantenfix clamps for cylinder to round section curved rail junction.

◆ Design considerations

WITH TODAY'S NEW AND UNUSUAL DESIGNS, assembly and gluing up must be given ongoing consideration during the detailed design stages. It is possible to predict a lot of potential problems as early as at the drawing stage.

If you employ a radical construction, the value of a mock-up or a test joint gives you the opportunity to glue up and test the construction dynamically. It might even back up your product liability insurance if the construction is to be included in the making of a chair, for example. It will certainly enable you to work out the sequence of assembly, bearing in mind such important factors as directions of pressure and clamping blocks to distribute load efficiently. In short, the motto of gluing should be: plan and leave nothing to chance.

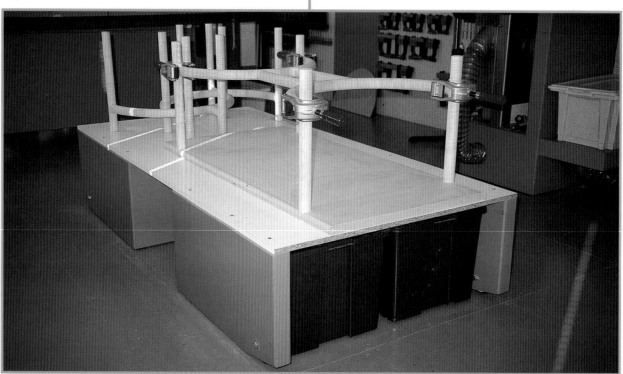

▲ Organization and planning are everything when it comes to gluing up – make life easy for yourself, have a dedicated table at a comfortable height.

◆ Cramp costs

WHILE IT IS TRUE THAT YOU CAN NEVER have too many cramps, economics often dictate otherwise as cramps can be expensive. In reality, it is often necessary to compromise, and applying some thought and discussing your requirements with established cramp makers can save you money.

Base your choice of cramps on the type of work you are planning to do, not forgetting that you can expand your collection as you go along. It is also worth shopping around to get the best deals. Look out for special deals at trade shows, where discounts are often offered to encourage people to attend.

Remember the maxim: 'nothing ventured nothing gained'. Ask for a discount if you are buying more than just a couple of items. I once went to a tool supplier intending to buy four 24in (600mm) sash cramps and came away with a dozen after negotiating a substantial discount. There are cramps for all kinds of situations. It takes time to build up a comprehensive collection and buying some of the specialist cramps can be put off until later.

◀ Good preparation, like spending the time making special blocks, will pay dividends.

▲ A carefully selected range of clamps and cramps.

Sash cramps

Probably the most indispensable cramp is the sash cramp. These are available in sizes from 24in (600mm), increasing in 6in (150mm) increments to 6ft (1,830mm). The ultimate goal is to have a selection of all the sizes, but a realistic start would be to think about the scale of work that you envisage carrying out and buy accordingly.

Also, bear in mind that sash cramps are used in pairs in many situations and that some sizes are used more often than others. I would recommend investing in six 24in (600mm) and six 36in (900mm) to start with.

When used in cabinetmaking, it is not necessary for sash cramps to have heavy-duty bars or T-section bars as joints should not be so tight as to require the extra force. However, if you require increased capacity it is possible to bolt two cramps together to achieve this. Use two bolts and screw the two cramps together so that they behave as one.

New sash cramps need to be cleaned thoroughly as they are liberally covered in oil. Be sure that you clean the screws, too, or you can be certain that oil will get onto that beautiful sycamore surface! Alternatives to the sash cramp are available, particularly the well-engineered deep-jawed versions that are popular in Germany and America. I personally don't favour these for assembling carcass furniture because of their excessive bulk.

In addition, I like the inner edge of the bar to contact the surface of the component being cramped and this is more difficult to achieve with deep jaws. Because it is impossible to tighten up all the cramps involved at the same time, in almost any situation that requires the internal corners of an assembly to be square it is likely that some adjustment will have to be carried out. This is done by moving the cramps towards the longer of the two diagonals. It is easier to do this progressively if one point of contact with the outside face of the assembly can be maintained. This is much more difficult to achieve with deep-jawed cramps.

However, with the inner edge of the bar in contact with the component it is quite likely that it will also come into contact with the glue, resulting in a rust mark on the surface. This can be prevented by covering the bar with masking tape. Better still, I use pieces of extruded plastic channel, which I cut from file binders. This U-shaped strip of plastic can be bought from any office supplies or stationery shop. The plastic strip can be slid along the bar to any desired position to prevent contact with glue, thus avoiding any rust on the cramp or stain on the wood.

Making your own cramp stands

It is also worth making cramp stands. The jaws of sash cramps have a small foot that is intended to prevent the cramp from falling over sideways when placed on a work surface. Sadly, the foot is often not wide enough and whole sets of cramps fall over at the most inopportune times. I have made my own cramp stands from MDF squares with a ¼in groove (cramp bars are still made from imperial stock) routed into the face. It is easier to rout a groove into a strip of MDF 2in x ½in (50mm x 12mm) and cut it into squares after routing the groove.

While talking about sash cramps I should mention cramp heads, which are bought in sets for which you make your own bars from wood. While this might seem an inexpensive way of solving the problem you will find that they are bulky and cumbersome to use.

G-cramps

G-cramps are extremely convenient for clamping small components together and for generally holding down components while working on them. Drop-forged from steel, with a powerful screw, they are available in a variety of sizes from 1in (25mm)

▲ Glue-up using F-clamps and G-cramps, also showing a glue spreader.

▼ Glue-up using a sash clamp, G-cramp for mitred corners and Kantenfix edging clamps for curved component.

upwards. I have some monster G-cramps with a 12in (300mm) capacity, which I use for laminating, where the force needed to hold thick laminations in tight curves is difficult to achieve with a bag press.

Very often the appropriate size of clamp depends on the scale of work being held, which suggests that owning a selection of G-cramp sizes should be the long-term aim of most furniture-makers. Deep-throat G-cramps are also available but my preference is for the more recently popular F-clamps.

F-clamps have also been popular in Germany and America, and have been manufactured by leading German makers for quite some time. They are now readily available in this country, too. The main advantage of F-clamps is the speed and ease with which they can be adjusted to suit the capacity being clamped. Unfortunately, over a period of time, the bar serrations wear and the grip is liable to slip. It's frustrating – to say the least – when you come to take the clamps off after the glue has set, only to find that the joint was not fully closed. This problem is now being addressed by some makers with a redesign of the bar and its serrations.

F-clamps are also available with deeper throat capacities than G-cramps, which make them more suitable where pressure needs to be applied well in from the edge

of a component. Be prepared to pay accordingly for the deeper-throated sizes. Another practical advantage with F-clamps is the provision of plastic shoe covers, which very often obviate the need for protective clamping blocks. One word of warning: when buying F-clamps, avoid the economy versions sold from market stalls. They are flimsy and badly made!

◆ Wooden-jawed cam clamps

For lightweight holding, Klemmsia wooden-jawed cam clamps are a good substitute for metal G-cramps and F-clamps. They are quick and easy to set and are ideal for holding down components, but are not really strong enough for gluing up where sustained force is required. Because these wooden Klemmsia clamps are very light in weight they are ideal when the combined weight of components and clamps would cause distortion to the assembly.

◆ Quick-grip

In recent years an assortment of quick-grip and single-handed action clamps have become available. They come with accessories offering a versatile range of options. They can be useful for occasional use but, in my opinion, are not a suitable alternative to G-cramps and F-clamps for sustained application of pressure when gluing up a construction.

◆ Edging cramps

I use veneers for most of my carcass pieces. The edges of man-made substrates require lipping, sometimes before veneering and sometimes after veneering. For straight-edged situations the lipping can be glued on and pressure applied with sash clamps. If the lippings are curved, however, gluing up becomes more complicated. To avoid curved cramping blocks I use edging cramps.

I am not keen on the type of edging clamp that has a G-clamp with a secondary clamping screw set at 90°. The hold of the G-cramping action tends to slip and the edge clamping direction, because of its fixed position, is not always centred on the edge of the component.

A few years ago I came across the definitive edging clamp from Würth. This is a well-engineered clamp, consisting of a sturdy diecast frame and a pair of double-acting cams, faced with rubber. The cams open like jaws to hold the thickness of the component, while a screw-driven foot applies pressure to the edge. The foot is virtually self-centred on the edge, despite the alignment of the cam jaws. It's ideal for applying pressure to a curved edge. With a little bit of imagination, you can use these clamps to apply pressure from one side to more situations than just edgings. Although fairly costly items, their versatility offsets the price.

▼ Kantenfix edging clamps used to glue on straight lipping.

Edge press clamps

FOR EDGE JOINTING SOLID WOOD TO PRODUCE wide panels from narrower boards, most craftsmen use sash cramps. With clamps alternately placed at intervals applying pressure to the edges from above and below the boards, the work can be held flat at the same time. I have a set of six Plano press clamps for this purpose.

These clamps hold the boards flat and align the faces while applying pressure to the edges. The clamp consists of two extruded aluminium bars that press on both faces of the boards. When edge pressure is applied from the end-screw, the bars in turn apply pressure to the faces, ensuring surface alignment, producing perfect butt joints, without the need for splines or biscuits. These clamps are definitely only justifiable if you are doing a substantial amount of butt-jointing in solid wood. Axminster Power Tool Centre's panel clamps – though not as sophisticated – perform the same function at a more modest cost.

Other clamps

THE CLAMPS I HAVE DESCRIBED FORM THE mainstay of my arsenal of clamping hardware. I also have six jet clamps, which are ideal in situations when pressure cannot be applied due to the screw being restricted by the position of other components. A typical example would be a partition in a box. Jet clamps apply pressure from the outside, rather than the end of the clamp.

For small, lightweight, additions I use spring-cramps. These operate like bulldog clips used for organizing paperwork. They are versatile and simple to use, with an amazing amount of strength in their springs.

Masking tape

I CANNOT END THIS SECTION ON HARDWARE without paying tribute to masking tape. Not quite hardware, it is nonetheless a fantastic way of holding components together, whether small or large. I have successfully assembled coopered edge joints with wide masking tape and lipped the edge of ⁵⁄₃₂in (4mm) thick MDF with a ⅛in (3mm) thick lipping using masking tape. What makes it work successfully is the elastic quality of the crêpe backing paper which, when stretched over a joint, contracts sufficiently to apply pressure.

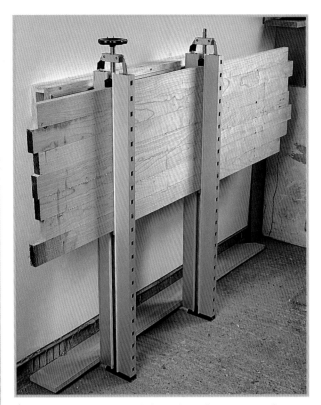

▲ The Plano clamps are superb if you glue up large amounts of solid board.

DEFINITIONS

Any clamp with a screw thread is actually a cramp – such as a G-cramp. Any clamp with a lever or cam is a true clamp.

STRAP CLAMPS

Strap or band clamps are usually associated with assembling mitred frames. Personally, I do not favour this system for mitred joints as I find that the pressure is not distributed at 90° to the surfaces being glued. However, I do use band clamps to apply pressure to a curved surface, which in turn is in contact with a curved edge to hold the components in place while the glue sets. Band clamps have been adapted for use in the assembly of components and have been associated with the haulage industry for many years. They consist of a flat strap of a low stretch material and you provide the tension by using a ratchet handle, which locks in position when you have applied the desired amount of pressure.

Glues

I have tried a variety of glues and adhesives and have learned to be selective. Here, I will explain the basic terminology used for the main groups of adhesives, before expanding on my own preferences.

◆ Urea formaldehyde resins

UREA FORMALDEHYDE (UF) RESINS ARE essentially of a two-part formula. The bulk is made up of a resin, to which a curing agent is added. This is certainly the case with industrial application. However, the introduction of Cascamite One-Shot back in the 1950s saw the resin and hardener mixed together in powder form. The addition of water released the chemical action of the hardener or curing agent resulting in a stated pot life of about 30 minutes. The pot life, however, was further affected by room temperature. Warmer temperatures reduced the pot life and open assembly time. For most situations the open assembly time is adequate.

The plus side of heat-accelerated curing was that UF resins can be thermally set by a variety of methods. Radio Frequency (RF) heating is used to cure bonds rapidly for joints and direct heating through metal plates is used for veneering. Not only is the glue set by the application of heat but the bond is also cured in a very short period of time. It's ideal for large-scale production.

I stopped using UF resins some time ago when I found that the shelf life was rather short. The shelf life was also affected by the container lid being removed from time to time, in a shared situation, especially if the lid was not replaced quickly, causing the powder to absorb atmospheric moisture. Joint failure and veneers lifting were common problems associated with moisture

▼ Choosing the right glue for the right application is critical to the success of a piece.

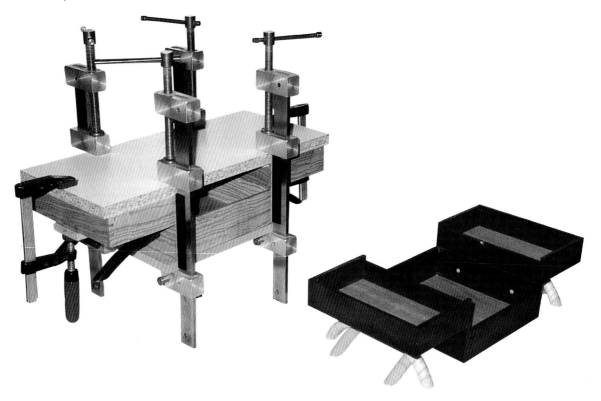

GLUE: A BRIEF HISTORY

The oldest form of glue known to craftsmen is animal glue. Early craftsmen refined the process of extracting gelatine from a variety of animal tissues, such as hooves and hide, by the application of heat, to produce an efficient and strong method for bonding wooden components.

The Egyptians used casein glue, made from milk. It was a cold cure glue with a good open assembly time and decent water-resistant properties. It never achieved the popularity of hoof and hide glues, probably because milk was relatively scarce before the establishment of a commercial dairy industry, and its value as a nutrient was most important.

▲ Animal glue has been the mainstay of furniture-makers for hundreds of years.

When cabinetmaking came of age in the 17th century, the complexity of structures that developed and the treatment of surfaces with veneers, relied upon animal glue. It is versatile stuff. Perhaps its most valuable asset is that the bond can be reversed by heating – a factor that is exploited to the full by antique restorers.

---

absorption. I came to the conclusion that UF was an uneconomical and inconvenient adhesive. It had to be mixed and there was almost always some left over, which was wasted.

There is no doubt that UF resins are strong, but I have found that the water held in the wood fibres after laminating takes some time to evaporate. This results in changes in the shape of the laminated form, which can lead to problems. In fact, any adhesive with a water base suffers from this problem. My final criticism of UF resins is the hardness of the cured resin: it dulls cutting edges. Planing the edge of a laminated component, results in the immediate loss of edge sharpness, blunting the blade.

▼ Very often, urea formaldehyde glues can cause spring-back, due to evaporating moisture.

◆ Polyvinyl acetates (PVA)

PVAs ARE PROBABLY THE MOST POPULAR adhesives. A white suspension of chemicals in a water base, they are available ready-mixed and ready to use. Whereas UF resins were developed mainly in the UK, the development of PVA was accelerated in Germany, mainly for industrial use. The bond is formed partly by the application of pressure and partly by evaporation of the water base.

The resultant glue layer is actually thermoplastic, but it is difficult to reverse the bond in the same way you can with animal glues. The cured glue is quite flexible and in some situations the subsequent movement of timber produces a phenomenon known as 'creep', when the glue can actually be felt as a line on the surface. This flexibility can be a positive advantage when dynamic movement, such as that experienced when sitting in a chair, is essential to the structure.

I have found in practice that the shelf life and pot life, which are essentially the same, make PVA a good, all-round glue. The open assembly time is rather short, so if you use PVA you need to be well organized and apply it quickly. It is slightly pressure-sensitive but there is time to manipulate joints before the bond starts. Clamps can be removed after a couple of hours but, as with all adhesives, the working strength is not achieved until the glue is cured. The cured glue film is opaque and if it is not cleaned off the surface it will eventually show as a pale mark when the wood oxidizes and changes colour.

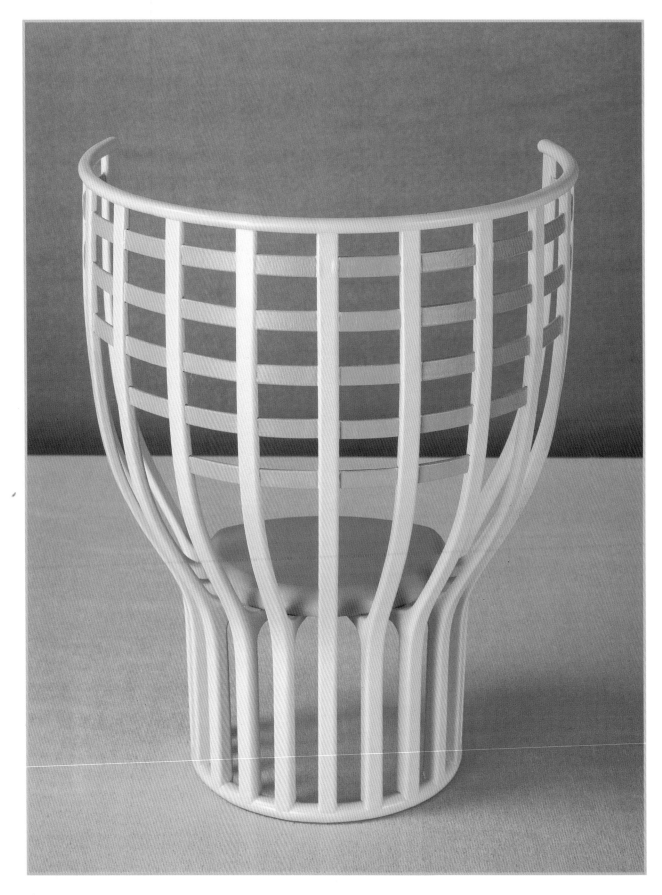

▲ PVA glues have a flexibility that can be an advantage, for instance in chair construction.

◆ Aliphatic resins

MY FAVOURED GENERAL-PURPOSE WORKSHOP glue is an aliphatic resin. For me, it has the primary advantage of convenience, being ready to use, with no need for mixing, no problems with ratios and no waste as a result of trying to judge how much to mix. As the solvent used to keep the glue liquid is water, it is necessary to keep it in a reasonably airtight container to benefit from its quite extensive shelf life. Kept in the containers in which it is supplied the lids ensure a good seal when stored. However, as it is available in different-sized containers I find it most economical to buy one gallon at a time and decant smaller quantities into the dispensers that I use to apply the glue.

The next advantage that attracted me to aliphatic resin is that it requires a short pressure time (although sometimes this can also be a disadvantage). Even after a few minutes the bond is strong enough to prevent repositioning as in the case of a joint that has to slide to a final position. The short pressure time, which is the result of the glue being distinctly pressure sensitive, is an advantage for rapid turnover of assembled components – ideal for batch production. I make batches of small boxes, which would be slowed down in terms of production if I were using a UF resin. With this glue I can clean up a set of dovetail joints quite safely after the box has been glued up for half an hour. Here, it is necessary to make a distinction between the setting time and curing time for the effective handling of assembled components. Although it is possible to remove a joint from clamp pressure after as little as 15 minutes and, with care, work on the assembled components, the final strength of the glue will not be realized until it has cured. In my experience a curing time of 24 hours seems to apply to all the glues generally available.

To reduce the problems experienced with a joint that needs to slide to final position, I try to design it in such a way that its location is positive in two directions, needing movement only in the third direction for assembly. As aliphatic resins are water-based, dispensers, brushes, rollers and any excess squeezed from joints can be easily cleaned off with water.

SHELF LIFE

While talking about shelf life one has to take into consideration how long the container may have stood on a shelf at the suppliers. There is usually no way of knowing this, so it is advisable to buy your glue from a major supplier with a high turnover. If the shelf life is not actually stated on the original container, you will know when you have exceeded it if you begin to notice that the glue has become more viscous with a very short open-assembly time.

▼ Spreading glue with a roller.

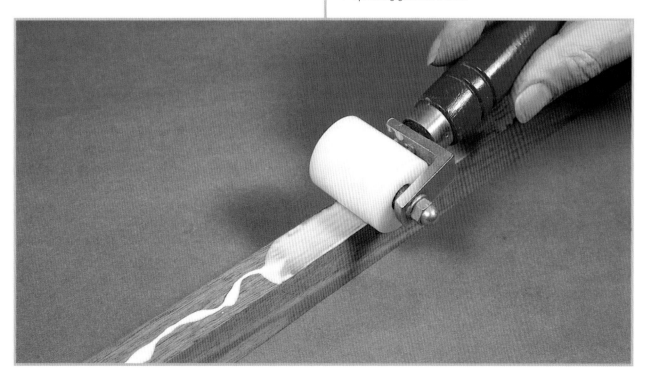

Another positive advantage is that, although the glue sets hard, providing a rigid bond, the glue line is not hard enough to damage cutting edges when being worked on later. It is also available in a water-resistant version suitable for outdoor work but, it is not suitable for immersion in water or in situations of continuous wetting and is therefore not suitable for boat-building.

◆ Epoxy resins

E VEN WITH THE POTENTIAL INCREASED OPEN-assembly time of aliphatic resin, I doubt if it would be long enough for laminating. The complexity of the process, coating several layers that have then to be positioned on a mould before pressure is sequentially applied, either with cramps or a vacuum bag press, demands a considerable open assembly time. In these circumstances I favour an epoxy resin. However, I must add that I do all of my flat veneering with aliphatic resin, speeding up the application of glue with a reservoir-fed roller and thus reducing the open-assembly time. The panels can be taken out of the press after as little as half an hour. I have not as yet researched some of the aliphatic resins currently available in America, which are reported to have long open-assembly times that are suitable for laminating. One further technical advantage makes epoxy

resins preferable for laminating: there is no water to dry out after the chemical curing process and as a result little distortion to the shape being formed.

Epoxy resins are two-part systems consisting of a resin and a hardener or curing agent. The shelf life, though quite extensive, is critical and the duration is clearly marked on the container. Mixing is also critical so the manufacturer supplies a metering device, usually in the form of a simple hand-operated pressure pump that is inserted into the container in which the pieces are stored. In theory it should be straightforward to use but I have found that if the pumps are not fully primed before delivering the resin or curing agent, the wrong ratio of mix occurs, resulting in potential failure. Also, for small quantities, it can be difficult to measure the amount that is needed.

When failures were experienced by my students in the past due to lack of cure, my assumption was that insufficient curing agent had been used in the mix. In such cases, my solution was to add more, but I found that it did not improve the result. After contacting the technical help line for the product I discovered that too much curing agent is worse than too little. The ratio is critical, so I took the advice of the scientist I spoke to and now

▼ After hours of preperation, careful gluing and clamping is called for or all that hard work will be for nothing.

I use a set of digital kitchen scales, which allows me to mix amounts as small as 0.2oz (5g) with accuracy. For even smaller amounts I use hypodermic syringes.

Why am I so critical about quantities? It's a question of cost and waste. The long open-assembly time makes it easier to mix up a little more if you run out rather than mixing too much in the first place and throwing away whatever is left over.

Exothermic reactions

EPOXY RESINS APPLIED STRAIGHT FROM THE bottle are too thin for most timbers, meaning that the glue soaks into the wood to such an extent that the actual surface-to-surface bond is starved of resin. This can be overcome by the addition of a colloidal silica filler, which thickens the mix and retards excessive penetration. The technical information supplied with these products stresses the fact that once mixed the resin is subjected to an exothermic reaction, producing intense heat, and dramatically shortening the pot life if held in bulk. However, it isn't until this actually happens and you finish up with a solid block of hardened plastic in a few minutes that the danger and waste of this phenomenon is fully appreciated!

The easiest way to overcome this problem and extend the pot life is to pour the mix into a shallow dish, so the heat produced is dissipated over a larger surface area. I use a small Teflon-coated baking dish, which can be cleaned out by peeling off any remaining glue once it has cured, so that I can use the dish again. Although West System produces a solvent for cleaning uncured resin off surfaces, containers and applicators, it is possible to use methylated spirits for this purpose. Meths is not suitable as a thinner but as I mentioned earlier thinning is not necessary.

Finally, there is the question of applying the resin to surfaces. For small surfaces economy paint brushes are suitable but when you need to cover a large surface, for example when laminating, a thin-walled plastic foam paint roller is ideal. Don't even try to clean them after use – buy them in bulk and throw them away when they have done their job.

Cyanoacrylate adhesives

BETTER KNOWN GENERALLY AS 'SUPERGLUE', cyanoacrylate adhesives are probably the most versatile adhesive system available today, capable of bonding dissimilar materials quickly and with great strength. They are available in different viscosities, from water thin for rapid penetration to very thick for longer open-assembly times, meaning that there is a viscosity for almost any range of bonding requirements. Bonding times vary from 'instantly' to 90 seconds. A spray-on accelerator is also available to produce an immediate cure. Because of the cost and the speed of bond, Superglue is mainly suitable for bonding small areas and is ideal for repairs.

The main drawback, particularly with the super thin viscosity, is its tendency to migrate beyond the area being glued and stick to other surfaces, usually your fingers! This requires very careful metering of the amount necessary: very often just one drop is enough. I use an old scalpel blade onto which I apply one drop and then carefully offer it up to the place that is being glued. Often it is possible to assemble the components and flush the glue in, relying on capillary action to draw it into the joint, rather like soldering. If pressure needs to be applied, use a piece of polythene sheet between the pressure block and the work piece as any squeeze-out will not adhere to the polythene. I even make my own filler for repairing surface damage with Superglue and fine sanding dust to match the colour. It sets hard in seconds and can be planed down and sanded in a couple of minutes. The resultant repair hardly shows after a finish has been applied.

Double-sided tape

THERE ARE MANY OTHER GLUES ON THE MARKET, in addition to those that I have referred to in this section. I have to say that these are the glues that I have used and I am able to emphasize the advantages that make them part of my adhesive arsenal. However, I cannot end without singing the praises of double-sided tape. It is ideal for rapid assembly of components involved in jig-making. At one end of the bonding spectrum I use it for the fabric linings of boxes and at the other end for the rapid inclusion of a stop block on my router table. Its versatility is without limits.

Using cramping blocks

The complex process of gluing up can be greatly eased by using cramping blocks. Here, I outline the positive contributions they make in addition to protecting your work from damage.

CRAMPING BLOCKS PERFORM TWO ESSENTIAL functions. The first and most obvious is to protect the work from damage. The second function is to distribute the pressure or load from the clamp to the contacting surfaces of the joint being assembled. Where possible, the contact surface area between the cramping block and the external surface of the component should be the same as that of the joint's surface area of contact. Any larger and there is the risk of distortion beyond the joint. You may have experienced this when assembling a carcass. The sides tend to bow inwards, making checking for square difficult. I will investigate the processs of 'checking for square' later.

▼ Gluing up 68° mitres with glued-on cramping blocks, using sash cramps for main pressure and G-cramps with ⅜in 9mm thick MDF blocks for surface alignment. Parcel tape on these blocks aids glue release.

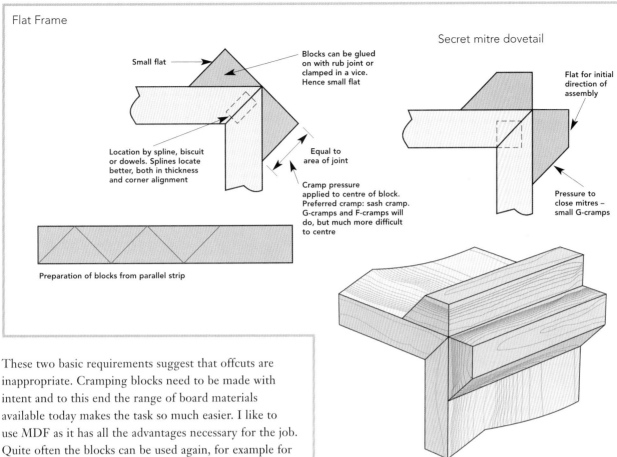

Flat Frame

Small flat

Blocks can be glued on with rub joint or clamped in a vice. Hence small flat

Location by spline, biscuit or dowels. Splines locate better, both in thickness and corner alignment

Equal to area of joint

Cramp pressure applied to centre of block. Preferred cramp: sash cramp. G-cramps and F-cramps will do, but much more difficult to centre

Preparation of blocks from parallel strip

Secret mitre dovetail

Flat for initial direction of assembly

Pressure to close mitres – small G-cramps

These two basic requirements suggest that offcuts are inappropriate. Cramping blocks need to be made with intent and to this end the range of board materials available today makes the task so much easier. I like to use MDF as it has all the advantages necessary for the job. Quite often the blocks can be used again, for example for gluing on lippings, so the effort that goes into preparation can be spread over more than one job. While considering lippings, make sure that the cramping block you use for this purpose is thick enough to spread the pressure effectively on the area between the clamps, otherwise there is the risk of localized distortion, resulting in an undulating wave on the outside edge.

◆ Surface protection

IN MOST SITUATIONS, YOU WOULD GLUE UP THE joints before treating the piece with a surface finish. If, however, you intend to pre-finish components before assembly, you may need to apply a strip of cork sheet to the face of the cramping block. This is easily done using double-sided tape. When seeking to prevent cramping blocks sticking to the joint, avoid the use of a release agent, such as wax. There is a risk that the release agent could contaminate the surface of the component and render its removal difficult at a later stage. I overcome this problem by covering the contact surface of the cramping block with parcel tape – even epoxy resin will not adhere to it!

◆ Mitred joints

ANOTHER PRINCIPLE THAT IS COMMON TO assembly of most joints is the application of pressure at 90° to the contacting surfaces. This is an essential requirement for mitred joints. The pressure face of the cramping block needs to be parallel to the surface of the mitre. I have found it better to glue the cramping block onto the corresponding outer surface of the component. The joint can then be assembled and the cramping blocks behave as part of the component and pressure can be applied directly to the mitred faces. When the glue has set, the block has to be removed, but do not split it off with a chisel as the split will go below the surface of the component. Remove the cramping block with a saw and then plane the surface clean. A quick-release system employing a strip of newspaper glued between the cramping block and the component works well. After the glue in the joint has set, use a chisel to split the newspaper joint and the cramping block will come off without damage to the component. This system also works for mitred carcass joints and secret mitre dovetails.

◆ Through dovetails

IF A DOVETAIL JOINT IS CUT CORRECTLY, THE tightness of fit should be such that when the joint has been glued up the cramps and block can be removed soon after the pressure has been applied and the joint closed. After all, it is an interlocked joint. In practice, however, cramping blocks are left on, to be removed when the glue has set. In this case a release agent is necessary and any contamination is effectively removed during the cleaning up process on the surface of the joint. To apply pressure to the tails of a dovetail you need to cut recesses into the face of the cramping block. I refer to these as 'bridge blocks'.

When I first started making batches of small boxes the prospect of making large numbers of bridge blocks that could only be used once was a daunting prospect. I examined the question of assembly and came to the conclusion that the entire outer surface of the box should be planed clean in addition to the removal of the projecting pins and tails. If the pins and tails were proportioned to be less than the thickness of the sides and ends of the box, there would be no need to apply pressure with bridge blocks!

Flat, reusable cramping blocks, covered in parcel tape, would make assembly a breeze. This works effectively on dovetailed carcass pieces that are small enough to be supported horizontally while cleaning up, where you can plane the entire outer surface easily. On large pieces, however, this would require a great deal of effort so it would be better to concentrate only on cleaning up anything that is projecting. You can then clean up the rest of the outer surface by sanding.

▼ The professional result of careful gluing up, using cramping blocks, is well worth the preparation involved.

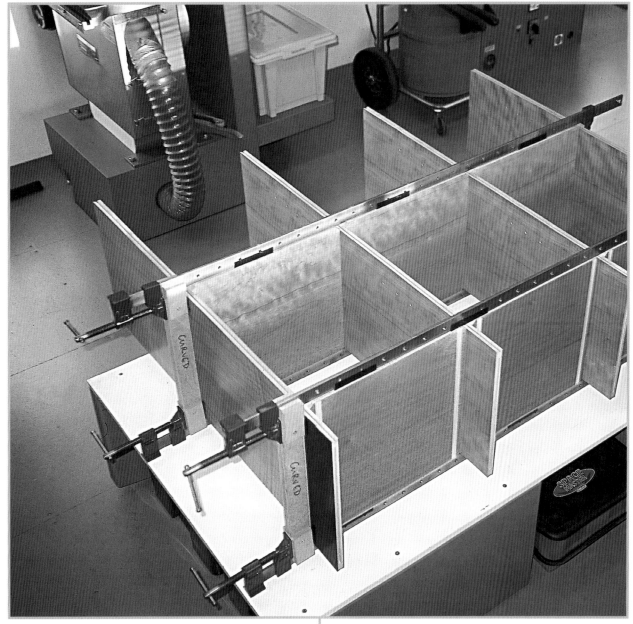

▲ Gluing up carcass shelves, using curved cramping blocks with location shots.

◆ Curved cramping blocks

STAYING WITH CARCASS ASSEMBLY, IF YOU include partitions or shelves in the construction, you may experience the problem of pressure away from the outer edges. To overcome this, the inner edge of the cramping block needs to bear a gentle curve, so that when pressure is applied to the ends the stiffness of the block applies pressure in the middle as the curve is straightened out.

Curved cramping blocks are best made from solid wood or thick plywood, rather than MDF, as they need to be quite stiff. I mark out a sprung curve and remove the waste on my disc sander. Alternatively, you could do this with a jackplane. You need to make matching pairs of curved blocks, which is quite a challenging job! Another refinement that I have introduced into my curved blocks is a location slot at each end. The bar of a sash clamp fits into these slots, making location and positioning more controllable.

Final assembly

Having discussed cramping, cramping blocks and glues, it is now time to run through how you can make assembling your work faultless and stress-free by following some simple guidelines.

G LUE CAN BE DIFFICULT STUFF TO HANDLE.
It has the annoying ability to get on surfaces other than those that form the bond. Many problems arise from using inappropriate application tools, an offcut from the waste box for instance! Brushes are a better bet, giving a convenient and controllable way of applying glue. I have an assortment of different sizes and shapes. However, the main problem is in trying to judge the right amount of glue to apply so that the excess that squeezes out when you apply pressure is kept to a minimum. In general I

use brushes to distribute glue on internal surfaces, such as a mortice or between the tails of dovetails. For more accessible surfaces, such as the shoulders of a tenon or the edges of a butt joint, I use a comb spreader. Ideally I re-use spreaders supplied with impact adhesives. Alternatively, you can make your own from sheet plastic, just make a series of shallow bandsaw cuts on the edge,

▼ Gluing up layers for stack laminated underframe using a comb spreader and glue bottle. Mitres are glued together and held with masking tape.

▲ Brushes will help spread glue in a controlled manner.

about 1/16in (1.5mm) apart. Make a few different sizes to handle anything. It is often easier to use a comb spreader than get out the veneering glue spreading roller. With a comb spreader you can control the amount of glue and spread it on the surface evenly and quickly.

▼ Glue-spreading aids – stiff artists' brushes, spatulas, toothed spreader and photographic rollers.

What container you use depends on how you buy the glue. I buy glue in bulk then decant it into small glue bottles and cylinders equipped with nozzles that I have saved previously. Nozzles make it easy to direct the glue carefully in controlled quantities. If you use glue that needs to be mixed before use, it's best to pour it straight onto the surface – if you decant it, it will set in the bottle.

◆ Dress rehearsal

I STRONGLY RECOMMEND A DRY RUN, PARTICULARLY for an assembly sequence you have not tried before. It is like a dress rehearsal. A dry run gives you a chance to foresee and solve problems without the panic engendered during the limited open-assembly time of a glue-up. It also helps you to work out the optimum assembly order and fine-tune difficult aspects, such as chamfers on the ends of tenons or splines. Lastly, it gives you time to fix cramping blocks in place with masking tape. Cover the blocks in shiny brown parcel tape so that they repel glue. Before dismantling the dry run, check joint identification marks – mine are on masking tape, to be removed later.

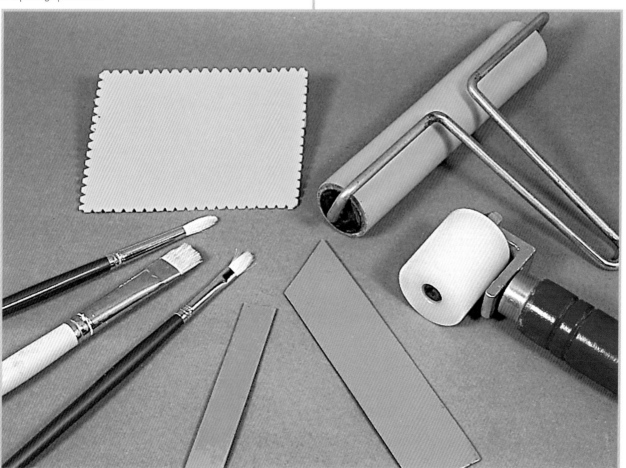

◆ Gluing up

Wᴛʜ ᴇᴠᴇʀʏᴛʜɪɴɢ ᴛᴏ ʜᴀɴᴅ, ɪɴᴄʟᴜᴅɪɴɢ cleaning materials in case of spillage, you are ready to start. If you can coat all surfaces from the first joint to the last within the open-assembly time then you can complete the whole glue-up in one session. Otherwise, break the sequence into shorter stages, but assemble all related components dry to assure alignment.

You needn't wait until the glue has cured before going on to the next stage. Once a bond has formed, you can gently dismantle the dry-fitted components and glue them. End-grain absorbs glue faster than face-grain so, if you need to coat both surfaces of a joint, cover the face-grain first. It is not always necessary to cover both surfaces, providing you assemble the joint before the glue forms a surface skin. Doing this shortens the assembly time, giving you time to apply pressure and squeeze out the excess glue, resulting in glue-line-free joints.

For a mortice and tenon, for instance, put glue in the mortice and spread it with a small, flat brush. Then apply a thin line of glue to each shoulder and spread it with a comb spreader. The joint should not be so tight as to piston the glue to the bottom of the mortice.

◆ Tight joints

Tɪɢʜᴛ ᴊᴏɪɴᴛꜱ ʙᴇᴄᴏᴍᴇ ᴛɪɢʜᴛᴇʀ ᴡʜᴇɴ ᴛʜᴇ ᴡᴏᴏᴅ absorbs moisture from the glue and swells. For an edge joint, spread glue to one surface with a comb spreader before bringing the two edges together. Unless the strength of the joint is of critical importance I do not think you need to apply glue to biscuits or splines (their primary function is location). The strength of a joint is often shared by other joints in the construction. If you have a complex construction to assemble in one go, you can use a slow-setting glue, such as an epoxy resin. Pour the mixed resin into a shallow container to prevent the build-up of heat that occurs after mixing in volume.

◆ Checking for square

Nᴏ ᴍᴀᴛᴛᴇʀ ʜᴏᴡ ᴀᴄᴄᴜʀᴀᴛᴇʟʏ ʏᴏᴜ ᴄᴜᴛ ᴊᴏɪɴᴛꜱ the construction is likely to be out of square after gluing up. This is because it is impossible to assemble all the joints that go together in one direction and apply pressure all at the same time. I check the diagonals, rather than using a try-square, as it is not unusual to find some bowing or distortion, especially with a carcass. Measuring

diagonals with a rule is tricky when outer edges are obscured by cramping blocks or cramps, so I have made various sliding internal diagonal testers, using Veritas bar gauge heads.

Correct out-of-squareness by moving cramps towards the long diagonal. The jaws of cramps are parallel to each other, so if you move a cramp slightly sideways, moving one end more than the other, tightening the cramp moves the corresponding pair of components in turn. Small movements can effect substantial change. Pairs of cramps are used, so you need equal amounts of movement to control the diagonals. I favour the type of sash cramp made by Record Tools because the small jaws allow the inside edge of the bar to make contact with the component, be it the outside of a cabinet or the rails and stiles of a frame. This makes it easier to control the squareness. If the construction is out of square I can judge

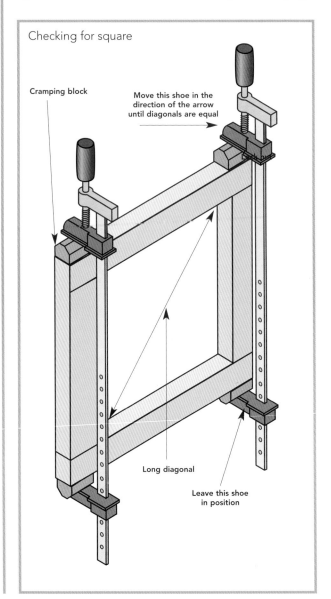

Checking for square

Cramping block

Move this shoe in the direction of the arrow until diagonals are equal

Long diagonal

Leave this shoe in position

the amount of movement needed by the distance the inside edge of the bar has to be moved. The time window for carrying out adjustments is quite generous – just do it before the glue begins to set.

Cleaning off excess glue

T HE AMOUNT OF EXCESS GLUE THAT SQUEEZES OUT should be minimal, but there will inevitably be some to remove. I mentioned earlier the value of pre-finishing, particularly surfaces that will be difficult to get at after assembly. When the glue has set, pick off the excess with a chisel or scalpel. If you prefer to wash the glue off, bear in mind that you could end up rubbing the glue into the surface. This will show up when the wood matures with age and changes colour due to ultraviolet light and oxidation. The water will also raise the grain and there is a risk of rust staining if the metal surfaces of cramps get wet. If you are gluing up with epoxy resin, you must clean up with methylated spirit, or the solvent provided, before the glue goes off. Once it has set the only way to remove it is with a chisel.

Removing cramps

O NCE THE GLUE HAS SET, REMOVE THE CRAMPS. You needn't always wait until the glue has cured. If cramps are left on too long, distorted components may not spring back to their original alignment. For instance, dovetailed constructions are best taken out of cramps as soon as the joints have been closed. Don't rush when you remove the cramps – gently ease the pressure on all the cramps before removing them completely.

Dealing with problems

G LUING UP PROBLEMS CAN BE KEPT TO A minimum with careful planning. However, if they do occur you need to assess the situation quickly. It is often best to stop and dismantle the assembly, clean off the glue as best you can and check out the problem calmly. Once it has been resolved you can resume the glue-up process.

▼ Good planning is usually the best way to avoid problems at gluing-up stage.

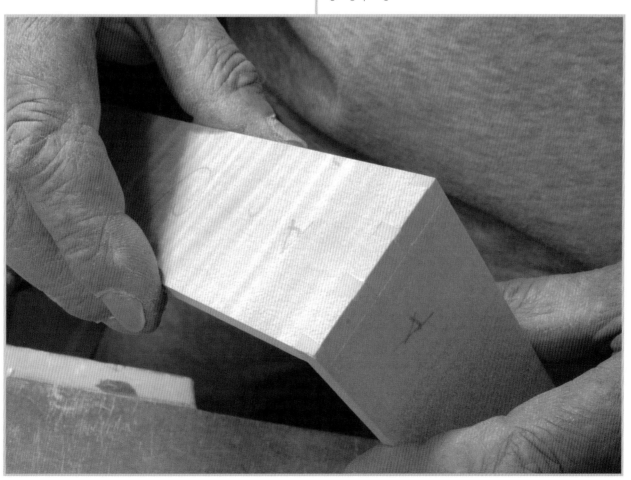

Part Two:
Pushing the Boundaries

Building a workbench

The workbench is central to the organization and efficiency of the workplace. At Parnham College my bench formed the central focus in the workshop and evolved as needed over the years.

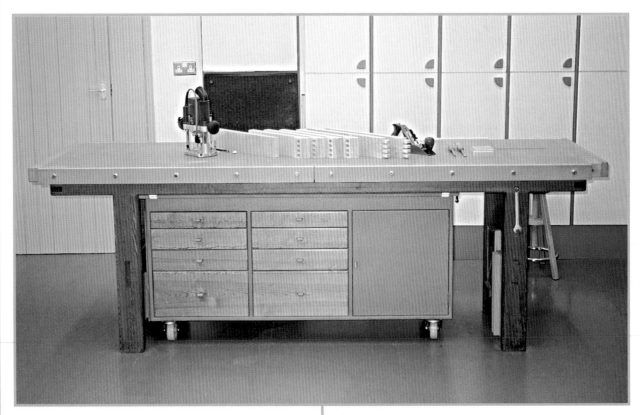

▲ Workbench and tool cupboard.

MY WORKBENCH WAS FIRST DESIGNED TO BE used as a dedicated router station for the production of a chaise rocking chair (pictured on facing page). It was 8ft (244cm) in length and dictated by the dimensions of the rocker. The main structure was made from recycled pitch pine beams from a school gymnasium.

This pine was straight-grained and extremely stable, and was sufficient to make a bench with a long upper frame and four legs. The construction and strength of components was such that it was not necessary to include any lower stretcher rails. Although its primary function was that of a router station, it made sense to install a vice, so it doubled as a workbench. The top consisted of a series of drop-in panels, one of which had a router mounted from underneath.

◆ Top

I DID NOT HAVE TIME TO MAKE A SOLID-WOOD TOP for the bench when the college opened so I bought a heavy-duty fire door. It was absolutely flat and perfectly stable, and even though it was not as long as the bench, it prompted me to use the exposed area of the original top for my tool-sharpening station.

It is paramount that a worktop bench is flat. It provides a reference for the accuracy of almost every stage in the making of a piece, from timber preparation and marking out to cutting joints, assembly and subsequent cleaning up. This became very apparent to my students, who were expected to complete all their timber

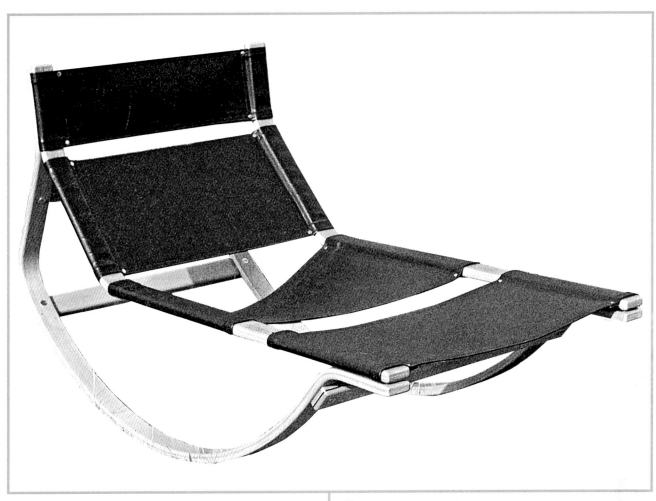

▲ The chaise rocker that the bench was built to accomodate.

▼ The edge strips are used as stops.

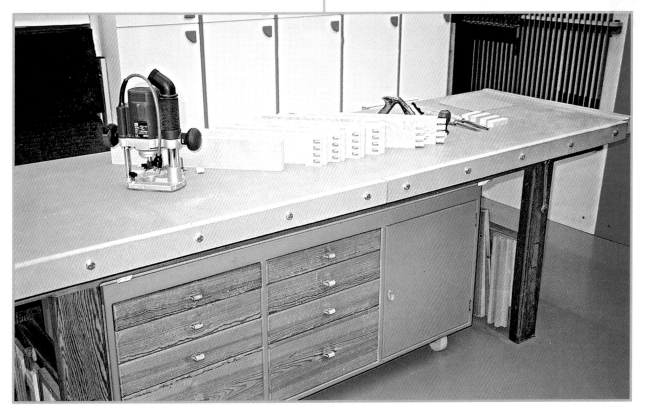

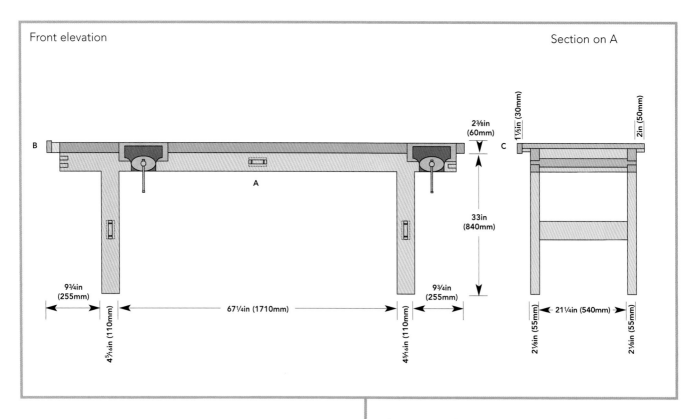

Front elevation

Section on A

preparation with a hand plane during their first term. The beech bench tops required frequent truing up and it prompted me to question the appropriateness of the timber for this purpose. I calculated the stability coefficient between radial and tangential shrinkage of beech (using a table published by FIRA – Furniture Industries Research Association) only to discover that there was a disproportionate difference between the two. A single board of crown-cut timber was never going to be stable enough for a workbench.

After a few years, many of the tops had become so thin that the fixing bolts holding the end cleats in position had begun to show. We had no choice but to remake the tops, but this time we chose a readily available material that was hard and stable enough for the purpose.

I know that purists will cringe at the thought of MDF being used for bench tops, but from my experience the choice is totally justified. I chose 1in (25mm) thick MDF – it is readily available and the surface was treated with teak oil to seal it and improve stability, bearing in mind that only one surface was exposed to the fluctuations of humidity and temperature in the workshops.

◆ Bench improvement

AFTER THE MACHINES HAD BEEN INSTALLED IN my workshop, I decided to improve my bench – starting with the top and was fortunate to find a sheet of 1⅛in (30mm) thick MDF at my local builders' merchants. I then set to work reducing it to the right width. This dimension was slightly wider than that of the upper frame as I decided to exclude the tool trough. From previous experience, the trough does little to help organize the workbench. It just gets filled up with shavings.

I realized that an end stop of some sort would be necessary. In the past I had used a single stop that was inserted into a square hole and was held in place with a wing nut and bolt through a slot, to enable vertical adjustment. The single stop was only suitable for the planing of narrow pieces of wood and a supplementary block had to be clamped in place for wider pieces.

This time I decided to make the stop the entire width of the bench top by using a piece of the 1⅛in (30mm) thick MDF with four slots to provide ¼in (6mm) of vertical adjustment. Four ⁵⁄₁₆in (8mm) hexagon-headed bolts with large washers held the stop in place and these were inserted into nuts that I concealed in the end of the bench top. I reinforced the ends with cleats made from hard maple. Before these were glued in place. I drilled the holes for the end-stop bolts and inserted the nuts into counter-bored holes from the inner face.

◆ Frame

I REMEMBERED THE FRUSTRATION I EXPERIENCED in the past when cleaning up the surface of a construction such as a four-component frame. The change in grain direction from rails to stiles meant that the frame had to be turned round to be held against a single stop, or be clamped down onto the bench to be held in place.

The clamps then had to be removed so that the frame could be repositioned for the next change in direction and so on. I installed another stop strip along the back edge of the top, using the same system of bolts and slots. For convenience in use I cut the strip into two 48in (122cm) lengths – in many cleaning-up situations the dimensional requirements would be much shorter than the length of the bench. I did not reinforce the long edges of the top with maple so I embedded the holding nuts into a strip of MDF glued onto the underside. This reinforcement gave the top more strength to resist the forces and loads that would be imposed when clamps were used to hold components down onto the bench. Although the new MDF top was heavy enough to hold itself down, being trapped in all directions by the cleats, I decided to fix it in place with screws inserted from underneath. The top was then treated with two coats of teak oil and for a few hours after the oil had dried I just could not bring myself to put anything on top. It looked so beautiful!

◆ In use

THE VICE I INSTALLED WHEN THE BENCH WAS used as a router station was a Record No.52 ½in with a quick-release mechanism. It is strong with a generous capacity, and I have fitted it with 1in (25mm) thick MDF jaws. The top edges have been reinforced with lippings made from hard maple. This, in turn, has been covered with a strip of white plastic to reflect light onto the surface of components when I cut dovetails.

I was fortunate to be offered a very good price for a job lot of Record vices some time ago so, together with my students, we bought the entire stock and I finished up with two spare vices. I decided that, in addition to having a second vice, the option of its position on the same edge as the main vice gave me quite a lot of possibilities for its use, not least that of holding a long piece of wood firmly in two places.

Another practical feature in the bench design is the substantial overhang at each end. The space underneath enables an assembled construction, such as a coffee table, to be positioned so that the surface being worked is supported on the top and the rest of the construction can hang below.

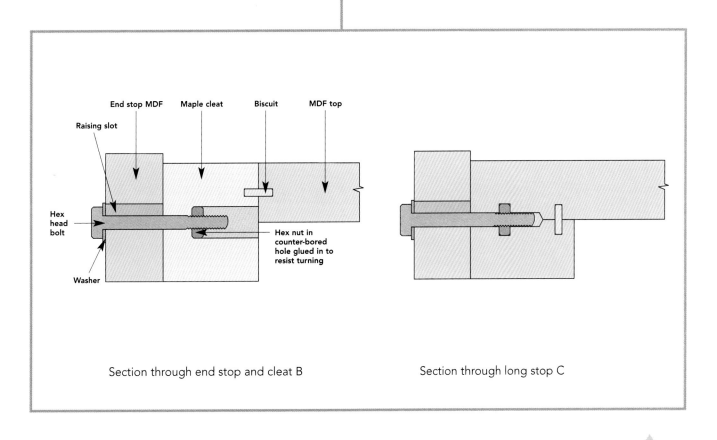

Section through end stop and cleat B

Section through long stop C

◆ Tool cupboard

WHEN I SHARED A BENCH WITH FELLOW students at college my entire tool collection could fit into a toolbox small enough to fit under a bench, together with three others. I now have a plethora of woodworking toys that could fill a shop! Storing this collection so that I could use them efficiently was another challenge that I faced when I set up my workshop.

My tool cupboard is mounted on castors and can be wheeled out of the way. In fact, everything that stands on the floor at the bench site in the workshop is on castors, apart from the bench itself. This enables me to clear the floor so that I can bring down a backdrop and use the space as a photographic studio. The bench itself can be moved by slipping a pair of carpeted box slides under the feet.

Another feature that emerged by chance is the support that I can receive when working on a long component that can only be held on one side of the vice. The drawers can be pulled out to support the projection. With two banks of four drawers, I have a selection of options. To increase the surface area of contact I have made a cover that slips onto the top edge of the projecting drawer front.

◆ Siting and lighting

MY MACHINES ARE POSITIONED AT ONE END OF the workshop, with the bench and hand processes at the other. I decided to build a bank of cupboards against the far wall of the workshop to house tools such as my routers, large marking tools and hand saws. I was tempted to hang many of these items on a show board but decided against it for two reasons.

This method of tool storage is often associated with a set-up where the bench is against a wall and it is convenient to reach them. I have the space to position my bench away from any walls so that I can gain access to the ends and the sides. Moreover, the extra storage that a tool cupboard with plenty of height provided made it the better option.

The second reason for the cupboards was to prevent the tools from becoming covered in dust. Despite the presence of dust extraction systems, exposed items hung on walls will gather dust. The cupboards are made from 6in (150mm) wide melamine board, which is cut to size accurately and quickly on my Felder. The depth of the cupboard is dictated by the largest item to be stored which is the depth of a router.

▼ Three of the four drawers in the bench.

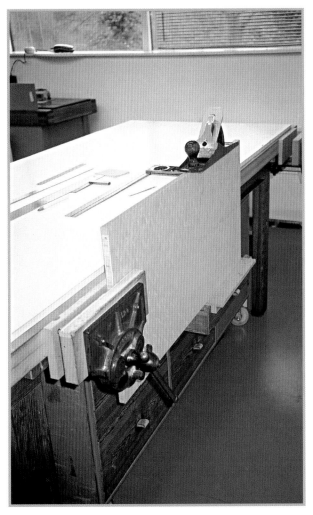

▲ Another mobile piece of equipment – a chest for hand tools. The drawers are used to support long components.

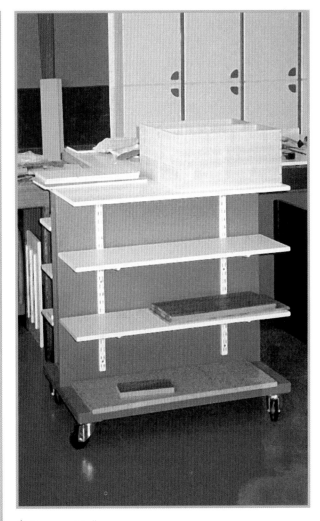

▲ Component trolley.

◆ Component trolley

Lighting the workshop was something to which I gave a lot of thought. I chose fluorescent strips fitted with daylight-corrected tubes which are mounted on the single plane sloping ceiling and can be switched on in various combinations. The light bounces off the white ceiling, white walls and white cupboard doors, illuminating the workspace evenly with a soft, bright light.

To complete the efficiency of the bench area I made a component trolley Although the bench itself is quite large, there is insufficient space to store the components being made for a complex piece such as a chest of drawers.

The trolley consists of a top and a series of shelves separated vertically by an upright divider, which also has a large storage slot through it. The upright and base are made out of MDF constructed into torsion boxes for strength and rigidity, and the shelves are fixed onto height-adjustable brackets. Mounted on castors, it can be moved to the machine shop end while components are being prepared and back to the bench area for the construction stages.

Ripple cherry and bog oak sideboard

Planning a commission is a case of matching the materials and design to the client's needs; considering both function and form.

OVER THE YEARS I HAVE COLLECTED AN assortment of interesting boards of wood and packs of veneers. From time to time I look through my collection and wonder what I can make from an inspirational board and for whom. I have a bundle of cerejeira veneers – not a name that slips smoothly from the tongue! What makes these veneers so special is their stunning crotch pattern and the colour. Imagine my

excitement when a customer approached me to design and make a sideboard and a china cabinet (see page 146). A visit to the client's amazing house on the banks of Loch Tay provided me with the information that is essential for a site-specific design. A very important consideration was the space that the pieces should occupy, as the proportions were critical to the relationship between object and surroundings.

▼ Contemporary design is combined with state-of-the-art cabinetmaking to create this stylish sideboard.

My disappointment was overwhelming when I got back to my studio and discovered that the leaves of cerejeira veneer would not be long enough for this project. They will have to wait for another opportunity. Fortunately, I had a bundle of beautifully marked ripple cherry (*Prunus avium*) that took the customer's fancy. Coupled with bog oak (*Quercus michauxii*), the combination turned out to

produce a very successful duo of pieces. I sent the customer the rendered presentation drawings and a sample of the timbers lacquered to convey the finished result and soon got the phone call confirming the order. It required no further discussion other than a confirmation of the dimensions. It doesn't always happen like this, but when it does it is very pleasing.

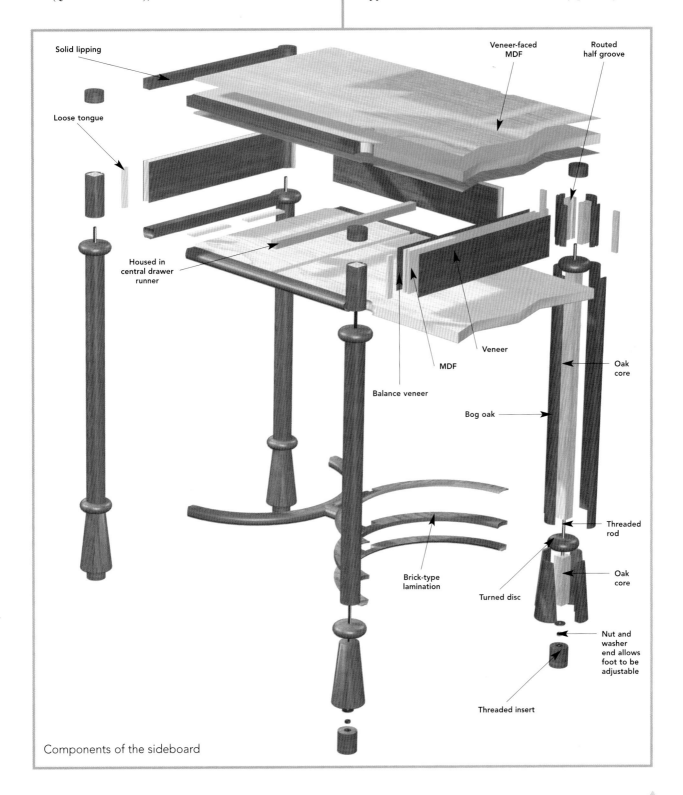

Solid lipping

Loose tongue

Housed in central drawer runner

Balance veneer

Brick-type lamination

Turned disc

Threaded insert

Veneer-faced MDF

Routed half groove

Veneer

MDF

Oak core

Bog oak

Threaded rod

Oak core

Nut and washer end allows foot to be adjustable

Components of the sideboard

◆ Workshop drawing

ALTHOUGH THE IMPORTANT DECISIONS NEED to be addressed before a design can be presented to a customer, the very nature of a designer-crafted piece benefits from the opportunities that present themselves as the work progresses. You need to keep an open mind for these chances but it is essential to make a clear statement of intent with which to monitor progress. In other words you need a working drawing. I use a sheet of melamine-coated board and in this case the sheet was large enough to cover my bench and remained there for the duration of the project. A full-size drawing is essential, providing an excellent double-check for dimensions and a valuable

CUTTING LIST

With any piece I make I prepare a cutting list and it was of paramount importance in this case, with so many components. I broke the list down into sub-sections aiming to use the materials economically and to save time by identifying components with dimensions that can be prepared earlier. The cutting list helps to organize the aesthetic contributions of colour, grain and pattern.

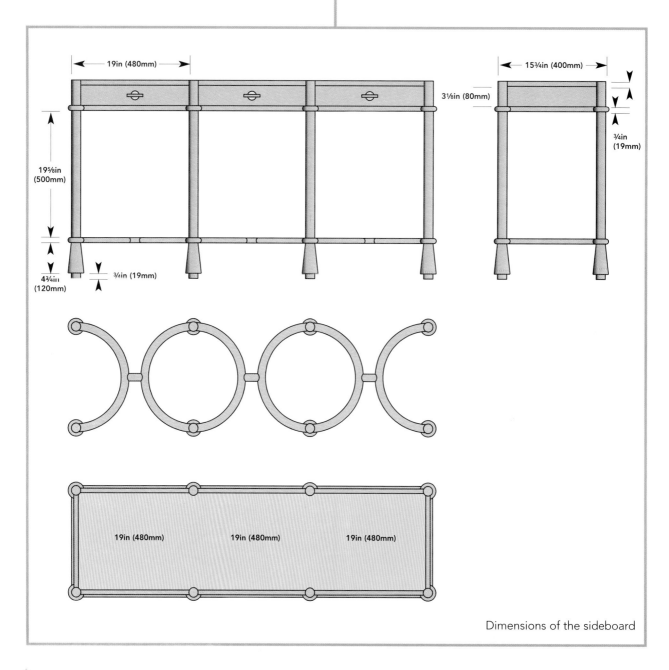

Dimensions of the sideboard

way to confirm proportions. The two pieces have much in common so I was able to superimpose one on the other. It also made sense to work on both pieces simultaneously as quite a number of processes were duplicated.

◆ Drawers and doors

THE PIECES THAT MAKE UP THE DRAWERS FOR the sideboard and doors for the china cabinet can be conveniently divided into three layers:

◆ The upper part – a cabinet for storage;
◆ The lower section, which includes the feet and stretcher rails;
◆ The legs, which form the connections.

I do not intend to describe these pieces as a step-by-step account on how to make them. Instead, I would like to focus on some of the practices that have evolved in my work and the equipment and thinking that contributes to them. I do not claim that they are unique or unusual, but I do feel that by sharing them with other makers I can contribute to the importance of the personal approach necessary to progress the craft.

▼ Legs – gluing on the bog oak facing strips.

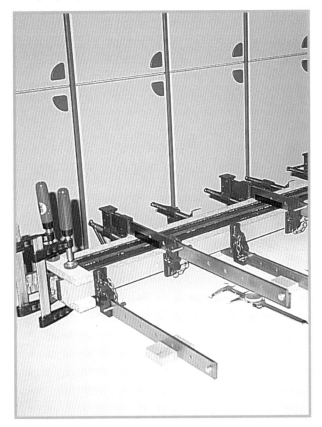

The legs

THE CHINA CABINET DOORS ARE THE MOST striking aspect of the piece. They are like paintings, asking to be framed. I wanted to do this in such a way as to emphasize the painting and play down the frame. This also suggested that it would be inappropriate to use projecting handles.

Also, a hard edge to the 'picture frame' jarred with the architectural feature of strongly rounded corners to the dividing walls that broke up the otherwise open-plan space of the dining room and sitting room. As such, cylindrical uprights to divide the storage space seemed to be the most appropriate solution. This was both an aesthetic and constructional challenge, the main problem being the connection between rectangular section horizontal rails and cylindrical vertical stiles. There was also the problem of hinging the doors. Some time ago I developed a door-hanging system that used concealed, spring-loaded pegs as pivots. This was to overcome the very obvious appearance of hinges, which spoiled the line between the door and the carcass. I decided to use this system again.

To overcome the problem of the junction between rectangles and cylinders I decided to scribe the shoulders of all the joints that had this need. This, in turn, dictated that the legs of the sideboard and the legs and vertical components of the china cabinet should be cylindrical. I will come back to the joint later on. Having decided on the rounded section my next thought was the construction of these cylinders. I had experienced problems of stability in the past using solid bog oak so I decided to build up the cross-section. I had also considered making both the sideboard and china cabinet so that the legs and feet could be taken apart to make delivery of the two pieces easier.

▼ Legs and door rails.

▲ Rounding over the legs on a router table.

Complexities

I BUILT THE LEGS UP WITH THE CORE MADE FROM two sections of clean, straight-grained oak with a half round groove in the joining faces. This would enable me to run a length of studding through the leg for the main assembly. I then built up the final diameter by the addition of four facing strips to bring the cross-section to the necessary size. I made the legs well over-length to make handling the rounding of the corners on the router table easier and to give me a piece of the same size of cross-section with which to make an end-hole-boring jig. This jig would enable me to drill holes accurately for

▼ Boring master template for disc hole routing jig.

the doorpost pivots, which would be too long to position on the pillar drill. All joints between the legs and rails had to be cut before the rounding process could be carried out. I used a loose tenon for these junctions. I felt it was not necessary to cut the mortice slots deeply into the ends of the rails or the legs so I was able to cut these using a simple holding jig on the router table. Once all the joints were cut and sized to length I was able to scribe the shoulders of the tenons, once again with a holding jig on the router table. I used a round-nosed cutter that matched the cross-section produced by a rounding-over cutter to scribe the tenon shoulders.

The key to success was the time and care taken to adjust the depth of cut and the fence setting, using a piece of wood prepared to exactly the same dimensions as that of the components. Once I had rounded over the leg cross-section and set up the router table to scribe the tenon shoulders I could get on with the carcass.

The carcass

THE BACK AND SIDES CONSIST OF RAILS WITH cylinders at the corners and at intervals along the front and back to line up with the legs. These give the visual impression that the legs are penetrating through the bottom overhang of the carcass. Careful dimensioning of

▲ Routing spline grooves and drawer dividers.

the back and side rails was easy to control using the reliable sliding table of my Felder saw. I fabricated these rails from MDF with a facing of sawcut bog oak balanced on the inside with ¹⁄₁₆in (1.5mm) constructional mahogany veneer. The atmosphere of the house in which these two pieces will reside is very dry so I could not take a chance with excessive shrinkage.

I veneered the top with ripple cherry veneer, balanced with mahogany on the inside. All the constructional joints were either biscuits or splines made from MDF. As the legs appear to continue on up through the top, their profile is seen at the edges and corners of the upper surface. A profiling jig was made to index with the spline grooves of the carcass divisions, which could then be modified for the corners. I made a master template by boring the profile hole through a piece of MDF, using my engineering lathe. By doing this I could carefully size it so that the leg cross-section was a tight fit in the hole. Without my toolmakers' quality engineering lathe much of this precision would not be possible.

Gluing up

AFTER PRE-FINISHING THE INNER SURFACES, the whole piece was assembled and glued up in my veneer press. However, because of the complexity of the construction (due to number of components involved),

I glued it in stages but always made sure that all other components were in place to ensure alignment and control of internal squareness. With aliphatic resin, I did not have to wait long between stages and by using this approach I was never in fear of glue going off due to the short open-assembly time.

The underframes

THE MAIN FUNCTION OF THE SIDEBOARD WAS TO act as a serving table, with storage for cutlery. Further storage would be provided by the china cabinet which accompanies the sideboard (see page 146). A form of stretcher rail was necessary which gave me the chance to explore the visual contribution that this could add to the design. Circles and cylinders had already been expressed in the design and this seemed to be the theme to continue.

I had not decided how I would make the circles when I produced the working drawing. The obvious way was to build up each section with laminated half circles and then join them together where they met the legs. I started to prepare the laminations from solid bog oak (*Quercus spp*), only to discover that they would have to be very thin to bend around the curve. It would also be difficult to pull the combined number of laminations needed to achieve the desired width around the curve and this, along with

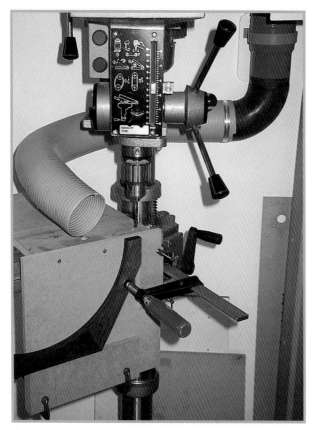

▲ Pillar drill holding jig for drilling threaded rod dowel holes – ends of half rings to leg disc junction.

▲ Gluing up layers for stack-laminated underframe using a comb spreader and glue bottle. Mitres are glued together and held with masking tape.

the huge amount of waste involved to make sufficient laminations for both underframes prompted me to rethink. I was also concerned that the change of curve that results from the spring of the laminated combination when it is removed from the mould would probably create some problems.

Finally, I decided to stack-laminate the rings in horizontal layers. Three layers, with staggered end-grain, mitred butt joints to provide a brick-like bond, would provide sufficient strength. I cut the 22½° mitres using the sliding table of my dimension saw with the fence set to the angle. The end-grain joints were glued and held together with masking tape to produce the three layers for each half ring. These layers were then glued and cramped horizontally to create the final thickness using an assembly jig to control alignment.

I formed the inside curve of each half ring using a router and trammel arm. A base board jig held the components in place; it was then adapted to provide an assembly jig for gluing each ring to its accompanying pair of leg joint discs. The outer curves of the rings were routed using a trammel arm after the ring–disc assembly had been completed This sequence ensured the contribution of flat surfaces and edges to the holding forces of cramps.

I turned the leg joint discs on my engineers' lathe, using the centre hole as the main reference. To do this, first drill this hole in the centre of a square piece of bog oak. Then feed the piece onto a mandrill, held in the chuck for turning. By starting with this hole it follows that every subsequent process will result in concentric alignment. The curved shoulder forming the junction with the discs

▼ Routing an inner curve/half ring for the underframe, using a trammel arm.

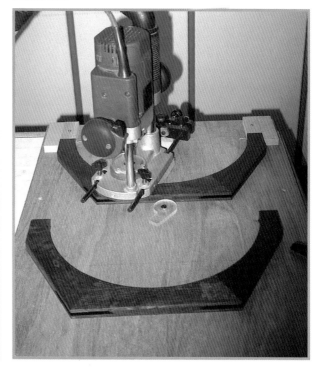

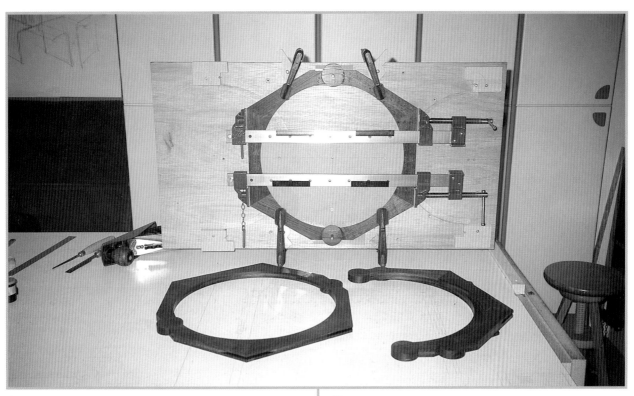

▲ Gluing up the base ring using a modified trammel arm jig.

▼ Rounding over the edges of the base rings.

▼ Assembled and sprayed base rings – underframes.

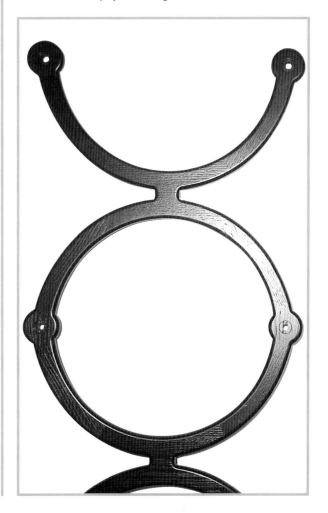

is shaped using a profile hole cut into the base board jig, used earlier for the trammel arm, together with a top-bearing router cutter. The discs are jointed to the half rings by dowels. Use threaded rod or studding for these dowels and bond the junction with epoxy resin. The resin bonds readily to the metal and penetrates well into the end-grain of the half rings, producing an extremely strong joint.

The short rails between the rings are simply jointed with mortice and tenons. Once the entire assembly of rings and rails has been assembled, use a rounding-over cutter to profile the edges. Rounded edges have become something of a detail signature in my work. When using this type of ball race-guided cutter on curved edges, it is highly likely that about 50 per cent of the wood removed will be cut against the grain. This carries the consequent risk of breakout and tearing. I overcame this problem by climb cutting or reverse feeding to remove the bulk of the waste and then feeding in a forward direction to finish off

the profile. I must stress the importance of hand-holding the router with the component clamped firmly down onto the bench when doing this. You will feel the router tending to run in the direction of the feed and can anticipate this movement to avoid losing control. Never carry out this type of routing on a router table as you run the risk of the work piece being torn from your grip. On pale woods, such as sycamore and cherry, quite a lot of scorching tends to occur – particularly when the feed is slowed down around corners. A very sharp router cutter is essential to keep this to a minimum. I keep a selection of sizes specifically for rounding over solid wood; as soon as they show signs of getting dull and any scorching becomes prominent I downgrade the cutters to less critical tasks. Having said all that, be prepared for quite a lot of delicate and sometimes tedious sanding to remove scorch marks. With practice, I have developed a sensitivity in using this technique that keeps the problem of scorching to a minimum.

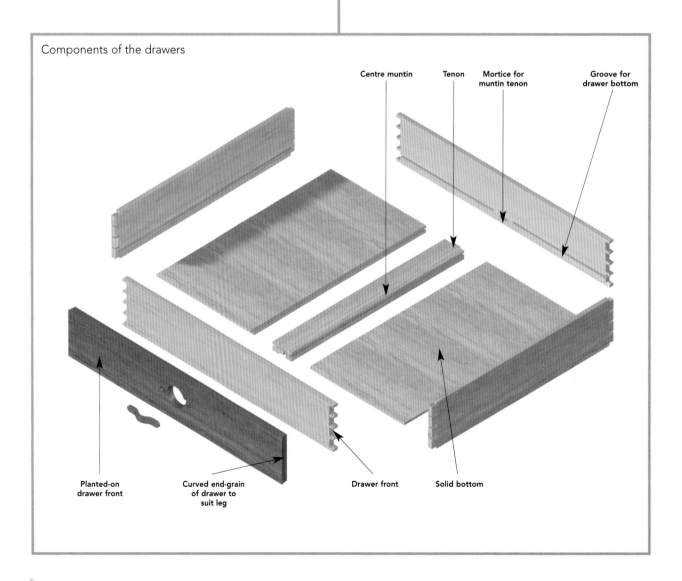

Components of the drawers

Centre muntin

Tenon

Mortice for muntin tenon

Groove for drawer bottom

Planted-on drawer front

Curved end-grain of drawer to suit leg

Drawer front

Solid bottom

▲ Assembling drawer bottoms and runners.

◆ The drawers

OVER THE YEARS I HAVE USED A VARIETY OF methods of making and running drawers in cabinet pieces. The main problem that is encountered is friction caused by surface-to-surface contact. The oldest and most popular method uses the entire surface of the drawer sides for lateral control and the top and bottom edges for vertical control. However, this represents a lot of surface area and further problems. One of these is the difficulty in sealing the sides to minimize moisture uptake and loss, resulting in drawers either jamming or shrinking and becoming too loose. Side runners work well for a while, but because of the narrow load-bearing edges in the grooves, wear is quite rapid and the fit deteriorates. The sides of the drawers also have to be thicker to accommodate the groove, making them look heavy.

Some time ago I came across a drawer construction that employed centre runners and this is the method I use today. The sides do not make contact with the inside of the carcass, enabling both the inner and outer surfaces to be sealed to improve appearance and stability. The top and bottom edges still provide vertical control and can be kept quite thin, reducing wear both to the sides and to

the corresponding running surfaces of the carcass. The centre runner provides all the lateral control necessary, with a shallow groove and no wear due to minimal side forces. To achieve this, machine a groove into a central muntin that is tenoned into the front and the back. The runner spline itself, which is fitted into a groove in the carcass, can be adjusted to fit into the runner to produce a perfect sliding fit before it is glued in place.

Muntins were common in the past in large drawers, to take the storage load that was carried by the drawer bottom. I still prefer to use solid wood for drawer bottoms; I like cedar of Lebanon (*Cedrela odorata*) because of its pleasant perfume. The solid drawer bottom runs with its grain from side to side, held in grooves in both the drawer sides, the front and back and the runner/muntin. It has to be able to expand and contract due to timber movement and as such should not be glued in place. Do, however, put a small amount of glue in the centre contact between the drawer bottom and the grooves in the edges of the runner, to stabilize and strengthen the construction.

▲ Maple inserts for the top and bottom edge drawer bearing strips.

▼ The final assembly of the drawers – showing false fronts and finished drawers.

The corner joints, both front and back, are through dovetails. Lap dovetails for the front joints are not appropriate as the whole drawer is narrower than the carcass opening. Prepare the material for both the front, back and sides to the same width and reduce the top and bottom clearance of front and back after marking out and cutting the corner joints and fitting the runner. This sequence enables you to align the top and bottom edges of all the drawer components and rout the grooves for the bottom before losing common reference edges.

◆ False front

BECAUSE THE OVERALL WIDTH OF THE ASSEMBLED drawer is narrower than the carcass opening a false front is necessary to fill the space. The false front is fixed to the drawer front with screws inserted from the inside. It is easier to drill and countersink the screw holes before assembling the drawer. The false front is carefully fitted to the opening ensuring sufficient clearance between the edges. The clearance I used was equivalent to the thickness of two layers of masking tape between the top and bottom edges and the sides. These layers of tape are applied to the corresponding surfaces. The drawer is then inserted into the carcass and the false front offered into place with two small tabs of double-sided tape between them. Once contact has been made, the false front and drawer can be pulled out together. It is quite likely that the screws, when inserted, will drift off-line, causing misalignment. To overcome this possibility, I drill two additional holes from the inside of the front through to the false front to accept precise diameter dowels, made from drawn brass rod. They are a tight fit in the holes and ensure perfect alignment when the screws are inserted. The first time the dowels are tapped into the holes, make them long enough to be extracted with the aid of pliers or pincers. Cut them to length for the final assembly. With the dowels in place insert the fixing screws, push the assembled false front and drawer into the carcass to test the fit. I have used this system many times and not once have I experienced any misalignment. Next, you can remove the holding screws and locating dowels and carefully separate the false front to remove the double-sided tape. The main reason I go to the trouble of making the false front removable is to gain access to the top and bottom edges of the drawer sides, should they ever need to be adjusted. Otherwise it could be glued.

▼ Finished drawers for the sideboard and the china cabinet.

Ripple cherry and bog oak china cabinet

This china cabinet accompanies the sideboard from page 134 and has much in common with it, both in construction and appearance.

◆ Carcass strength

In many ways the carcass of the cabinet is similar to the upper part of the sideboard, albeit extended upwards to increase the storage potential. However, because of the increased vertical dimensions and the subsequent problems of rigidity, I had to

▼ The china cabinet in ripple cherry and bog oak that forms a set with the sideboard from page 134.

incorporate new aspects into the construction to stiffen the carcass. Some time ago I came across the principle of the torsion box. This consists of a frame with thin sheet material glued on to the upper and lower faces. If a twisting load is applied to the upper surface the tension transmitted to the plywood of the lower surface counteracts the load. This means that compression forces are counteracted by tension forces.

The aesthetics of the china cabinet meant that it was not possible to include a complete torsion box. Instead, I was able to get close to the principle by making the lower section housing the drawers into a torsion box

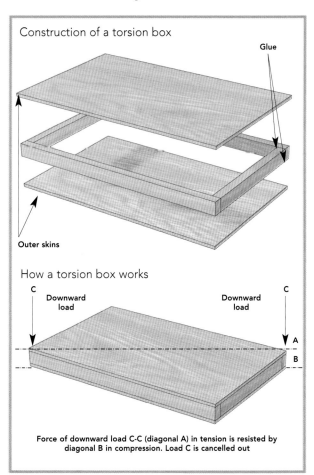

Construction of a torsion box

Glue

Outer skins

How a torsion box works

Downward load

Downward load

Force of downward load C-C (diagonal A) in tension is resisted by diagonal B in compression. Load C is cancelled out

Components of the china cabinet

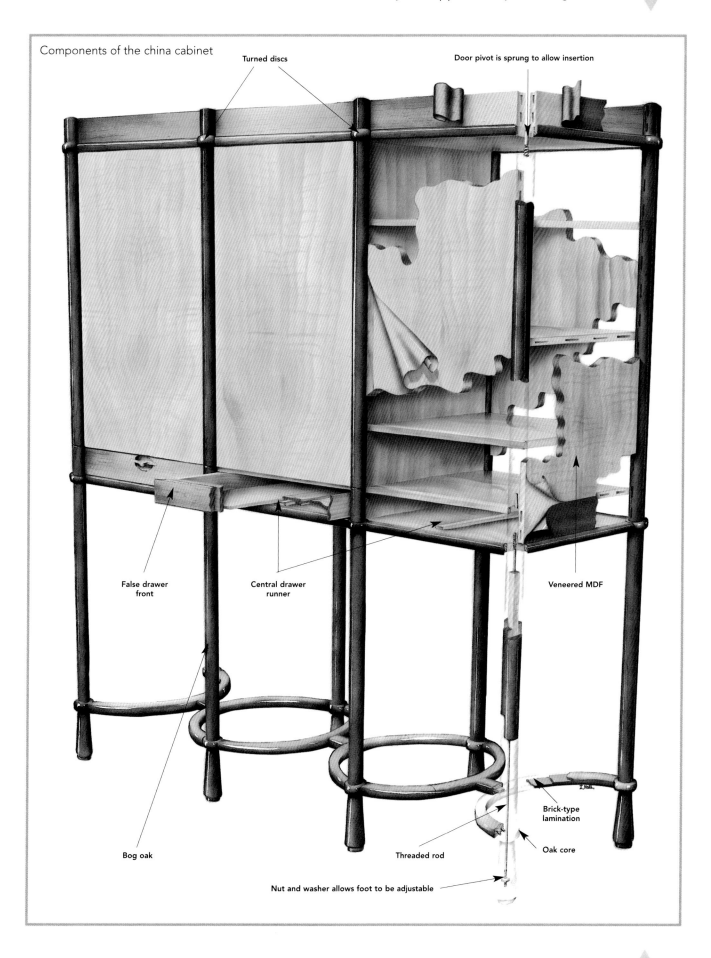

Turned discs

Door pivot is sprung to allow insertion

False drawer front

Central drawer runner

Veneered MDF

Bog oak

Threaded rod

Brick-type lamination

Oak core

Nut and washer allows foot to be adjustable

with one element missing and the upper section into a torsion box without the upper skin. The combination of these two constructional features contributed positively to the rigidity of the carcass. I felt that, structurally, the vertical dimensions of the carcass would result in flexibility that would negate the torsion box effect so I decided that I could overcome this weakness by gluing in the back panels.

◆ Scribed joints

I MENTIONED EARLIER THAT YOU SHOULD SCRIBE all the joints between the cylindrical components of the legs and their corresponding rails. Also use this method of construction for the sides and the back of the china cabinet. Scribed shoulders, splined and glued, produce a very strong, twist-free construction. For extra strength, joint and glue in the middle set of shelves, leaving the remaining shelves free to be positioned on adjustable pegs. It seems like a belt and braces approach but I have found in the past that any lack of stiffness in carcass construction often leads to the misalignment of doors when the carcass settles.

I knew that the piece would stand on a stone floor, which – although recently laid by a specialist flooring company – would not be perfectly flat. I made the feet adjustable to overcome the problem of distortion of the carcass, which could result in misalignment of the doors.

▼ Rows of leg and foot components.

◆ Gluing up

GLUING UP THE CARCASS WAS NOTHING SHORT of a challenge. As with all my case furniture I pre-finished the inner surfaces before the glue-up. It's easy to denib and burnish these surfaces to a good standard as flat components. Remove any excess glue that oozes out from cramp pressure after it has dried as it will not adhere to the pre-catalyzed lacquered surfaces. Break the gluing into a number of stages to overcome the relatively short open-assembly time of aliphatic resin. Make sure that all the relevant components are in position with unglued joints to ensure correct alignment.

◆ The doors

FOR THE DOORS YOU NEED TO USE A BOARD material that is both dimensionally stable and free from distortion. This is particularly important if the entire surface of the door is covered with veneer. MDF is suitable but is heavy and can put a strain on hinges. The lighter version, known as low-density fibreboard, is acceptable and as the door is not subject to horizontal load bearing, it would serve the purpose well.

In my opinion the ideal material is laminboard, but this is very difficult to source nowadays. Laminboard is a type of blockboard with very narrow core strips. These strips can be as narrow as ¼in (6mm). No single strip can impart individual movement to a board sufficient to influence the surrounding strips and cause distortion. The result is a very stable material that, because of the low resin content present in the construction, is also very light. It is ideal for the type of doors I designed for this cabinet. The question is, where can you get it? Because of the relatively low demand suppliers of board materials tend not to stock it. They will, however, import it for you if you buy in bulk. I got a range of sizes from Germany and now I have a supply for future projects.

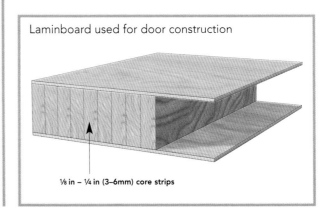

Laminboard used for door construction

⅛ in – ¼ in (3–6mm) core strips

Dimensions of the china cabinet

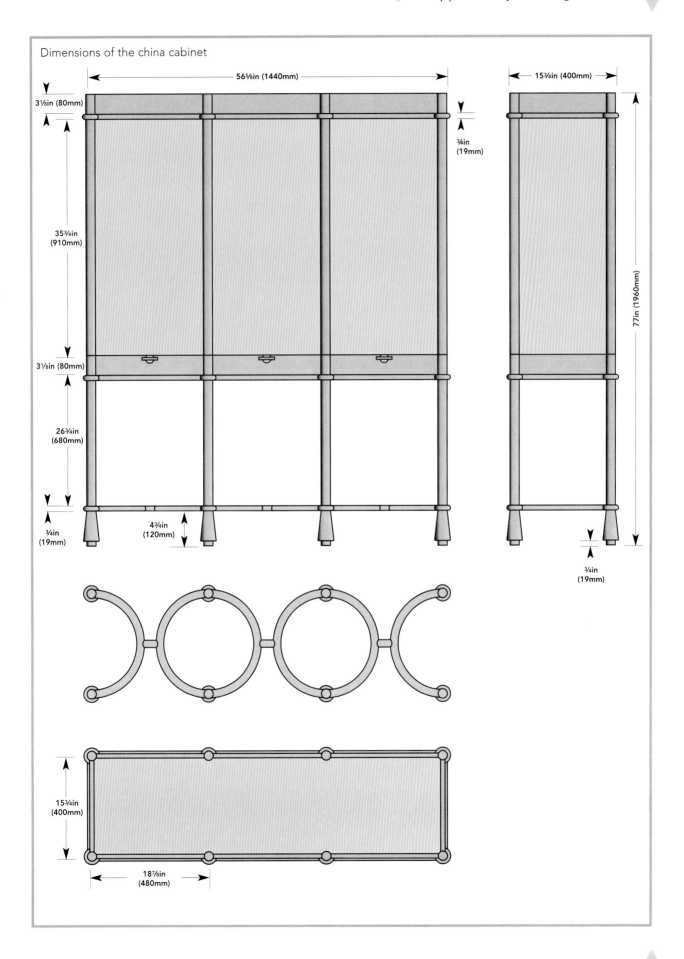

56⅝in (1440mm)

15¾in (400mm)

3⅛in (80mm)

¾in (19mm)

35¾in (910mm)

77in (1960mm)

3⅛in (80mm)

26¾in (680mm)

¾in (19mm)

4¾in (120mm)

¾in (19mm)

15¾in (400mm)

18⅞in (480mm)

Box jig for drilling pivot bush holes

Brass or stainless steel bush

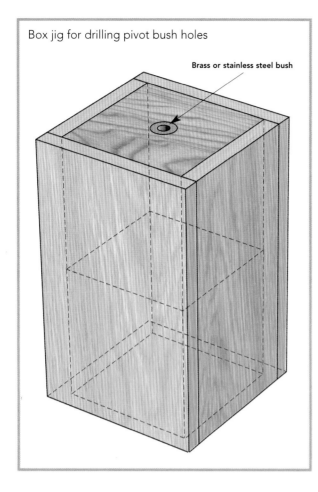

◆ Hinge pivots

I DEVELOPED MY DOOR-HANGING SYSTEM FOR two reasons. Generally speaking, the quality of commercially produced brass hinges leaves a lot to be desired. Poor alignment of the leaves and inconsistent accuracy of the screw holes can cause a lot of frustration when they are being installed. The second reason is an aesthetic one. The brass punctuation that breaks up the line between carcass and door can detract from the visual relationship between them. The pivots that I make to respond to these limitations overcome the problems.

Use pivots made from drawn stainless steel rod, which is accurately dimensioned during manufacture. They are carried in the doorposts in brass bushes. The upper pivot is spring-loaded, while gravity holds the lower pivot in. Machine some slots into the doorpost, to give access to a small shoulder, enabling the pivots to be retracted with a screwdriver.

Make the corresponding location in the carcass by using another brass bush with a flange that governs the upper and lower clearance of the door and also acts as a washer. Drill the carcass bush holes before assembling the cabinet. Then drill the holes for the lower pivots while holding the component in the four-jaw self-centring chuck on an engineering lathe. The upper holes are the centres for turning the discs.

◆ Doors

DRILLING THE HOLES FOR THE PIVOT BUSHES in the doorposts presents a challenge. The post is too long to form the hole using a drill press. It is also difficult to hold the post in place during this process. To solve the problem I developed a jig that uses a square-sectioned offcut from the doorpost before it was rounded.

Drill a hole through this block, holding the piece in a four-jaw self-centring chuck. Then line the hole with a metal bush that resists damage from the drill that eventually forms the hole in the doorpost. For short runs I use brass for this bush but, if the box jig is going to be used, I often use stainless steel.

You have probably come across the problem of holes drifting off-centre when drilling into end-grain. The drill takes the line of least resistance and follows the grain if it is not parallel to its rotating axis. This is due to the small section of the core of twist drills that are not stiff enough to resist flexing. To overcome this problem I tend to use metal-cutting end mill drills, which have a stronger core and resist drifting. This only works if both the drill and

The edges, including the hanging edge, have to be lipped before veneering to protect the vulnerable laminboard and to give the door the visual continuity it deserves. The lippings are not load bearing so you can scale down their thickness. Even the hanging edge, which is further strengthened by the cylindrical upright, has to be lipped so that the sharp edge created by the scribed junction between the two will not be damaged easily during subsequent handling.

For lightweight lippings I do not use any form of location such as splines or biscuits. There is sufficient surface area here to rely on a butt joint that does not require the force of cramps to hold it in place while the glue sets.

Instead, attach strips of masking tape at frequent intervals. The elastic quality of the tape imparts enough load to the lipping to allow you to lip several edges in rapid succession. Once the doors have been lipped, they can be veneered with the stunning ripple cherry.

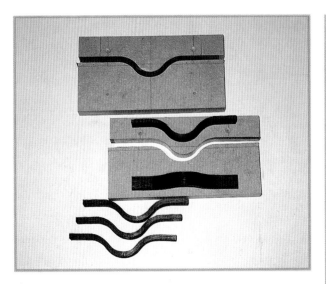

▲ Handle laminating jig.

work piece are held firmly and would not be suitable for hand-held work using a drill press as the mill drill has no spur centre.

Once you have drilled and lined the centre hole, face the block on four sides with MDF, ¼in (6mm) thick. This produces a box that can be placed over the end of the doorpost and held in place with a small cramp to facilitate boring the hole with a portable power drill.
Use a slow speed and light feed pressure to gain all the benefits of good alignment.

◆ The handles

FORM THE SMALL, GENTLY CURVED HANDLES BY laminating strips of bog oak veneer in a two-part mould. This is easy to make using a profile template developed from the inner curve of the handle. Shape the two sections of the mould using a router with a template bush and a cutter that is equal in diameter to the thickness of the combination of veneers that forms the handle. Insert the handle into a routed groove that spans a hole in the drawer front. In addition to creating more clearance behind the handle, the hole is a visual signal to the position of the handle as the pale-coloured cherry of the false front of the drawer shows through. This works well on the sideboard. However, I did not want to use the curved handle on the doors of the cabinet. By moving the position of the hole until it broke the upper edge of the drawer I gained access to the lower edge of the door. Routing a recess in that location was sufficient to form a positive pull.

◆ Finishing

SAND ALL SURFACES BEFORE GLUING UP SO THAT fussy corners and difficult access situations present fewer problems later. I sand large flat surfaces using a Festo random-orbit sander that produces an excellent result. I use 180 grit, sufficient to produce a quality surface on which I then spray a base coat of cellulose sanding sealer. I have an assortment of cork-faced blocks, which I coat with an adhesive-backed silicon carbide paper, and use to hand-sand the surfaces that cannot be done by machine. The random-orbit sander has an efficient dust-collecting system and I keep a vacuum cleaner by the bench for dust produced by hand-sanding.

The first application of a sprayed base coat always gives me a buzz. To see the fantastic colour and grain patterns that have been so dull and subdued until this moment is something worth waiting for.

Lightly denib the base coat with 400 grit and finally spray it with two coats of pre-catalyzed lacquer. Spray drift is a problem, particularly when finishing the outer surfaces of cabinet pieces. I use cardboard masks, strategically placed, to avoid this. The extra bit of effort is worth it in the long run – it is a nuisance if you have to denib and burnish the inside of a cabinet. Once the topcoat has cured – and I leave this as long as possible – very lightly denib the surfaces with 400 grit, if they need it. I prefer a matt finish and even though I spray a matt lacquer I find it necessary to enhance the result with Webrax. I no longer use steel wool as the remains of the ferric filaments have a habit of turning up later. On pale timbers and in the presence of water the results can be catastrophic. For flat surfaces, I again use it on a random-orbit sander – the result is an even, matt finish. Where the sander would over-buff corners, or for curved surfaces, I use strips of hand-held Webrax sheet.

▼ Spraying a door – a step towards the 'Wow' factor.

Ripple sycamore chest of drawers

I try and make at least one speculative piece every year such as this chest of drawers. Its design was inspired by the architectural concept of supports featuring on the outside of buildings.

▼ My Placet chest in weathered sycamore with ebony posts and plinths, patinated brass handles and outriggers.

FROM TIME TO TIME A DESIGNER'S OWN BRIEF can be a springboard for personal expression. It enables us to indulge in ideas that may have been building up for quite some time. This is one such piece and its design was inspired by the architectural concept of supports featuring on the outside of buildings. Hence the block that contains the drawers appears to hang between four cylindrical uprights, connected by what seem to be flimsy metal outriggers. I chose to use a bundle of very tight, weathered ripple sycamore (*Acer pseudoplatanus*) that dictated the control of pattern and the mitred chevron effect of the four show surfaces of the cabinet. This in turn influenced the configuration and spacing of the drawers and the pattern created by the handles.

I had sketched the pattern of the chevron on squared paper to develop the idea before converting it into a full-sized drawing. I always produce a full-sized drawing on white melamine board to work out the exact proportions and to ensure that the construction and dimensions are precisely recorded. This drawing remains near my bench as a constant source of reference. It confirms timber preparation dimensions and reminds me of the sequence of the processes.

◆ Carcass construction

THE CHOICE OF VENEER FOR THE SHOW surfaces could only be carried out successfully if it was laid on man-made board. The debate of solid versus veneer for case furniture is often argued but a big factor in the argument is the method used for laying the veneer. I am very aware of the fact that much of the furniture made today will go into overheated houses and this affects the stability of solid wood. I also like to use the patterns of wood grain that can be exploited effectively with veneers.

Working drawing of the chest of drawers

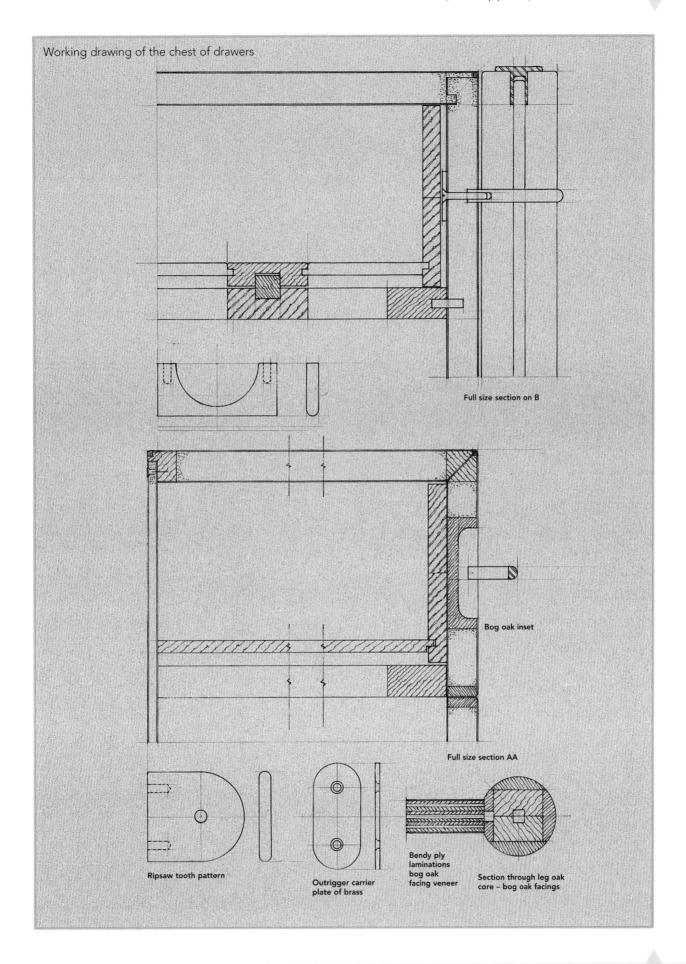

Full size section on B

Bog oak inset

Full size section AA

Ripsaw tooth pattern

Outrigger carrier
plate of brass

Bendy ply
laminations
bog oak
facing veneer

Section through leg oak
core – bog oak facings

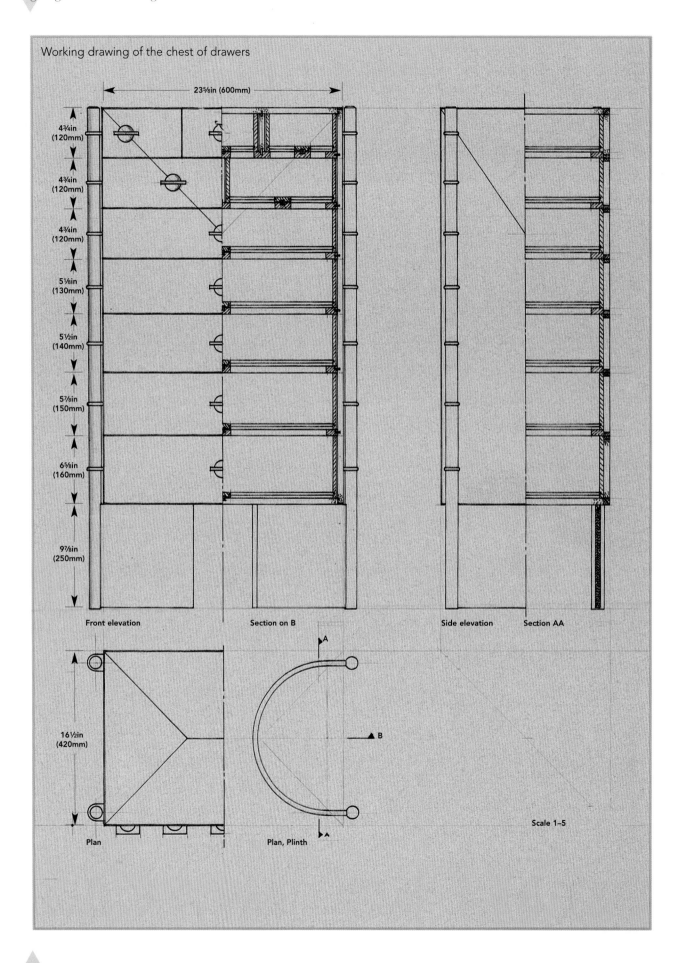

Working drawing of the chest of drawers

23⅝in (600mm)

4¾in (120mm)
4¾in (120mm)
4¾in (120mm)
5⅛in (130mm)
5½in (140mm)
5⅞in (150mm)
6⅝in (160mm)
9⅞in (250mm)

Front elevation

Section on B

Side elevation

Section AA

16½in (420mm)

Plan

Plan, Plinth

A

B

A

Scale 1–5

◆ Lippings

AFTER DIMENSIONING THE MDF TO SIZE
I applied the lippings. They perform two functions,
both protecting the edges and creating grain and colour
continuity. The lippings were glued on before laying the
veneers. Only the front and back edges needed lipping –
the front edge would be heavily chamfered to accept the
corresponding outer edges of the drawer fronts and the
back edge would be rebated to accept the back panel.
Because the lippings were going to be installed before
veneering and because they were not load-bearing
components, I glued them straight onto the edges
of the MDF without tongues or biscuits.

◆ Veneering

THE VENEERS WERE SIZED AND EDGE JOINTED TO
create a linear pattern based on the available width
of the leaves and the intended width of the carcass
components. I then cut the mitre angle of the chevron
pattern and shot the edges using my veneer edging jig.
Great care was exercised to ensure perfect alignment
of the linear joints where they meet on the mitred edge
joints. All the edge joints were taped and glued and the
tape removed after the glue had set.

As I used masking tape I was able to remove it before
laying the veneer. The inner surfaces were then veneered
with khaya (*Khaya invorensis*) backing veneer that was wide
enough not to require edge jointing to make up the width.
To make sure that the mitred effect of the show veneer
aligned perfectly with the corners of the lipped panel, I
placed the carefully dimensioned rectangle face down on
the lower caul. The surface of the substrate was then
coated with aliphatic resin, using a roller to speed
up the process. This was then carefully positioned on

▼ Edge jointing veneers for top.

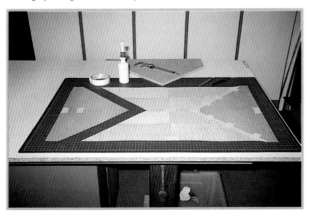

the veneer and pressed down using hand pressure.
Aliphatic resin grabs when contact is made so I could
be quite sure that it would stay in place when the slightly
oversized backing veneer was laid down and the upper
caul and platen was lowered. The overhang could then
be removed later with a router-driven edge trimmer.

◆ Drawer frames

DRAWER FRAMES PERFORM TWO IMPORTANT
functions. They provide runner control for the
drawers and stiffen the carcass while helping to keep
internal corners square. I decided to make the drawer
frames from hard maple (*Acer saccharum*) in the knowledge
that it would respond well to the wearing between the
runner components and the top and bottom edges
of the drawer sides. I also inset strips of maple into
the corresponding surfaces of the insides of the top
and bottom, which had been veneered with khaya,
a stable, but fairly soft, tropical hardwood.

Mortice-and-tenon joints were used to form the
corners of the frames and to position and hold the
intermediate rails to house the centre runners. The
grooves for the centre runners were cut on my router
table before the frames were assembled. Holes were
drilled in the back edges of the front rails to take the
screws for the internal drawer stops. These holes were
drilled before the frames were assembled, as access to
these surfaces would be very difficult after gluing up.
Likewise, holes were drilled from the inside edges of the
side runner rails so that these could be screwed to the
inner faces of the carcass sides. The working drawing
helped to anticipate this sequence of processes.

▼ Routing mortices for the drawer frames using two fences.

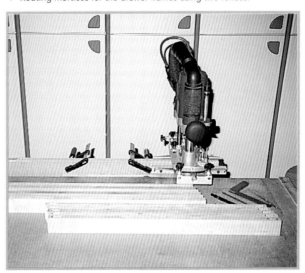

▲ Sizing tenons for the drawer frames using router table and slide.

◆ Splines

The drawer frames were connected to the carcass sides with splines made from ¼in (6mm) MDF. Although using biscuits would have been a quicker solution I chose splines to give me precise control in two directions. I cut the grooves for the bottom frame with a router, running the fence off the bottom edge of the carcass sides. This ensured that the grooves were parallel to the edge.

The remaining grooves were routed using the first set as a reliable reference. A pair of splines was inserted into the first two grooves and a spacer was placed against them and held down with G-cramps. The width of this spacer was equal to the width of the drawer side minus the distance from the cutter to the edge of the router base plate. The ¼in (6mm) diameter cutter matched the

▲ Inside carcass; detail showing outrigger fixings and drawer stops.

splines perfectly. This process was repeated for each drawer frame and the width of the spacer was changed to accommodate the reduction in the drawer sides as they progressed from the bottom to the top of the carcass sides.

The spacer was made from ¼in (6mm) thick MDF and dimensioned to width on my table saw. This method of routing the spline grooves ensured that the runners of the drawer frames would be parallel. After routing, the spline grooves were accurately set to length using a pair of cutting gauges to mark out the end lines; these were then squared up with a chisel. I repeated this process for the spline grooves in the edges of the drawer frames, certain in the knowledge that they would align perfectly when the carcass was assembled.

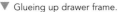

▼ Glueing up drawer frame.

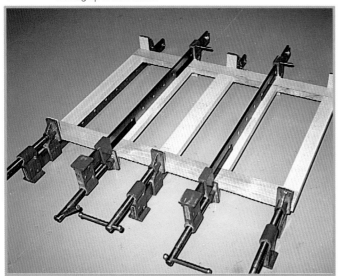

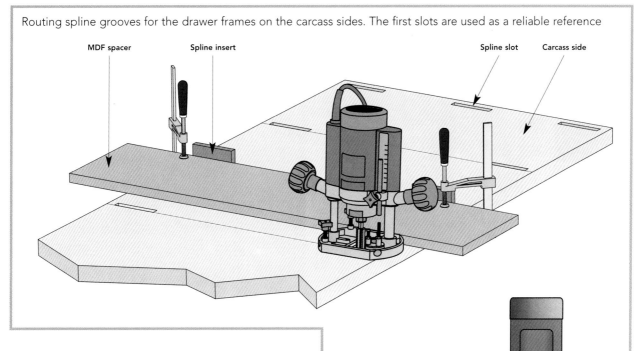

Routing spline grooves for the drawer frames on the carcass sides. The first slots are used as a reliable reference

MDF spacer   Spline insert

Spline slot   Carcass side

Router base

Spline insert

MDF spacer

Cutter

◆ Corner joints

ONCE AGAIN I CHOSE TO AVOID BISCUITS FOR THE corner joints. The most suitable joint seemed to be a simple lap joint that would have been easy to cut with a router. The only problem was the lack of positive location in two directions, which would have caused additional problems during assembly. Therefore I decided to include stub tenons in the configuration and these gave me the location both from the front and back edges, and from the outer corner of the joint. The thickness of the lap was determined by the size of the oak (*Quercus spp*) beading evident on all the corners of the finished carcass.

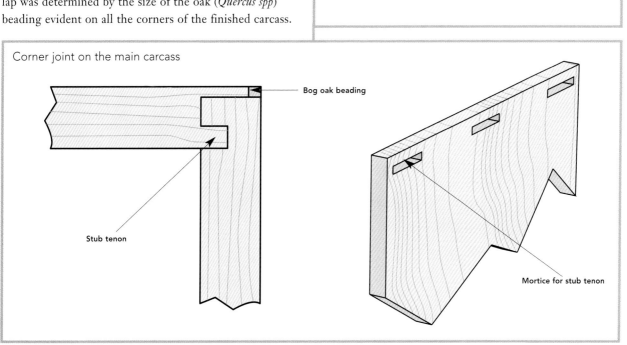

Corner joint on the main carcass

Bog oak beading

Stub tenon

Mortice for stub tenon

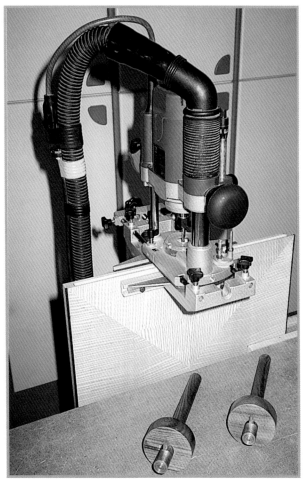

▲ Routing groove to form lap and tenon strip – carcass corners.

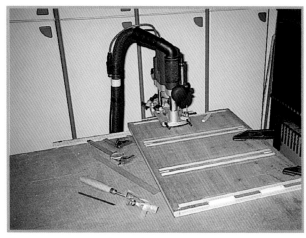

▲ Routing out waste to form stub tenons – carcass corners.

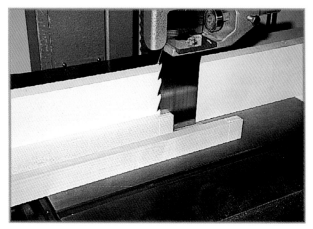

▲ Bandsawing tenons.

◆ Outrigger slots

I MENTIONED EARLIER THAT THE CARCASS WAS suspended between the legs and was held in place with patinated brass outriggers. To ensure a strong enough connection between these components it was necessary to insert the base of each outrigger into a slot in the carcass side.

To cut these slots I used a jig that I'd developed for routing housings and grooves that had to be cut at 90° to the edge of a component. The jig consists of a wide strip of ³⁄₁₆in (5mm) thick Perspex with a slot cut through it to accept a router base bush. One end of the jig is fitted with a fixed stock, set square to the slot, and the other end carries a moveable stock that traps the jig in place. Stops were also in place to control the length of the routed slot accurately.

This dimension and its position relative to the front and back edges of the carcass sides was critical, so the effort to control this accuracy was justified. After routing a slot from the front edge I turned the jig round and set

the fixed stock against the back edge to cut the rear slot. A small location block was then dropped into the front slot and the jig was positioned over it; this ensured accuracy and avoided additional marking out.

▼ Routing outrigger slots using housing jig.

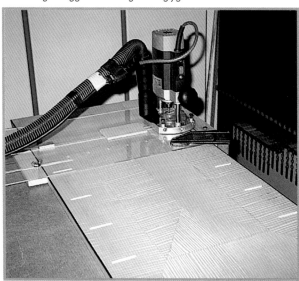

◆ Details

THE FRONT EDGES OF THE CARCASS HAVE A mitred profile that accepts the mitred edges of the drawer fronts, necessary to show the bog oak beading that defines all the corners of the carcass. A ⅛in (3mm) square beading was glued into rebates in the front and back edges of the carcass top, bottom and sides and the inner edges were profiled using a mitre router cutter. The back edges were then rebated to accept the carcass back.

◆ Inner surfaces

ONCE ALL THE CARCASS COMPONENTS HAD BEEN constructed I sanded all the inner surfaces with a random orbit sander using a 180grit disc. The drawer frames were hand-sanded using 240grit on a cork block. I carefully covered all surfaces that would eventually be glued with masking tape prior to spraying the interior with cellulose sanding sealer. I did not denib these surfaces before spraying a second coat of acid-catalyzed lacquer. The purpose of finishing the insides of the carcass is twofold. Firstly, it seals the surfaces and balances them with the outer surface finish. Secondly, it makes the removal of any glue that is squeezed out after assembly easier. Once the glue has dried it can be picked off with a chisel, or a scalpel, as it will not bond with the lacquer.

◆ Gluing up

TO GIVE ME TIME TO WORK WITHIN THE OPEN assembly period of aliphatic resin, I dry-assembled one carcass side and all its corresponding components. The other side was then glued, and the cramps put in

place. The assembly was checked for square by measuring the diagonals and it went together square, first time. Once the glue had cured the cramps were removed and the top and bottom rebates were cleaned up with a router cutter. This was to remove any glue and to define the final size before the bog oak beadings were glued in place.

The outer surfaces were then sanded and sprayed with basecoat. This application would balance the inner surface finish and protect the carcass during later stages. Because the basecoat is not catalyzed, it can be left for quite some time before final finishing. The solvent in the topcoat will etch into the basecoat, forming a chemical bond when it is eventually sprayed.

I made the uprights and curved sections, which carry the carcass, of bog oak; both for visual contrast and to differentiate between the function of storage and support. I chose to fabricate the cross-section from layers of wood to ensure stability and to enable the hole that runs down the length to be produced accurately. I know from bitter experience how difficult it is to drill long holes into end-grain – the long-reach drills follow any variation in grain density and the hole drifts off line.

I built up the core, which was made from clean, straight-grained English oak (*Quercus robur*), from two pieces. A half-round groove was routed into the joining surfaces and a waxed rod of stainless steel was inserted into the grooves to align the strips during gluing up. Once the glue had set, the rod was pulled out. The core was then faced with strips of bog oak and the result was like a solid piece of wood with an accurate hole running through the length of each component. Care exercised in the preparation and assembly of the facing strips meant that only the squeeze-out of glue had to be removed, resulting in an accurate square cross-section.

▼ Gluing on bog oak facings – uprights.

▼ Spraying inside of carcass sides – note the masking tape.

The final round section was achieved with a rounding over cutter and a router table. Due to the large radius, and the risk of tearing and breakout, I removed most of the excess wood by chamfering the corners on my bandsaw, with the table set at 45°.

All that remained to be done was to subdivide the uprights into pieces long enough to fit between the outriggers. I did this in two stages: a primary cut with the bandsaw and crosscut slide, slightly oversize; and two finishing cuts per component on the dimension saw to ensure accuracy and prevent breakout. Even with a crosscut blade on the dimension saw, the falling piece often suffers breakout as it is not supported when the saw bursts through. With a rounded cross-section this effect can be even worse, so the two stages in dimensioning the uprights using a slow feed speed were justified.

The lengths of the uprights fit in between the outriggers, so this measurement had to be transferred from the slots in the carcass to the crosscut slide of the dimension saw. I took this measurement with dial callipers and transferred it directly to the adjustable stop of the crosscut fence. Once cut, each piece was given an identification number to ensure grain continuity, bearing in mind that there are four uprights and each one is cut into eight sections.

◆ The curved sub-base

THE FOUR UPRIGHTS AND OUTRIGGERS WOULD not be rigid enough to support the carcass without an additional sub-base. In conventional cabinetmaking, stretcher rails would provide the support needed. I explored many various options to address this problem and in the final analysis, aesthetics played a big part. The curved sections are laminated from bendy-ply and faced with bog oak veneer. The core is formed of three layers of 3⁄16in (5mm) thick ply; this was so that I could build up the thickness quickly and effectively when laying the veneers and laminations in the bag press.

I used epoxy resin, which has a long open-assembly time and the formed section does not spring or change shape when it is removed from the mould. The resultant curve is more stable because the resin is cured chemically and there is no water held in the glue layers that has to dry out after curing. Epoxy resin is also much more benign to cutting edges that are involved in subsequent machining processes, particularly those of planer knives.

Laminated forms, because of their curved surfaces, present problems of handling and holding during later stages of canstruction. It is therefore necessary to

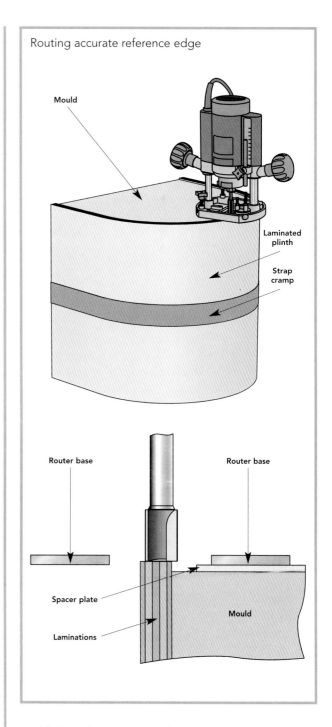

Routing accurate reference edge

Mould

Laminated plinth

Strap cramp

Router base

Router base

Spacer plate

Laminations

Mould

establish a reference edge and I do this with a routed end cut from one flat face of the laminating mould. I hold the laminated form onto the mould with a strap cramp and position the assembly on the bench with one flat face uppermost. The edge of the laminated form projects above the flat face.

A spacer plate is attached to the router base with double-sided tape so that the cutter can project enough to skim the laminated edge without damaging the face of the mould. The surface that is produced is accurate enough to then be cleaned up on the planer. This reference edge can

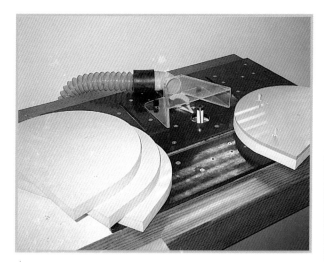

▲ Routing sections for laminating mould.

be used to dimension the section to width using a high fence on the table saw. The ends of the laminated forms also need to be squared up and cut to length. Once again, I used the mould and a router. This time, I held the laminated form in place with sash cramps and cut through it with a router-driven slitting saw mounted on an arbor. A ½in (12mm) diameter bearing gave me sufficient depth

of cut to go through the thickness of the section without too much penetration into the surface of the mould. I had modified the teeth of the cutter, changing it from a ripping action to a crosscutting action, to prevent breakout of the surface veneers. This is easily carried out with a small green-grit grinding wheel held in a lathe chuck.

After dimensioning the laminated sections to size I lipped the bottom edge with four strips of bog oak and trimmed off the excess with an end-bearing laminate trimmer held in my router table.

◆ Jointing the laminated sections to the uprights

THERE ARE TWO OPTIONS WHEN A RAIL IS JOINED to a rounded section. Either you scribe the shoulders of the tenon or you produce a flat, into which the mortice is cut, and leave the shoulders square. I chose the second option because it would have been very difficult to scribe the long shoulders of the ends of the laminated section to

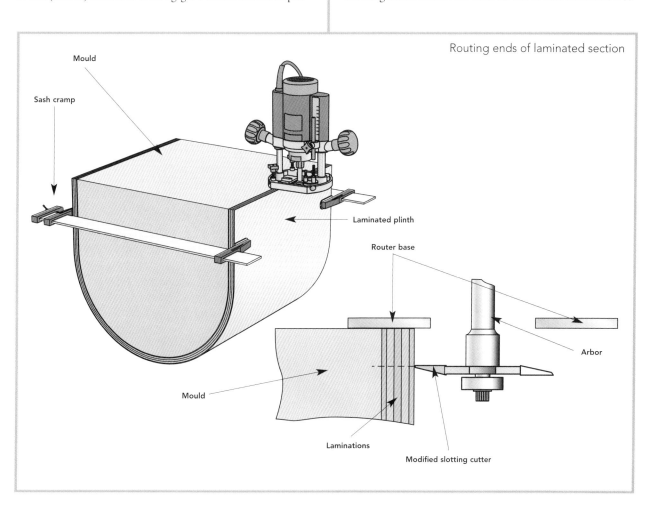

Routing ends of laminated section

Mould

Sash cramp

Laminated plinth

Router base

Arbor

Mould

Laminations

Modified slotting cutter

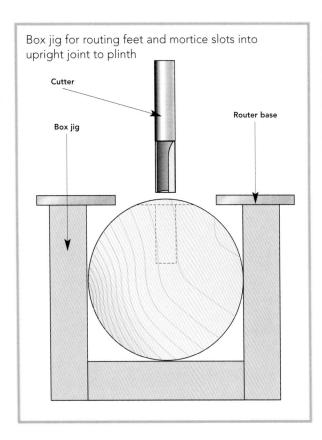

Box jig for routing feet and mortice slots into upright joint to plinth

Cutter

Box jig

Router base

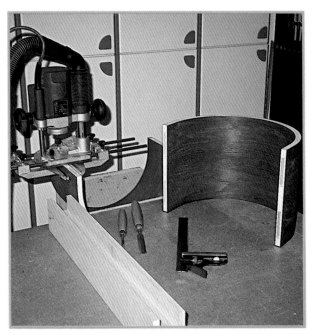

▲ Routing mortice slots in curved sub-base. Note also the box jig used for routing mortices in corresponding sections of uprights.

fit the curve of the uprights. Having already cut the ends square and knowing that the bendy-ply would not be strong enough to make continuous tenons, I used ¼in (6mm) MDF for loose tenons. The mortice slots into the laminated section were cut with a router and two fences

and the corresponding slots into the uprights were cut using a box jig, which was also used to rout the flat faces. These joints would have been very difficult to glue up before the advent of the cam-type edging clamps made by Kantenfix. They are so effective that I didn't even have to use any cramping blocks to pull the joint together.

▼ Gluing up sub-base to upright, using Kantenfix cam cramps.

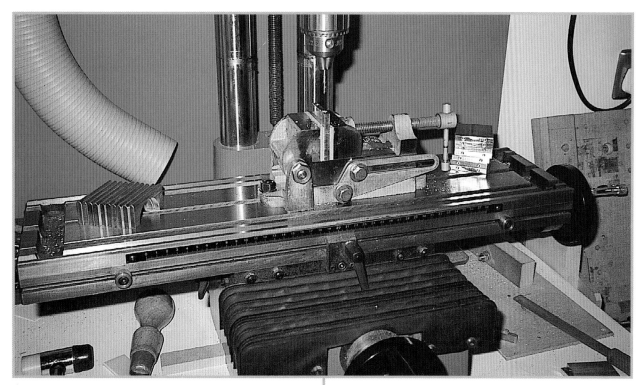

▲ Drilling fixing holes using a milling machine.

◆ The outriggers

A FEATURE OF MANY OF MY PIECES OF FURNITURE is the use of custom-made metalwork. It is possible to design the parts and have the metalwork made by an engineer. Obviously, there are costs involved and sometimes they can be high, especially for unusual components, as the set-up time can be quite long. The alternative is to invest in metalworking equipment and make the fittings yourself. In the main the skills necessary are not substantially different from those involved in removing material to shape wood, but the bonus is the options that are available when interesting designs are undertaken.

In fact the only specialist machine that was involved in making the outriggers was a milling machine, which was used to square up the ends that fitted into the carcass slots and to drill and tap the threaded holes for the fixing screws. The half-round profile was shaped using a disc sander and pivot jig after the excess material was removed with a bandsaw.

I chose half-hard free-cutting brass for the outriggers because it is easy to machine and does not require cutting fluids when it is being worked. The half-round cross-section was cut on a router table with a ⅛in (3mm) radius ball-race-guided rounding-over cutter. Make sure to note the carrier plate for safe handling of small components. Because of the small size of each outrigger and the possible risk of injury in handling it, I made a carrier

▼ Forming profile of outrigger using pivot jig and disc sander.

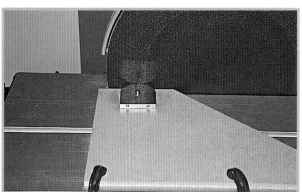

▼ Rounding edges of outriggers on router table. Note the carrier plate for safe handling of small components.

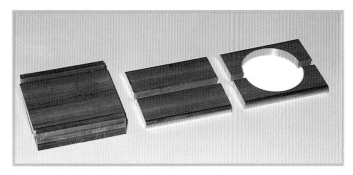

▲ Stages in making the drawer pulls.

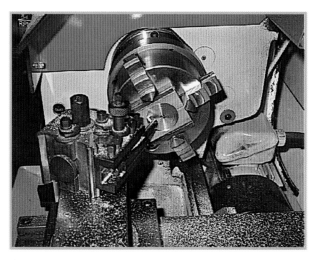

▲ Two drawer pulls held in four-pair self-centring chuck – boring a hole to produce profile.

plate that also served to register the contact necessary from the ball-race. The cuttings, which are very fine, were picked up by the dust extraction system that is fitted to my router table, and the spindle speed was reduced to prevent overheating. The cut was so good that the rounded edges needed no further polishing before the outriggers were patinated. This was done with solution of copper sulphate dabbed onto the brass, which was heated to a low temperature with a hot air gun. This type of patination works on any alloy that contains copper, but the colour will eventually rub off, so it is necessary to seal it with lacquer.

The drawer pulls were made in a similar way. The half-round internal edge was cut on my engineering lathe. I held two pieces of brass strip together in a four-jaw self-centring chuck and bored out the centre until the internal curve was formed. The screw fixing holes were drilled and tapped once again with my milling machine and the rounded front edge was profiled with the rounding-over cutter in my router table.

◆ The drawers

SOME YEARS AGO I CAME ACROSS A METHOD OF constructing drawers that incorporate centre runners for lateral control; only the top and bottom edges of the sides are involved in horizontal load bearing (see drawing on page 154). I built up the width of material for drawer sides, backs and false fronts from strips of edge-jointed wood that were resawn from crown-cut boards. As this is how most commercially available timber is sold, and thin boards that would be suitable for drawer making are difficult to locate, I have evolved this approach to overcome these limitations.

By resawing strips – usually from 2in (50mm) stock – working from the edge of the board, each piece is as close to quarter-sawn material as possible. The board was surfaced and planed to thickness before being resawn into strips, so the edges of each strip were already planed.

With my Hitachi band resaw I get very clean surfaces, so I taped and glued the edges to produce the desired depth of the drawer components before thicknessing. With aliphatic resin, the edge-jointed components needed only a short time in the cramps to get a glue-line-free result before they were surfaced and finally thicknessed to the required size.

My choice of timber for the drawer components on this occasion was maple, partly for its pale colour but also for its wear-resistant properties and stability. The centre runners, also made from maple, were tenoned into the inner faces of the front and back. As they are load-bearing components, they need to be strong enough to support the contents of a filled drawer. For this reason the drawer bottom could not be inserted from the underside of the drawer back as is possible in conventional construction. Therefore the through dovetailed corner joints, both front and back, could be identical. I set out the arrangement of dovetail pins so that the top and bottom

▼ Underside view of drawer, showing centre runner.

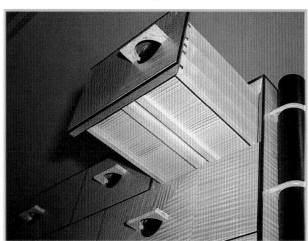

half pins did not go right to the edges. This enabled me to reduce the width of the false front and back by a couple of millimetres, resulting in sufficient clearance from any contact that would foul the action of the drawer. The only contact in the drawer running is between the top and bottom edges of the sides and the inside edges of the centre runner and guide rail.

Once the material for the drawer was prepared I fitted the sides to the internal dimensions of the carcass. I used to plane the top edge of each side until it was a tight fit in the carcass. These days I take the measurement of the drawer opening with dial callipers and transfer it directly to the ripping function of my dimension saw.

Working from the bottom edge of the drawer side – the face edge – I passed the component through. The trapezoidal-tooth saw blade created a smooth, clean edge. I knew from experience that when the drawer was assembled a shaving off the top and bottom edge would be sufficient to give a good running fit.

The false front was fixed to the show front of the drawer with screws inserted from the inside. These holes were drilled and countersunk before the drawer was glued up. After all the corner joints and drawer runner mortices were cut, the back and false front were reduced in depth to allow for carcass clearance, and the inside surfaces lightly sanded with 180 grit and a cork block.

The drawer was then dry-assembled and the area around the runner mortices protected with masking tape, before the insides were sprayed with sanding sealer. Any glue that subsequently squeezes out after the drawer is finally assembled can be easily removed with a chisel, as it will not adhere to the sanding sealer. After the lacquer had cured, I routed the grooves that accept the drawer bottoms. This ensures that there is no lacquer in the grooves that might inhibit glue bonding later in the assembly of the drawers.

◆ Drawer bottoms

THE DRAWER BOTTOMS WERE MADE OF CEDAR OF Lebanon (*Cedrus lebani*) and were ¼in (6mm) thick, so they had to be prepared from thicker stock. I divided the width of the drawer bottoms into quarters and prepared strips of wood to achieve these dimensions. They were then planed to thickness and edge jointed. Once again the method of holding the joints together was with glue and masking tape. The bottoms were cut to size, allowing for timber movement from front to back. The edges were rebated to fit into ⅛in (3mm) grooves in the sides, front, back and edges of the drawer runners.

◆ Gluing the drawers

THE FIRST STAGE IN THE SEQUENCE IS TO GLUE the bottoms into the grooves in the runners. Because of the differing grain directions it was not possible to glue the entire length of the joint, so I applied the adhesive to the middle third of the groove and the corresponding shoulder of the rebate. This stiffened up the construction, making the drawer rigid and less prone to distortion. After the glue had set I sanded with a random orbit sander.

The drawer bottom and runner was then glued into the mortices in the front and the back components; I took extra care to avoid getting any glue in the grooves so that expansion and contraction can take place later on. Finally, the dovetail joints were glued up, and the assembly was checked for squareness. Because the sides were fairly thin and could potentially flex, I checked the diagonals.

▼ Three stages of glueing up drawers: bottoms and runner (at the rear), front and back to runner (centre), and corner joints (foreground).

◆ Cleaning the outer surfaces

THE BIGGEST PROBLEM ENCOUNTERED WHEN cleaning up a box or container after it has been glued up is that of supporting the surface area that is being planed. I had offcuts of melamine-coated board that was thick enough to withstand flexing. I clamped a piece onto the bench with sufficient overhang to support each inside face of the four drawer surfaces. I chamfered the back corners and planed towards them to prevent breakout. This works well if the grain direction is taken into consideration when the components are first marked out.

The back could be planed from either corner. The front joints needed to be left square so that they fitted cleanly with the inside of the show front. Cleaning up the outer face of the false front was done by planing inwards from both corners. When doing this, constantly check the squareness of this surface to the centre runner, or the show front will not align with the front edges of the main carcass.

When all this was done the surfaces were sanded and sprayed with base coat to balance the finished inner surfaces. The cedar drawer bottoms were left unsealed for the resin oil aroma.

◆ The show fronts

THE SHOW FRONTS WERE MADE FROM MDF lipped with American cherry (*Prunus serotina*). The patinated brass drawer pulls were set into the fronts with a depression behind them to increase the amount of finger hold. I used bog oak for the circular depression.

▼ Routing depression for drawer pulls.

A rectangle of bog oak was inserted through the MDF before the veneer was laid, creating a framed effect when the depression was routed.

The most challenging aspect of making the drawer fronts was that of laying the show veneer so that the mitred effect and the upright edge joints lined up perfectly. To do this I made up a caul of melamine-coated chipboard and two fixed stocks to control vertical and horizontal alignment. I then laid the prepared assembly of edge-jointed and glued veneers face down onto the caul. This had been lined with polythene to prevent glue, which might bleed through and bond the veneers to the caul. The top drawer fronts were coated with glue and placed down onto the veneer, registering their position with the top and side stocks. A thin piece of card was inserted between the edges to keep them apart.

By using a roller spreader I was able to control the coating of glue so that very little went into the gaps created by the card inserts. When the last drawer front was in place the inner surfaces, which were now uppermost, were coated with glue and the backing veneer laid down. I then checked to see that nothing had moved. The second caul was put in place, and the entire package was carefully slid into the veneer press.

To separate the individual drawer fronts I cut through the veneer with a scalpel and straightedge, into the small gap created by the card inserts, and cleaned up the edges with a veneer trimmer.

▼ Drilling jig – locating pegs, false front to show front.

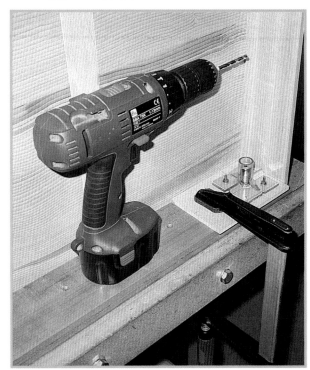

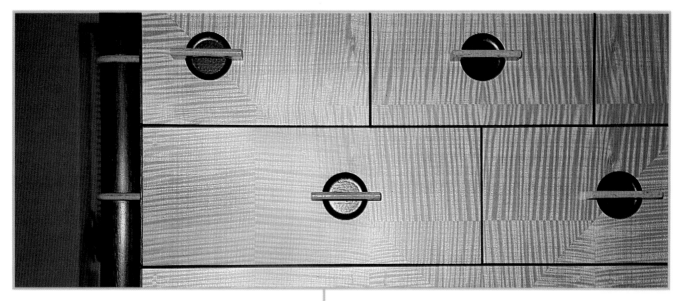

▲ Detail of front, showing alignment of veneers.

◆ Fixing the show fronts

I CUT THE DRAWER PULL WINDOWS WITH A
template and ball-end router cutter controlled by
a bearing. Slots were then cut and screw holes drilled
to accept the pulls. The outer edges of the show fronts
are mitred to fit into the carcass so as to connect visually
with the sides and pick up on the corner bead that runs
all the way around it. The bead was glued into its rebate
and cleaned up before the mitre was cut.

The show fronts were then fixed to the false fronts,
starting with the bottom drawer, as this makes contact
with three mitred edges of the carcass. Alignment and
location are the primary fitting concerns. With the drawer
in place and two dabs of double-sided tape on the false
front, the show front was positioned against the mitred
edges. This held it firmly enough to push the drawer
forward from the open back of the carcass until contact
was made. The connected assembly was then pushed out
carefully and the two fronts cramped together so that it
could be removed from the carcass.

Two location holes were drilled from the inside,
using a simple drilling jig to ensure continuity of position
in all the drawers and to make sure the hole was drilled
square to the surface. Temporary pegs were inserted into
the holes to make sure that nothing moved when the
fixing screws were inserted.

As mentioned earlier, the holes in the false front
were drilled before the drawer was assembled. This
process was carried out for all the other drawers, using
masking tape between the corresponding edges to create
the clearance necessary and to control alignment of the

veneer pattern on the fronts. The temporary pegs were
replaced by brass dowels made from the same diameter
stock to ensure one-to-one transfer of alignment for the
final assembly. Without these pegs I would have to rely on
the fixing screws for alignment and I know from bitter
experience that wood screws can drift off line.

▼ View of drawers pulled out.

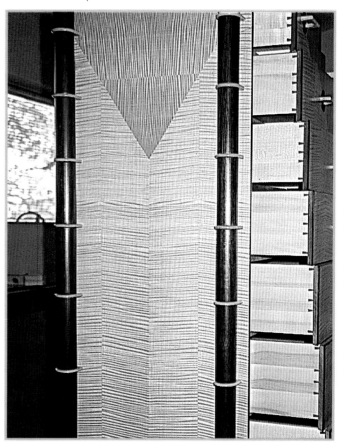

Laminated dressing table

This dressing table that I worked on as a commissioned piece can also be looked at as a masterclass in laminating as it covers all aspects of this fiddly, but rewarding, process.

MY CLIENTS FOR THIS COMMISSION wanted a dressing table as a showpiece for their bedroom. They had a dressing room next to their bedroom so the table did not need to contain a lot of storage space. The main requirements were a surface, a mirror and two drawers for small items such as make-up and jewellery, with lots of curves contributing to the form.

▶ This curved dressing table is a fine example of laminating.

Components of the dressing table

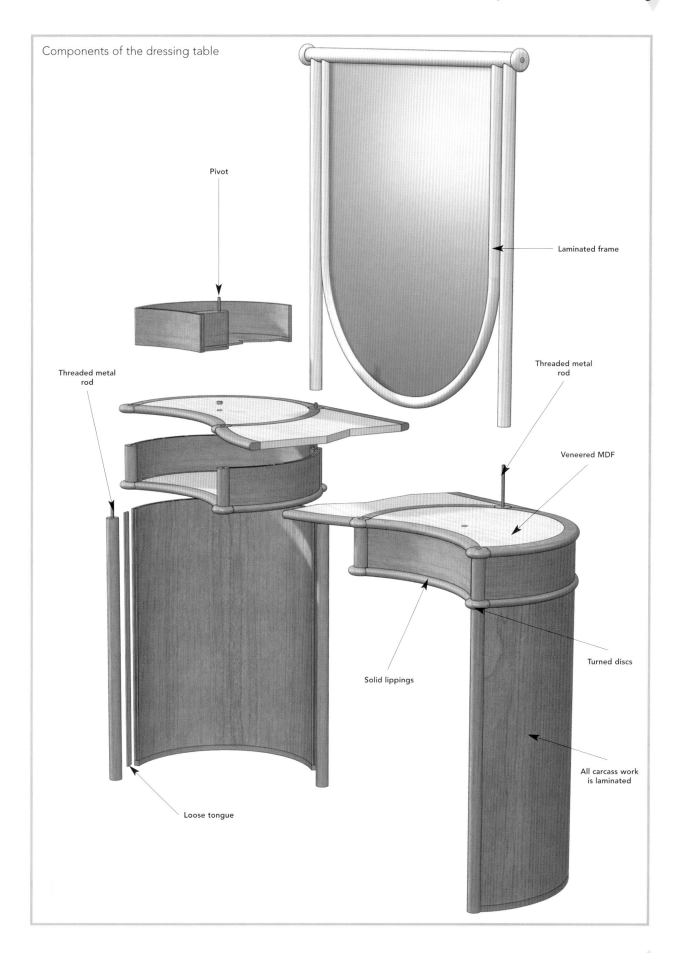

Pivot

Laminated frame

Threaded metal rod

Threaded metal rod

Veneered MDF

Turned discs

Solid lippings

All carcass work is laminated

Loose tongue

▲ The dressing table in situ.

◆ **Drawings**

STARTED BY MAKING A FULL-SIZE WORKING
drawing, which took the form of a large sheet of
white melamine board that would live my bench for
the duration. In addition to this, I drew a half-plan view
on a piece of MDF which became the reference base for
holding the components while the curves were being
formed, much of which was done with a router. The main
part of the construction consisted of two vertical sections
of a cylinder, made by laminating.

◆ **Bag press**

NOWADAYS, SMALL WORKSHOPS CAN AFFORD
vacuum presses and the scope of laminating has
moved out of the domain of large-scale manufacturing.
A bag press enables laminated shapes to be produced with
a single part mould as long as the cross-section is formed
in one plane. Thin layers of wood, which can be bent
easily, are glued and held in place onto a mould covered
with a layer of plastic until the adhesive has set.

  I have tried a variety of ways of making moulds, and
the one that I now use evolved through my interest in the
router. Whichever method you choose will involve a lot of

▼ An earlier piece using a similar idea for the base.

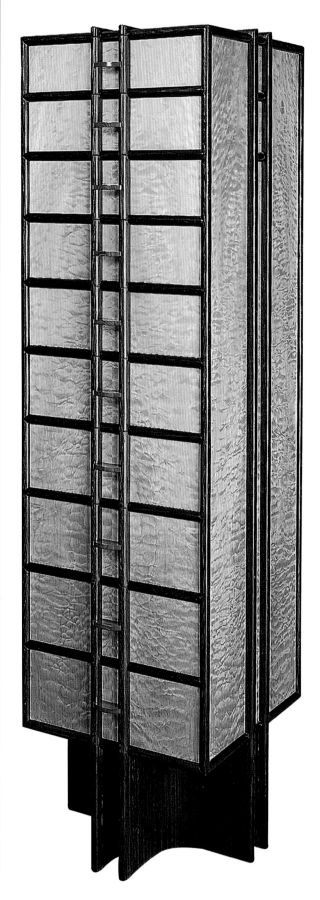

work, and this is often dedicated to the production of a mould for each individual shape. It does help if the design can utilize a single shape for more than one component, but there is the risk of compromise that might affect the aesthetics of the piece. I made two moulds: one for the uprights and another for the rotating drawer.

◆ Moulds

I MAKE MY MOULDS FROM LAYERS OF THICK LOW density fibreboard (LDF) – 1in (25mm) thick. Because of the high pressure generated by the vacuum bag, it is necessary to make the mould solid throughout. It is tempting to experiment with hollow, sectional moulds but the likelihood of collapse and distortion is not worth the risk. I managed to find some ultra-light LDF, which is strong enough to withstand the pressure and light enough to make a large mould relatively easy to handle.

I made a template from ⅜in (9mm) thick MDF. For this project the template was held down onto the MDF reference base with panel pins, making sure the centre hole that would be the pivoting point lined up with the centre hole in the base. I then routed the curve that would represent the inside of the laminated upright, using a trammel arm that I engineered myself.

◆ Calibrated

IN THOSE DAYS, I HAD NOT COME ACROSS THE MicroFence system; the production of this dressing table would have been a breeze with the precise adjustment of the MicroFence trammel arm. Although my version had a fine adjustment screw, it was not calibrated and it required much more care and effort to achieve precise results. The dimensions of the template allow for extra length and width, as it is almost impossible to prevent a small amount of slip when the mould and glued laminations are inserted into the vacuum bag.

The template was then fixed to layers of LDF and the profile formed with a top-bearing cutter set into my router table. I developed two refinements that ensured perfect alignment from one piece to the next. It was almost impossible to fix the sections together without misalignment. I drilled three holes through each layer and inserted lengths of studding – threaded rod – through them.

This raised the question of repetitive accuracy from one layer to the next. I drilled three holes in the template, into which I inserted brass bushes that have a ¼in (6mm)

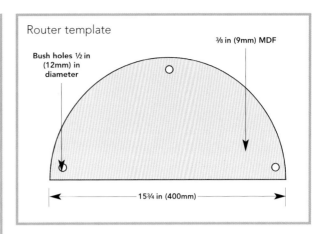

Router template

Bush holes ½in (12mm) in diameter

⅜ in (9mm) MDF

15¾ in (400mm)

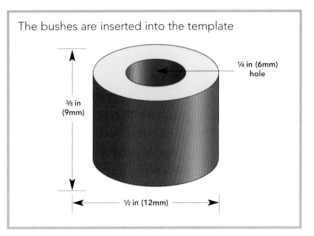

The bushes are inserted into the template

¼ in (6mm) hole

⅜ in (9mm)

½ in (12mm)

hole drilled through them. I made the bushes myself on an engineering lathe. Because free cutting brass rod is quite soft, it would be possible to drill these bushes on a woodturning lathe. If this option is not available, you will need to have them made by a small engineering company. The template was held down onto the blank with a few panel pins and holes were drilled through the bushes using a pillar drill, which has the benefit of reliable accuracy. The bushes also resist any damage to the hole from the twist drill.

◆ Extra support

FOR EXTRA SUPPORT DURING THE ROUTING process, I inserted two pieces of metal rod into the bushed holes and the combination was ready for the router table. To make routing easier, it helps to remove the bulk of the waste with a bandsaw. Bear in mind that board material will damage the teeth, so it is advisable to use an old blade for this purpose. Cut to within a couple of millimetres of the line that has previously been marked using the template. It also helps to identify the upper surface of each layer so that there is no

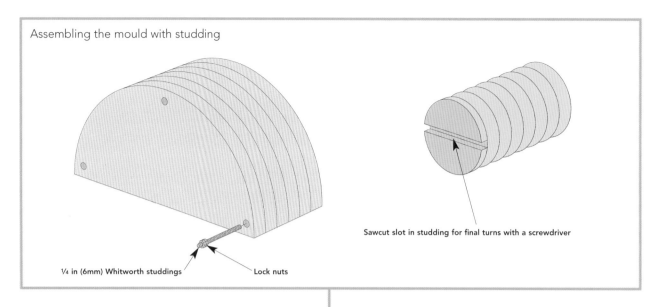

Assembling the mould with studding

¼ in (6mm) Whitworth studdings   Lock nuts

Sawcut slot in studding for final turns with a screwdriver

misalignment during the assembly process. I specifically stated that the holes drilled through each layer had a diameter of ¼in (6mm). This is because the studding I use to align and hold the layers together has a ¼in (6mm) Whitworth thread. It is still possible to buy this imperial studding from DIY stores.

The larger diameter not only ensures alignment, but the thread also holds the layers together and no glue is required. In the future it might be possible to recycle the LDF for the making of a smaller mould. Cut the studding to length with a hacksaw, so that it is ³⁄₁₆in (5mm) shorter than the combined length of the layers that will form the mould, and saw a small slot into one end of each piece, which can be used for the final stage of assembly. The other end needs to be slightly tapered so that it enters the holes easily.

Assembly

NOW TO THE ASSEMBLY STAGE. SCREW THE studding into the first layer until the tapered end projects enough to engage the holes of the next layer. As the studding had to be screwed through several layers, I put two nuts at the slotted end and tightened them to act as lock nuts. This enabled a spanner to be used to drive the studding. Lightly clamp the two layers together and screw the studding through until the tapered ends appeared again. Repeat this process until all the layers have been assembled.

Finally remove the lock nuts and finish inserting the studding with a screwdriver until it is completely concealed and there is no risk of sharp ends projecting and damaging the plastic vacuum bag.

Alignment

ALIGNMENT OF THE LAYERS SHOULD BE PERFECT but it helps to lightly sand the surface onto which the laminations will be laid before applying a layer of polythene. This acts as a release agent, preventing any adhesive from soaking through and bonding itself to the mould. I use heavy gauge polythene sheet, which is normally used for damp-proofing. This can be held in place with parcel tape, which is also resistant to adhesion from glue. Placing the mould and glued laminations into the bag is a challenge. I marked a centre line across the top of the curved surface and continued it down the two outer faces. This lined up with a corresponding line on the uppermost lamination, which was the show veneer.

Bendiply

BECAUSE THE EDGES OF THE LAMINATED FORM would not be seen, I used 'bendiply' for the core. Constructional veneers are normally available in ¹⁄₁₆in (1.5mm) thickness but with three ⅛in (5mm) layers of bendiply I was able to build up the thickness with fewer layers. It is possible to buy ⅛in (3mm) thick constructional veneers but it would have been uneconomic.

The show veneer was nicely figured steamed pear, but because bendiply has opened grain, it was necessary to include a sub-layer of khaya backing veneer. This became common practice after early plywood pieces, such as those designed by Marcel Breuer, showed signs of cracks in the surface. Double-veneering, as it was known, consists of laying an inexpensive veneer below the show veneer, set at 90° to the surface-grain direction of the ply.

Spreading the glue

EPOXY RESINS CAN BE MESSY TO SPREAD. THEY are also prone to an exothermic reaction if they are left in bulk in the container in which they are mixed. This can happen very quickly and the mix will soon set before your very eyes.

The ratio of five parts of resin to one part of hardener is critical. Do not be tempted to put in a little extra hardener for good measure. Strangely enough it will not set. I find the pumps supplied with the resin are not very reliable as the priming process can result in some extra material being pumped into the container. My solution is to use a set of digital kitchen scales and the risk of error is eliminated. As soon as I have mixed a batch I pour it into a shallow, non-stick baking dish.

The heat dissipates over a larger surface area and the pot life and open-assembly time is increased. I used a foam roller to spread the adhesive. Although these rollers can be cleaned with a solvent such as methylated spirits, they are cheap enough to be discarded after use as the cleaning process is quite messy.

It is not necessary to coat both contacting surfaces between two layers. Also, make sure that you do not apply any glue to the show veneers. Being thin, the glue will go right through making it very difficult to clean the outer surface after it has cured. I made sure that the surfaces were evenly coated with the thinnest application possible.

Slippery

WITH THE SURFACES COATED, THE COMBINATION was ready to go into the vacuum bag. This is quite a challenging task and for large moulds it helps to have the assistance of another pair of hands. Epoxy resin is also very slippery while it is still wet so I took the precaution of fixing a piece of masking over and on both exterior surfaces at the centre of the ends.

This also had the centre line marked onto it. The last thing I did before the assembly went into the mould was to fix the pack of laminations down onto the mould, once again with masking tape, thereby reducing the risk of movement as the bag pulled down. Leave the whole lot in the bag with the extractor switched on for the period of the setting time.

GLUING UP

The choice of adhesive is very important. With my early attempts at laminating I used urea formaldehyde resins. These were the glues used by industry where speed was necessary. They could also be set thermally. They were the most commonplace adhesives for the amateur and small manufacturers. They had a good open assembly but there were two disadvantages that I frequently came across. The cured glue line was so hard that it damaged cutting edges, particularly those of planers' blades. I also noticed that the shape of the lamination underwent changes as the moisture that was held in the wood fibres dried out over a period of time.

This prompted me to experiment with epoxy resins, which are now my adhesive of choice. They have a long open-assembly time and there is no water involved so the shape remains constant once the glue has cured. Epoxy resins do not dull cutting edges and their only slight disadvantage is their cost. With care, however, it is possible to mix these glues economically: thanks to the good open assembly time, if you do not mix enough you can always mix a little more, thereby avoiding waste.

The viscosity that is produced from a standard mix can be too thin, resulting in excessive penetration into the wood fibres. This can be overcome with the addition of a small amount of colloidal silica.

Spring back

WHEN LAMINATED FORMS ARE TAKEN OFF THE mould there is usually some spring, which causes the shape to open up a little, and it is difficult to predict how much spring will occur. I am told that it can be worked out using a mathematical formula but from my experience it is possible to anticipate the allowance that can then be built into the mould. Epoxy resins reduce the tendency for the shape to change, and in the case of the main laminated forms for my dressing table the use of 'bendiply' resulted in no change at all once they had been removed from the mould.

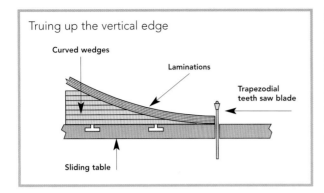

Truing up the vertical edge

Curved wedges

Laminations

Trapezodial
teeth saw blade

Sliding table

Most straight-edged components made from wood can be prepared with a simple system of face sides and face edges with a plane or a planer-thicknesser. Although the principle is basically the same here, the fact that curves are involved makes the establishing of reference edges a different proposition, particularly if other components with straight edges are going to be combined. The mould can now be used to check the accuracy of the reference edges of the laminated form. It is necessary to true up the ends, and this can be done on a surface planer.

The fact that there is bound to be some kind of misalignment of the layers can make it very difficult to establish a planed straight edge, which will also be square to the long vertical edges later in the truing-up process. I overcame this problem by using the ends of the mould and a router to true up the top and bottom edges of the laminated form.

◆ Form

HOLD THE FORM FIRMLY ONTO THE MOULD WITH a band cramp so that the rough edge is proud of the surface. Fix a sub-plate, made of ¼in (6mm) MDF with double-sided tape to the base plate of the router. A ¾in (19mm) parallel carbide cutter with a good end cut is big enough to produce a clean surface – set the amount of projection to just clear the end face of the mould.

Set the router to a low spindle speed and gently ease it into the laminations, bearing in mind that only half of the soleplate is in contact with the end surface of the mould. The depth of plunge is governed by a stop. This enables a series of progressive light cuts to be made, which reduces the likelihood of breakout.

The trued-up ends provide reference edges from which the straight, vertical edges can be cut. The sliding table of my Felder combination machine was the ideal tool for this. I made a pair of 'curved wedges' to support the laminated form which was also held down onto the sliding table with the cam clamp that fits into T-slots.

Hold the trued-up end against the sliding table fence. With everything firmly held, push the assembly against the rotating saw blade, equipped with 60 trapezoidal teeth. The result is a clean, straight, sawn edge that will require no cleaning up whatsoever.

◆ Cutting

WHILE I AM COVERING THE REQUIREMENTS for truing up the edges of the laminated vertical sections, it is necessary to look at the process of cutting across the shape to produce the upper and lower lengths that constitute the drawer compartment and the support below it. This is best done after the spline slots that locate the vertical edge to the round sectioned leg have been cut: it is easier to control the process on a long edge, there being a short spline for the drawer compartment and a long one for the legs.

Once again, it should be possible to cut through the laminations on a table saw. Because the curve is quite deep it is not possible to push the piece through in one pass, either on the sliding table or against the rip fence, due to the limitations caused by the diameter of the saw blade. A rolling action against the rip fence is also a safety risk. Another option is to use a bandsaw with the end running against the fence.

The rough saw cut can then be cleaned up using the technique I described earlier, with a router off the end of the mould. Instead, in this case I used a router and a slitting saw and arbor. This is another piece of equipment I made using my engineering lathe. The arbors available for use with slitting blades are too small and short. This dimension is determined by the shank size of a quarter of an inch. I used a piece of ½in (13mm) diameter stainless steel rod, which was stiff enough to get the extra length that I needed.

I turned a shoulder at one end, equal in diameter to the slitting blade hole and long enough to accept a ball race, and a thread was also cut to take a nut and washer. I also modified the carbide teeth of the slitting blade to produce a clean crosscutting action. This was done with a green-grit grinding wheel.

A problem often experienced when man-made boards are used in furniture-making is the appearance and risk of damage associated with edges. This is certainly the case with the bendiply core of the laminated form.

The top edge will be covered by the actual top of the dressing table, but the bottom edge, even though it cannot be seen, is liable to become damaged. I decided to apply a lipping which, because the curved shape of the

Cutting through the laminated form

Modified crosscut teeth

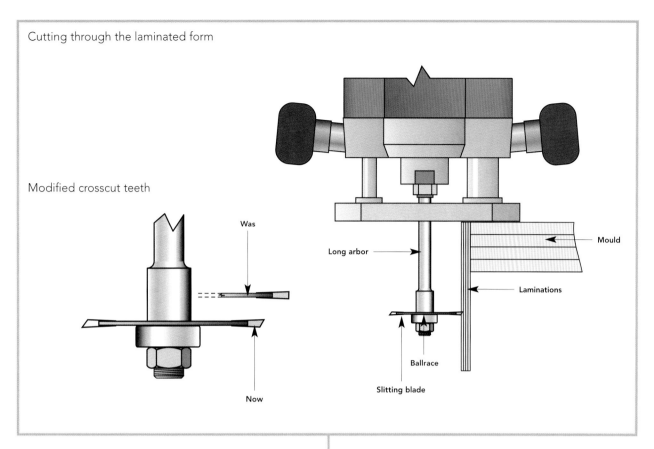

Was

Long arbor

Mould

Laminations

Ballrace

Slitting blade

Now

laminated form, had to be made from four strips that are mitred together. I cut the angles on my sliding table saw and assembled them with masking tape until the glue set. Even though the joints have end-grain contacts, they are strong enough to withstand handling until the lippings are glued onto the bottom edges. The overhang is then removed with a ball-race guided cutter mounted in the router table.

◆ Spline joint

I MADE THE FOUR LEGS BY CONVERTING A SQUARE section to a circular section with a rounding-over cutter and my router table. The timber was planed to a square section and the length left longer than required for the finished component. This extra length made the rounding process safer, especially on the last cut where the section could rotate as it was being fed through against the fence.

The square end also gave me more control when it came to holding the component in the jig that I used to rout the spline grooves. I cut off the excess material from the corners so that there was less material for the rounding-over cutter. This was done using the bandsaw with the table set at 45°. My router table is fitted with a feather board that holds the work against the fence. It is

Mitre butt joints making up the lippings for bottom edge of laminated form

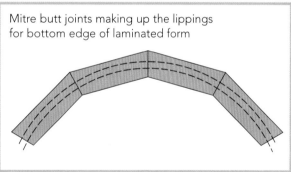

Box jig

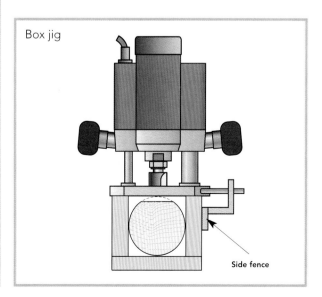

Side fence

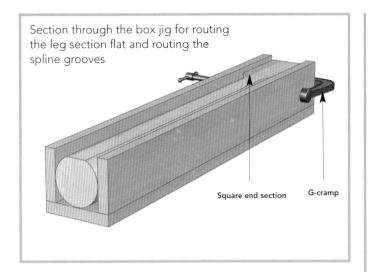

Section through the box jig for routing the leg section flat and routing the spline grooves

Square end section   G-cramp

There are two options for the surface contacts between the cylindrical upright and the edge of the laminated form; either to create a flat face on the curved section of the leg or to scribe the edge of laminated form with a hollow. I have used both methods for other pieces but, because of the difficulty involved in the holding of the components, I chose the former of the two options.

The groove in the edges of the laminated form was cut using my router table with the feather board providing extra control. I made a holding jig from MDF to cut both the flat face and the groove in the legs. The box section was formed from strips of MDF held together with double-sided tape, which is more than strong enough for the job – it is also quick and easy to use. I cut the flats first, using a cutter that was both wide enough and had a good end cut with the router held overhead controlled with a side fence. The extra length that I left with a square section ensured a positive alignment in the jig and provided a firm grip from a small G-cramp.

not a conventional feather board with a series of angled sawcuts that provide spring pressure. It has two opposing sawcuts that run parallel to the fence. This means that the work can be fed in both directions if necessary.

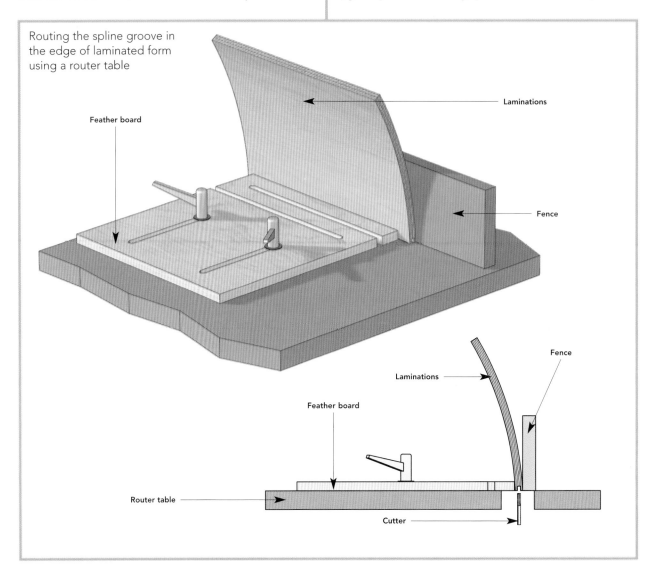

Routing the spline groove in the edge of laminated form using a router table

Feather board

Laminations

Fence

Laminations

Fence

Feather board

Router table

Cutter

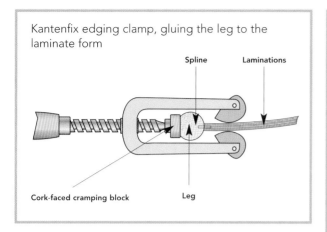

Kantenfix edging clamp, gluing the leg to the laminate form

Spline — Laminations — Cork-faced cramping block — Leg

Once all the flats had been machined I used the same set-up with the cutter that had been used to produce the groove in the edges of the laminated form. The spline was made from ⅛in (4mm) thick MDF which, although it contributed to the strength of the joint, was mainly to provide positive location. I often think of the potential of modern tools and of the problems I experienced before these were available. Cramping the assembled joint between the round sectioned leg and the vertical edge of the laminated form would be hard without Kantenfix edging cam clamps. The cramping block I made to centre the pressure has a curved inner surface which is coated with a strip of sheet cork, held with double-sided tape and the shallow curve cut on the router table. The friction created ensures the block stays in place during gluing.

◆ Lippings

THE TOP AND BOTTOM LAYERS THAT MAKE UP the compartments for the swivelling drawers are made from MDF, veneered with weathered ripple sycamore (*Acer pseudoplatanus*). This colour provides a gentle contrast with the steamed pear (*Pygrus communis*) that forms the laminated uprights, the mirror frame and the curved lippings.

Lippings are used to protect the edges of veneered board materials and to minimize the visual distraction that could affect the appearance of the piece. There are two ways that lippings can be used effectively; either as an edging strip, which is covered with the veneer to replicate the appearance of solid wood, or glued onto the edge after veneering, in which case a contrasting wood can be used, making a feature of the combination. I chose the latter approach – the lippings work like a picture frame surrounding the busy expanse of ripple sycamore.

The bundle of veneers that I had available were quite narrow, so the width from the back to the front is made up from four consecutive bookmatched strips. Because the four strips have a herringbone effect it could have been quite disturbing to the eye, appearing to move from left-to-right. Because of the powerful symmetry on either side of the vertical centre line, I felt it was necessary to repeat this feature on the plan view of the top to eliminate the feeling of unbalanced directional

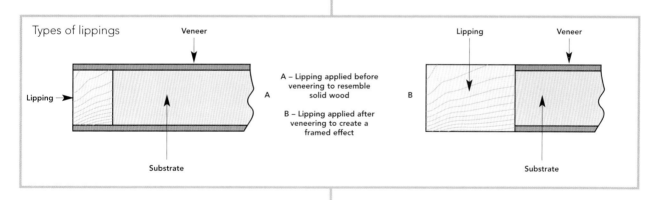

Types of lippings

Veneer — Lipping — Substrate

A – Lipping applied before veneering to resemble solid wood

B – Lipping applied after veneering to create a framed effect

Lipping — Veneer — Substrate

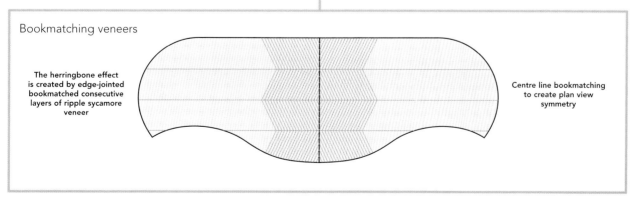

Bookmatching veneers

The herringbone effect is created by edge-jointed bookmatched consecutive layers of ripple sycamore veneer

Centre line bookmatching to create plan view symmetry

CUTTING LIPPINGS

I had two options when making the curved lippings; either to laminate them or to cut them from the solid. I chose the latter. Laminating the curves would have required the production of three moulds because of the different radii. This involves a lot of extra work. I was also aware that the striped effect would clash with the straight lipping at the back edge of the top, which is made from solid pear wood.

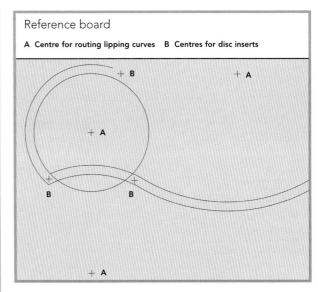

Reference board

A Centre for routing lipping curves   B Centres for disc inserts

movement. The veneers are cut and edge jointed before being glued and stuck together with masking tape. I prefer this method as it enables me to remove the tape before the jointed veneers are laid, which eliminates any risk of damage to the veneer after it is removed from the press.

◆ Reference base

I MENTIONED EARLIER THE REFERENCE BASE, WHICH is a piece of MDF with a drawn half-plan view. This is the multi-function jig that I used to rout all the curves for the lippings, the curved edges of the veneered section and the disc inserts that form the centres of the cylindrical uprights. The drawing provides me with an accurate image from which to control all of the router trammel arm settings. The sequence starts with drilling the centre hole of the main circle above the swivel drawer containers. This hole cannot be created using my pillar drill due to the limitation of the distance from the centre of the chuck to the front of the pillar. The hole has to be accurately drilled, which rules out the use of a power drill held freehand. Instead I made a simple jig from MDF with a brass insert to hold the drill at 90° to the surface. The jig is positioned accurately over the centre point on the drawing by pushing a ¼in (6mm) diameter spur centre punch through the brass sleeve. You can buy a set of punches but they are designed for use in metalwork.

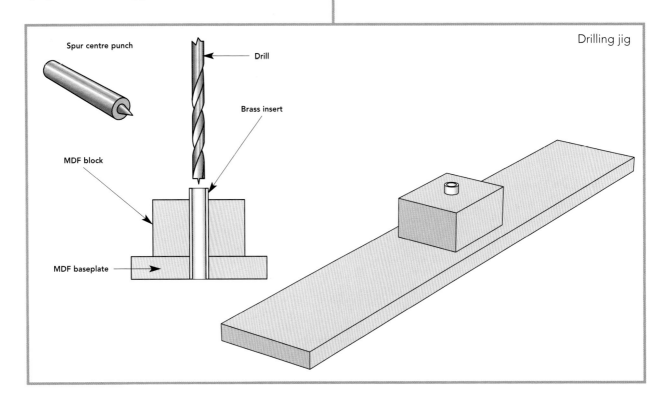

Drilling jig

Spur centre punch

Drill

Brass insert

MDF block

MDF baseplate

For wood, fine spur centres produce a better mark but as these were not an option I decided to turn my own from stainless steel rod. My set of punches ranges from ⅛–½in (3–12mm) in increments of one millimetre. With the drilling jig in place and held firmly with a couple of cramps the hole is drilled with a hand-held power drill driving a spur centre drill bit. The back edge of the dressing tabletop is a straight line – this forms the reference edge, from which the centres of all the radii that are necessary for the curves can be accurately marked.

The centres are then drilled with the jig that has been used to establish the centres on the reference board. The curves can then be marked out with a beam compass fitted with a fine click pencil. Instead of using the point supplied with the compass, I made a replacement stud from ¼in (6mm) stainless steel rod that fits into the slot holding the point.

This set-up allows all the control needed to draw the curves from the same centres that will be used for the router trammel arm. These two holes will eventually be used for the spindle that provides the centre for the rotating drawer. Now there is a clear visual diagram of the dressing tabletop shape.

◆ Routing the curves

I MENTIONED EARLIER THAT THE ROUTING OF THE curves for both the inner and outer joints between the lippings and the veneered section would have been very easy with a MicroFence trammel arm. I did not have one at the time so I decided to make my own. It uses the same principles as the MicroFence system but lacks the graduated dial for accurate transference of dimensions from an inner curve to a corresponding outer curve.

To reduce the problem of backlash common with screw thread driven movement, cut the male thread from free-cutting brass rod with a die set at the maximum adjustment possible and adjust it a little at a time until you achieve a fit that has the absolute minimum of backlash. The pivot for the trammel arm is made from stainless steel rod, which is a perfect fit in the centre hole of the reference board.

To rout the outer curves for the main circular forms of the drawer compartments, the bulk of waste is removed using a bandsaw, cutting very close to the pencil line. The veneered section is then centred onto the reference board and held in place with two screws driven in from the underside. These screw holes will eventually be on the inside of the drawer compartment so they will not show. The trammel arm and router are placed over the assembly

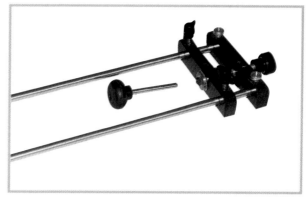

▲ Trammel arm with pivot pin removed.

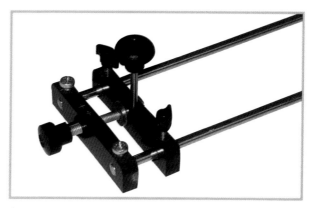

▲ Trammel arm with pivot pin in situ.

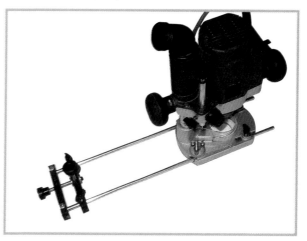

▲ Trammel arm installed in the router.

with the pivot pin inserted into the centre hole, and the cutter position adjusted to touch the line. Because the bulk of waste has been removed it is possible to make a cut that is slightly deeper than the thickness of the top. The entire cut is made in one pass around the curves at each end of the top.

The fact that the cutter produces a shallow track in the reference board is intentional as it provides the edge for the setting that will produce the inner curve for the lipping. The same method is used to cut the curve that forms the front edge of the top. The pivot hole will eventually be used to anchor the bottom curve of the mirror frame. The curves that form the front edges of the drawer compartment take their centres from a pivot point on the reference board. An offcut of veneered board with a hole drilled through is put in place to keep the trammel arm at the correct height.

◆ Routing the curved lippings

THE LIPPINGS ON THE OUTER CURVES OF THE drawer compartments are made from two pieces of pear wood. These are prepared initially as parallel strips, which are wide enough to contain the curved width. The junction between them is then cut on the dimension saw with the crosscut fence set at a 60° angle. It is, in effect, a mitre joint relying on a good fit that will be held together with glue. Even though the bonding surfaces are end-grain I decided not to introduce a spline into this joint as there would be no undue stress or any load being shared between other glued surfaces in the surrounding construction.

The trammel-arm setting of the router is changed to cut the inner curve of the lipping using the inside edge of the shallow track left by the previous cut for the radius. The lipping blank is then positioned on the reference board with two small dabs of double-sided tape and held firmly with two screws inserted from the underside to resist the cutting action of the router. In this position the beam compass is used to mark the curve with a pencil line. Also, the screws are removed and the waste cut off on the bandsaw to reduce the effort required for the router cut.

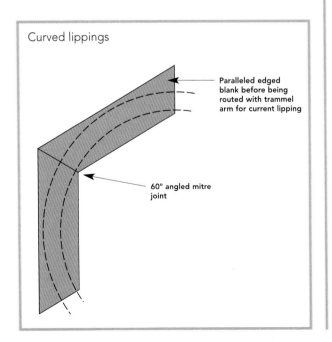

Curved lippings

Paralleled edged
blank before being
routed with trammel
arm for current lipping

60° angled mitre
joint

The solid wood lippings are cut even closer to the line to reduce the likelihood of breakout, as half of the curved edge cut with the router is against the grain.

This process is carried out on the inner edges of all the lippings but the outer edges are left straight and square which makes gluing up and cramping much easier.

The next stage is to control the alignment of the flat faces of the lippings with the flat face of the top and the under-sections of the drawer compartments. This is achieved with curved splines or loose tongues for which grooves are cut with a ball-race-controlled slotting blade and a router. I decided not to use my router table because the overhang of the top beyond the edge of the table is quite risky; not in terms of injury to myself but to the edges of the top. The safest option is to use a hand-held router overhead, fitted with extraction, particularly to catch the MDF dust.

◆ Gluing up

THE CURVED SPLINES ARE MADE FROM ⅛IN (4MM) MDF. The profile is drawn with the beam compass and the shape cut on the bandsaw. The main function of the splines is for surface alignment, so glue is not needed in the grooves. The lippings are then able to slide along the length of the curved edges of the top to position them before pressure is applied. Once again, this is achieved with Kantenfix edging cam cramps.

Once the glue has dried the surface is skimmed with a finely set smoothing plane before sawing off the excess and routing the outer curves to their finished shape.

The change in direction of each run of lipping is punctuated with a disc insert. The holes that accept the discs are cut after the lippings have been installed so it is not necessary to achieve a good fit at these junctions as the material is routed away later.

◆ Insert discs

INSERT DISCS PERFORM TWO FUNCTIONS. THEY provide a connection between the cylindrical uprights and the horizontal layers that form the drawer containers, and a visual link between the curved lippings. The discs are inserted into cylindrical housings that are cut with a router. I created a template from ¼in (6mm) Perspex.

The hole in the template matches the diameter of the insert disc. It is possible to purchase router template jigs with a selection of differently sized holes, but I required one with a single hole to place over the

Routing cylindrical housings for insert discs

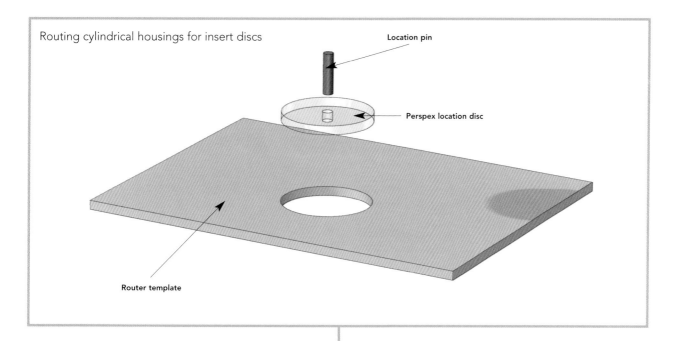

Location pin

Perspex location disc

Router template

lipped components to ensure the position is aligned with the reference base. My template is made by fixing a piece of Perspex with screws to a square of ¾in (18mm) plywood held in the four-jaw self-centring chuck of my engineering lathe. The hole is then cut with a drill and a boring tool to precisely the right diameter. Once the Perspex disc fits perfectly into the template hole, turn it on a mandrel so

that the centre hole is the same diameter as the holes in the reference base. This combination enables the template to be positioned in exactly the right place so that the disc holes can be routed with a top-bearing router cutter. After the template is made, zero the setting of the cross slide so that you can use it later to turn the wood disc inserts.

Mandrel for turning discs

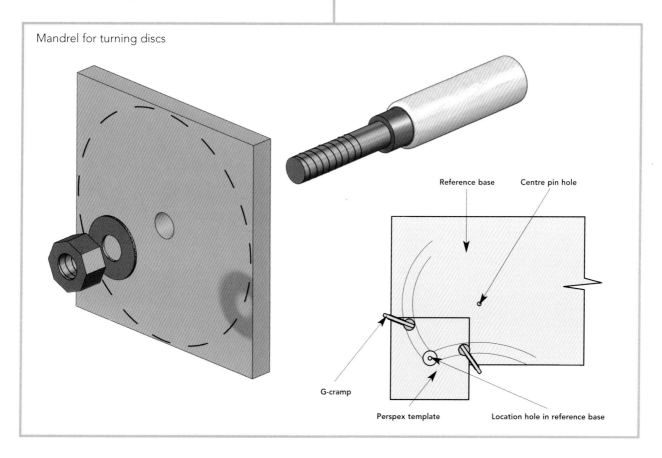

Reference base

Centre pin hole

G-cramp

Perspex template

Location hole in reference base

The tolerance of fit between the discs and the cylindrical housings is such that they can be inserted with finger pressure but are positive enough to avoid any lateral play. I did this to avoid the likelihood of expansion that can result from the glue being applied to the inner surfaces of the housing and the outer surface of the discs. The over-tight fit can actually result in glue starvation with the piston effect of the insertion. The discs are also slightly thicker than necessary and the excess is planed off after the glue has set. I also make sure that the grain direction of each disc is in harmony with the lippings.

Lippings

THE HALF-ROUND PROFILE OF THE LIPPING EDGES is both an aesthetic and practical feature. The general roundness of the form of the dressing table almost asks for any edges to be softened, and the use by the owner encouraged me to apply a rounded profile. In theory this is quite easy to achieve with a router and bearing-guided cutter. In practice, however, there are some problems of manipulation, this is particularly where an edge changes direction and in those areas where the grain changes direction. With the former problem there is a risk of scorching due to the friction from the cutting edge when the feed movement of the router pauses.

This is quite common with pale woods such as ash (*Fraxinus excelsior*) but is less likely to occur with the even-density grain of pear wood. It also helps if the cutter is sharp and to this end I keep a set of dedicated rounding over cutters that are only used for solid wood. As soon as they show signs of becoming blunt I downgrade them for use on board materials. It always surprises me how quickly TCT cutters lose that initial sharpness.

A slower spindle speed can also help to reduce scorching. With practice and confidence, the pause that takes place at a direction change can be minimized and the flow of movement that is necessary to prevent

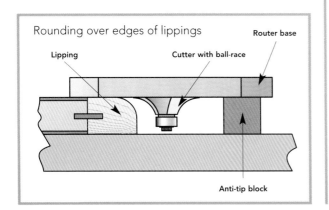

Rounding over edges of lippings

Lipping

Cutter with ball-race

Router base

Anti-tip block

scorching can be avoided. It also helps if the bulk of the material is removed with the depth set slightly less than the final cut and a second pass made with the depth reset to skim the absolute minimum to the finished profile.

Curved lippings

A ROUTER PASSED AROUND A DISC INSERT RESULTS in 50% of the material being cut against the grain. The same is true with a curved lipping. Feeding the router in the direction against the rotation of the cutter, which is regarded as good safe practice, can result in breakout in those areas where the cutter is rotating against the grain. A reverse-feed or climb cutting can do a lot to reduce breakout. To minimize the risk of the router running out of control, it helps to understand the practical principle of what is happening. The cutter behaves like a rack and pinion when fed in reverse and the tendency for it to run out of control is very likely with larger cutters. In the case of this dressing table, an 5/16in (8mm) radius rounding-over cutter, was much easier to control, particularly as the profile was achieved with two passes. Although I am prepared to take a risk by reverse-feeding to control the problem of breakout, I would only do this with the router hand-held in an overhead mode. I would never reverse-feed when using a router table as it is almost impossible to anticipate the speed of feed. The component is very likely to pull out of your hand with possible damage and risk of injury.

The component is held down onto the bench with cramps to prevent it from moving. Because only half of the router base is in contact with the surface at any stage during the cutting process it can tip over and damage the edge that is being cut. To overcome this problem fix a small block, equal in thickness to the component, to the underside of the overhanging half of the base with double-sided tape.

Before explaining the next process, I feel it is necessary to point out that some rounding-over cutters may have quite a large gap between the cutter and the ball-race. This will cause a small ridge when the second profile is being cut. For this reason I chose a cutter with a radius slightly less than half the thickness of the component so the rim of the ball-race is always in contact with the edge. Even though the profile is not a true half circle it can be blended in by sanding.

◆ Edges and surfaces

FOR SOME TIME I HAVE BEEN USING SELF-ADHESIVE abrasive sheets. It is available in all of the standard grit sizes and comes in rolls perforated to a handy size for the shaped hand blocks that are designed for its use – hard blocks for flat surfaces and foam rubber blocks for shaped work. The initial cost per roll might seem high but the convenience it has is well worth the outlay. Also, there is no waste – the abrasive sheet area is the same size as the hand block and there is no need to use a larger piece to hold it, which is necessary with a cork block.

I use a flexible foam block to sand the rounded over edges starting with 150grit and finishing with 240grit. As it is not possible to collect the dust produced while hand-sanding I keep my vacuum cleaner handy and suck up the dust at convenient times during the process. I prepare the flat surfaces using my Festool random orbit sander in order to mask and pre-finish any surfaces that are difficult to reach after the carcass has been assembled. This also enables any dried excess glue to be removed as it does not adhere to the lacquered surfaces.

◆ The carcass

THIS IS QUITE A STRAIGHTFORWARD PROCESS BUT to make it easier assemble the top and lower drawer shelves first before gluing the curved leg sections in place. Using aliphatic resin there is not long to wait between

stages as the pressure sensitive advantage of this glue forms a strong bond quite quickly. The short open-assembly time discouraged me from attempting to glue up the entire assembly in one session.

Instead of using cramping blocks I covered the faces of the cramp shoes with sheet cork held on with double-sided tape. It is not necessary to apply any additional pressure with blocks as the components are rigid enough, and their absence from the assembly process means one thing less to worry about. I did, however, use some spacers to ensure parallel alignment between the cramp bars and the surfaces that they span. This is to overcome possible damage to the projection of the rounded edges of the top and the drawer shelf, and to ensure the pressure applied is not out of square. The spacer blocks are made of MDF with a groove routed into them to slip onto the cramp bars.

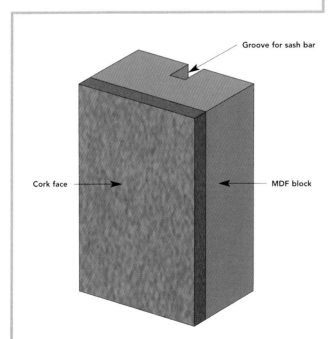

Groove for sash bar

Cork face

MDF block

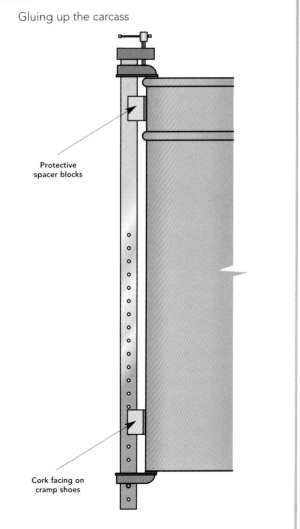

Gluing up the carcass

Protective spacer blocks

Cork facing on cramp shoes

◆ Mirror frame

THE CURVED SECTION OF THE MIRROR FRAME IS made up from three pieces of solid wood, which are cut to shape after the frame has been glued up. I decided not to laminate the curves for the same reason as the curved lippings on the carcass. 60° mitres are cut using a dimension saw with the crosscut fence set at the appropriate angle. The mitre joints are reinforced by inserting dowels made from ¼in (6mm) diameter threaded rod glued together with West System epoxy resin. It is difficult to align the dowel holes but using a %in (7mm) drill, which is slightly oversize, means you can align the surfaces during the gluing up stage – the epoxy resin will maintain the alignment when the glue has set.

Bearing in mind that cramp pressure needs to be applied parallel to the surfaces being joined, glue the cramping blocks onto the components – they will be removed when the curved shape is formed later. The two side uprights and the three pieces that form the curve are glued together in one operation. I used sash cramps for the joints to the uprights and G-cramps for the mitre joints. Surface alignment is achieved with small blocks held in place with G-cramps. To avoid the blocks adhering to the surfaces insert a slip of polythene sheet between the two. The shaping of the curves is carried out in a similar way to that of the curved lippings. The assembled components fixed onto a baseboard with screws inserted from the underside. The screw holes are removed once the rebates that receive the mirror and the back are cut. With the assembly in place the beam compass is used to mark out the curves. It is then removed so that the excess material is sawn off using a bandsaw. The baseboard is used again to form the curves accurately with a router and trammel arm. The junction between the frame uprights and the top rail is formed by scribing the ends with a round-nosed router cutter with the same radius as the cross-section of the top rail. A mortice and tenon with scribed shoulders is an alternative but it is a difficult joint to glue up after the rounded cross-section has been formed. I made a jig from MDF to hold the uprights in an inverted position and ran it over the cutter against the fence of my router table. The joint is held together temporarily with double-sided tape and a screw is inserted through a pre-drilled hole to pull it together.

The head of the screw is housed in a counter-bored hole filled with a wooden plug after the frame is finally assembled. Once again I used epoxy resin to glue up the joint. All this is completed once the rebates that accept the mirror and back have been cut. These are cut in two stages with a ball-race-guided slitter for the back because of the wider dimension and a ball-race-guided rebate cutter for the mirror. These two processes are carried out in this sequence on my router table. After the rebates have been cut the frame is held down again onto the backing board so that the rounded profile can be routed using the same method as that for the curved lippings. I made the back from ⅛in (4mm) thick MDF and fixed it in place with screws. It is essential to make provisions for replacement glass should it break or scratch in the future. Even though the dressing table is positioned against a wall and the back is not visible I lined the MDF with leather to finish it off.

Mirror frame: gluing up

Polythene-coated surface alignment blocks

Sash cramps

Glued on cramping blocks

Pressure

G-cramps

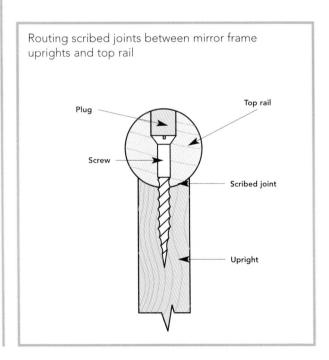

Routing scribed joints between mirror frame uprights and top rail

Plug

Top rail

Screw

Scribed joint

Upright

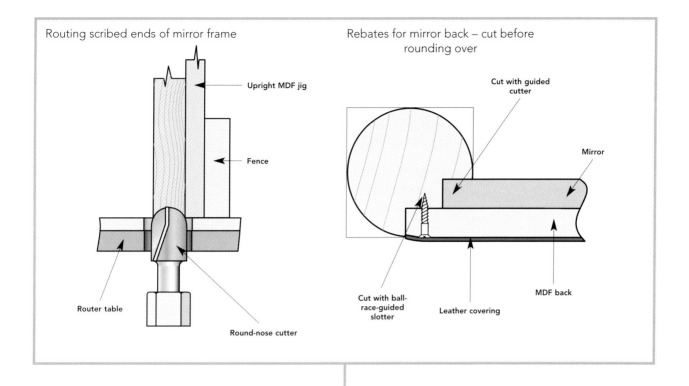

Routing scribed ends of mirror frame

Upright MDF jig

Fence

Router table

Round-nose cutter

Rebates for mirror back – cut before rounding over

Cut with guided cutter

Mirror

Cut with ball-race-guided slotter

Leather covering

MDF back

MAKING THE DRAWERS

Making the drawers is a challenge but the construction embodies many of the aspects that I have covered in the description of the piece so far. Because the edges will be exposed the curved front and sides are laminated using ⅟₁₆in (1.5mm) thick cherry constructional veneer. The front is also veneered with weathered ripple sycamore (*Acer pseudoplatanus*) to match the framed effect of the top. The junctions at the corners and the back are made with inserts so that a rounded flow can be formed and the location joints are made with splines. A central boss connected to the inside of the drawer front and the back ensures that the pivot is positively held in place. The edges of the drawer bottoms are inserted into grooves cut into the inner surfaces of the front and sides.

The most demanding task is the final assembly and glue up. This necessitates gluing on cramping blocks that then have to be removed later. I also included a melamine-coated baseboard held in place with the pivot spindle inserted through the central boss to ensure that there is no horizontal distortion.

The alignment of the drawer front when closed is achieved by the inclusion of a stop inserted from the underside of the carcass. I turned the stops from brass rod and cut threads onto their shanks, but left a small shoulder that projected enough to act as a stop when the drawer is closed. To avoid harsh impact the projection is covered with a rubber washer.

Part Three:
Gallery

▶ **Ged's chair**
Laminated seat and
back. Made with
American black walnut
core and faced with
steamed Swiss pear.
Frame in solid pear
with walnut inlay.

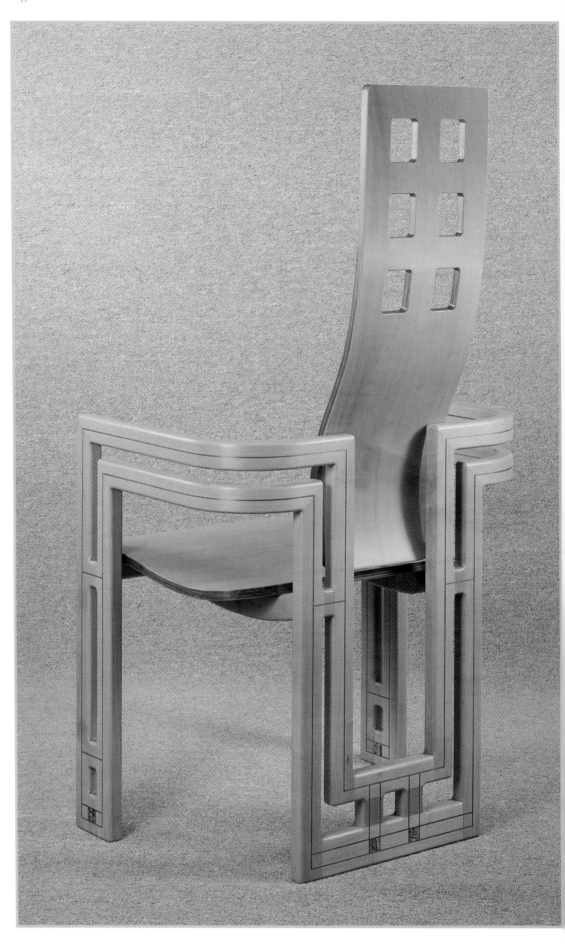

▲ **Dressing table**
A dressing table with
two chests of drawers.
Bleached ash and
English walnut.

▲ **Wardrobe**
Wardrobe with three
drawers. Weathered
ripple sycamore and
steamed Swiss pear.

▶ **Float**
Chest of drawers to
store a collection of
CDs. Birds eye maple
and English walnut.

▲ **Dressing table**
Designed to sit in the
corner of a bedroom.
Weathered ripple
sycamore and steamed
Swiss pear.

▲ **Bedside tables**
Birds eye maple and
ripple sycamore.

▲ Bedside tables
Ripple sycamore and
pear inlay.

**◄ Quatrain chest
of drawers**
Quilted maple and
wenge with malachite
handles.

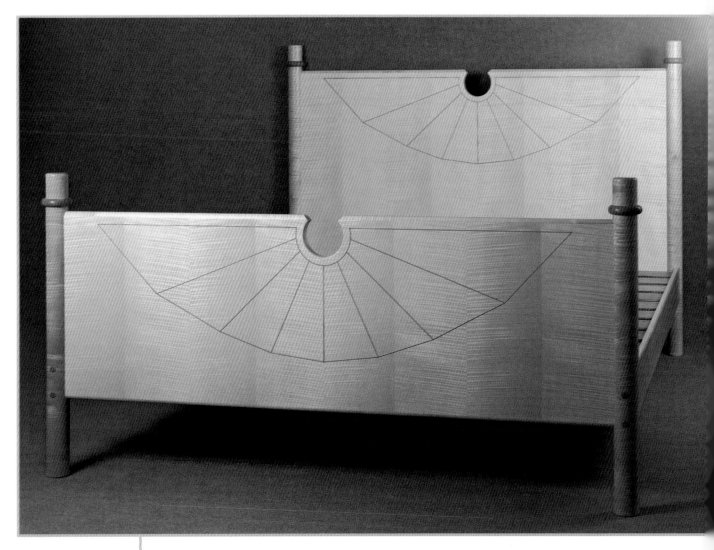

▲ **Double bed**
Ripple sycamore and
pear inlay.

◀ Chest of drawers
Ripple American cherry
and English walnut with
kingwood and coloured
titanium handles.

▶ **Lattice tower**
Chest of drawers in
ripple sycamore and
figured Australian
walnut.

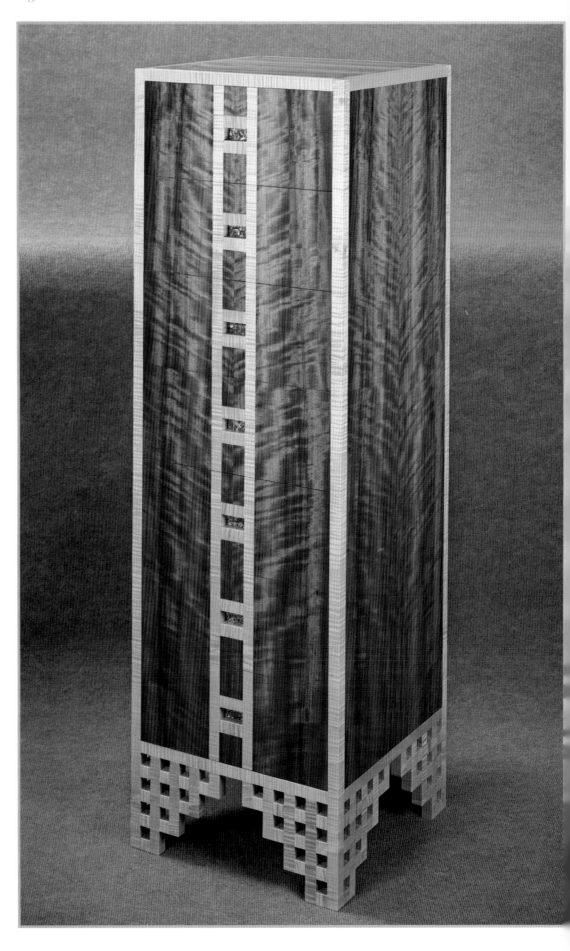

▲ **Jewellery chest**
Burr elm, bog oak and
ripple sycamore with
brass feet, stay and key.

▲ **Desk with
reversible top**
Bleached oak, burr oak
and ripple sycamore
inlay.

▲ **Curtsey**
Laminated wenge legs
and surround with
bleached burr oak top
and burr elm torus-
shaped feet.

▲ **Coffee table**
Bleached burr oak and
wenge with patinated
copper rods.

Nave altar
A nave altar for
St. Asaph Cathedral in
bleached and fumed oak
with a plate glass top. A
sand-blasted celtic cross
pattern decorates the
front glass panel.

Conversion tables

millimetres to inches

mm	inch	mm	inch	mm	inch	mm	inch
1	0.03937	26	1.02362	60	2.36220	310	12.20472
2	0.07874	27	1.06299	70	2.75590	320	12.59842
3	0.11811	28	1.10236	80	3.14960	330	12. 99212
4	0.15748	29	1.14173	90	3.54330	340	13.38582
5	0.19685	30	1.18110	100	3.93700	350	13.77952
6	0.23622	31	1.22047	110	4.33070	360	14.17322
7	0.27559	32	1.25984	120	4.72440	370	14.56692
8	0.31496	33	1.29921	130	5.11811	380	14.96063
9	0.35433	34	1.33858	140	5.51181	390	15.35433
10	0.39370	35	1.37795	150	5.90551	400	15.74803
11	0.43307	36	1.41732	160	6.29921	410	16.14173
12	0.47244	37	1.45669	170	6.69291	420	16.53543
13	0.51181	38	1.49606	180	7.08661	430	16.92913
14	0.55118	39	1.53543	190	7.48031	440	17.32283
15	0.59055	40	1.57480	200	7.87401	450	17.71653
16	0.62992	41	1.61417	210	8.26771	460	18.11023
17	0.66929	42	1.65354	220	8.66141	470	18.50393
18	0.70866	43	1.69291	230	9.05511	480	18.89763
19	0.74803	44	1.73228	240	9.44881	490	19.29133
20	0.78740	45	1.77165	250	9.84252	500	19.68504
21	0.82677	46	1.81102	260	10.23622		
22	0.86614	47	1.85039	270	10.62992		
23	0.90551	48	1.88976	280	11.02362		
24	0.94488	49	1.92913	290	11.41732		
25	0.98425	50	1.96850	300	11.81102		

1 mm = .03937 inch   1 inch = 25.4 mm
1 cm = 0.3937 inch   1 foot = 304.8 mm
1 m = 3.281 feet   1 yard = 914.4 mm

inches to millimetres

inch		mm	inch		mm	inch		mm
1/64	0.015625	0.3969	11/32	0.34375	8.7312	43/64	0.671875	17.0656
1/32	0.03125	0.7938	23/64	0.359375	9.1281	11/16	0.6875	17.4625
3/64	0.046875	1.1906	3/8	0.375	9.5250	45/64	0.703125	17.8594
1/16	0.0625	1.5875	25/64	0.390625	9.9219	23/32	0.71875	18.2562
5/64	0.078125	1.9844	13/32	0.40625	10.3188	47/64	0.734375	18.6531
3/32	0.09375	2.3812	27/64	0.421875	10.7156	3/4	0.750	19.0500
7/64	0.109375	2.7781	7/16	0.4375	11.1125	49/64	0.765625	19.4469
1/8	0.125	3.1750	29/64	0.453125	11.5094	25/32	0.78125	19.8438
9/64	0.140625	3.5719	15/32	0.46875	11.9062	51/64	0.796875	20.2406
5/32	0.15625	3.9688	31/64	0.484375	12.3031	13/16	0.8125	20.6375
11/64	0.171875	4.3656	1/2	0.500	12.700	53/64	0.828125	21.0344
3/16	0.1875	4.7625	33/64	0.515625	13.0969	27/32	0.84375	21.4312
13/64	0.203125	5.1594	17/32	0.53125	13.4938	55/64	0.858375	21.8281
7/32	0.21875	5.5562	35/64	0.546875	13.8906	7/8	0.875	22.2250
15/64	0.234375	5.9531	9/16	0.5625	14.2875	57/64	0.890625	22.6219
1/4	0.250	6.3500	37/64	0.578125	14.6844	29/32	0.90625	23.0188
17/64	0.265625	6.7469	19/32	0.59375	15.0812	59/64	0.921875	23.4156
9/32	0.28125	7.1438	39/64	0.609375	15.4781	15/16	0.9375	23.8125
19/64	0.296875	7.5406	5/8	0.625	15.8750	61/64	0.953125	24.2094
5/16	0.3125	7.9375	41/64	0.640625	16.2719	31/32	0.96875	24.6062
21/64	0.1328125	8.3344	21/32	0.65625	16.6688	63/64	0.984375	25.0031
						1	1.00	25.4

About the author

Robert Ingham has an unrivalled international status as a teacher, designer and craftsman. He trained at Loughborough College and Leeds College of Art followed by a degree at Leeds University. Then, together with his brother George, ran a successful furniture-making business in Thirsk, Yorkshire.

After deciding to pursue separate paths, Robert went to Dorset to assist John Makepeace in establishing the prestigious Parnham School and went on to become its principal for many years. Under Robert's tenure the school developed an influential international reputation with many of its graduates going on to become part of the British designer-maker elite.

In 1997, after 20 years at Parnham, Robert gave up full-time teaching in order to run his own highly acclaimed workshop in North Wales. Widely exhibited in the UK and America and with many important pieces in private collections and corporate pieces made to commission, he has achieved most of the major accolades awarded in the industry for excellence, including several coveted Guild Marks. Recently he has been invited to join the Worshipful Company of Furniture Makers, been granted the Freedom of the city of London and been made a Fellow of the Society of Designer Craftsmen.

Index

To place an order, or to request a catalogue, contact:

GMC Publications

Castle Place, 166 High Street, Lewes, East Sussex, BN7 1XU United Kingdom

Tel: 01273 488005 Fax: 01273 402866

Website: www.thegmcgroup.com

Orders by credit card are accepted